YOUR
LIFE
DEPENDS
ON IT

YOUR LIFE DEPENDS ON IT

WHAT YOU CAN DO TO MAKE
BETTER CHOICES
ABOUT YOUR HEALTH

TALYA MIRON-SHATZ, PhD

BASIC BOOKS

New York

Basic Books
Hachette Book Group
1290 Avenue of the Americas, New York, NY 10104
www.basicbooks.com

Printed in the United States of America

First Edition: September 2021

Published by Basic Books, an imprint of Perseus Books, LLC, a subsidiary of Hachette Book Group, Inc. The Basic Books name and logo is a trademark of the Hachette Book Group.

The Hachette Speakers Bureau provides a wide range of authors for speaking events. To find out more, go to www.hachettespeakersbureau.com or call (866) 376-6591.

The publisher is not responsible for websites (or their content) that are not owned by the publisher.

Print book interior design by Amy Quinn.

Library of Congress Cataloging-in-Publication Data
Names: Miron-Shatz, Talya, author.
Title: Your life depends on it : what you can do to make better choices about your health / Talya Miron-Shatz, PhD.
Description: First edition. | New York : Basic Books, 2021. | Includes bibliographical references and index.
Identifiers: LCCN 2021005929 | ISBN 9781541646759 (hardcover) | ISBN 9781541646742 (ebook)
Subjects: LCSH: Health—Decision making. | Health behavior.
Classification: LCC RA776.95 .M57 2021 | DDC 613—dc23
LC record available at https://lccn.loc.gov/2021005929

ISBNs: 9781541646759 (hardcover); 9781541646742 (ebook)

LSC-C

Printing 1, 2021

Wherever the art of Medicine is loved, there is also a love of Humanity.

—Hippocrates

The function of education is to teach one to think intensively and to think critically.

—Dr. Martin Luther King Jr.

This book will drive you to think intensively and critically about
your health and medical decisions.
To take a leading role in them.
And to make the best choices you can.

Let me tell you something—it's hard.
Oh, and your life depends on it.

CONTENTS

ACKNOWLEDGMENTS

WRITING ABOUT MEDICINE IS ONLY POSSIBLE BECAUSE THE PROFESSION IS phenomenal: people choose to dedicate their lives, night and day, to the health and well-being of others. My admiration and humble, heartfelt thanks go to all of you, healthcare professionals, and especially to my own doctors, who provided care, instilled trust, and actually cared.

Many researchers, from medicine, psychology, behavioral economics, sociology, history, and more, have produced the knowledge I discuss here. Thank you for your insights.

Many patients (whose names I changed to maintain their privacy) and many professionals (whom I present with their real names unless they asked otherwise) have shared their intimate, sometimes scary medical experiences with me. I cherish your words and silences, from the shortest, seemingly random exchanges to the deliberate encounters.

The best professionals stood by me and helped make this book happen. My agent, Rachel Sussman at Chalberg & Sussman, provided invaluable guidance. My acquiring editor, T. J. Kelleher, and my editor, Eric Henney, both at Basic Books, have shared the vision and assisted in bringing it forward forcefully. Thank you all so much.

My wonderful assistants: Nina Rabinowitz, Noa Tauber, and Danit Tarashandagan.

My friends Linda Adams, Shari Motro, Einat Niv, Gil Troy, and Kathleen Vohs. Writing with clever, loving souls around you ensures it is not lonely.

I was very fortunate to share my research with colleagues and collaborators, most of whom have become great friends—Stefan Becker, who was my partner in creating and leading the eHealth Venture Summit and Innovation award at MEDICA, Glyn Elwyn, Gunther Eyesenbach, Yaniv Hanoch, Margaret Hansen, Elissa Ozanne, Avi Tsafrir, and Mladen Vidovich. A special thank you to my colleagues at the Winton Centre for Risk and Evidence Communication, Cambridge University, who are unique in bringing their knowledge into wide application: Alexandra (Alex) Freeman, Mike Pearson, Gabe Recchia, and Sir David Spiegelhalter.

My friends and colleagues who have read drafts and generously shared their wisdom: Zackary Berger, Simona Botti, Mayer Brezis, Joan McIver Gibson, Tamar Hess, Jack Hoadley, Yash Huilgol, Deborah Jones, Yasmine Konheim-Kalkstein, Ayelet Meir, Barbara Mellers, Michal Rosen-Zvi, Michal Sagi, Talia Sagiv, Jacqueline Shire, Efrat Suraqui, Odette Wegwarth, and Matthew Willcox. Any lack of wisdom is purely mine.

My mentors, Gershon Ben Shakhar for his huge faith in me, Gerd Gigerenzer for his dedication to risk communication in medicine, and Dan Ariely for, wow, setting such an example.

My students at the Wharton Business School, University of Pennsylvania, at the Hebrew University, at the Mount Sinai Hospital, and at the Ono Academic College, for everything you have taught me.

Daniel Kahneman, for your kindness and honesty, for transformative years under your supervision at Princeton University, and later, for pushing me to write about something big.

Tamar Elad-Applebaum, a bright spiritual leader, for your enthusiasm. You defined this book as a humanistic endeavor, and you should know, being an unrelentingly inspiring beacon of humanism.

My family—Ariel, Itamar, Alona, Hammutal, Shir, and Rodrigo—has been a pillar of support, as has the Mamo family I am so lucky to belong to. My son, Itamar, in particular, has contributed to this work with great dedication and tremendous wisdom, which are so typical of him. Thank you, my beautiful family. I love you.

My parents, Nathan, who died many years ago but whose love still shines on me, and my mother, Ester (she goes by Etti, which she thinks sounds younger), a retired nurse, whose professional pride has set a stellar role model and whose love and care for me and my family are a lasting miracle. Thank you both for giving me life and so much more. With this book, and with my research on medical decision-making, I hope to pay back my debt to you.

WHY I CARE SO MUCH ABOUT HEALTH AND MEDICAL CHOICES

We all make health and medical choices every single day. We choose to take a vitamin supplement, go for a run despite a sore tendon, forego birth control pills, or have chemotherapy after cancer surgery. The more important these decisions are, the more vulnerable we are, and the tougher choosing becomes. This is why we need to build up skills to deal with these choices.

We need to know how to ask the right questions, distinguish information from misinformation, and make the best health choices for ourselves and our loved ones, at home, with our doctors, and in the hospital. Likewise, if we are the doctors. In fact, also, if we manage a health system.

I will show you how.

I am a decision scientist, with a PhD in psychology. I trained at Princeton University, taught at Wharton, and am a visiting researcher at the University of Cambridge. My research focuses on medical decision-making: looking at how doctors and laymen, in hospitals, online, and at home, make these choices. I also know the ins and outs of health and medical choices as a consultant for health advertisers and for medical device, pharmaceutical, and digital health companies. Few share my broad perspective, which I now share with you.

I DID NOT START MY JOURNEY WITH MEDICAL DECISION-MAKING AS AN expert—I started it as a sixth-grader, when the school nurse examined me and mumbled something I did not understand. In the following months, my father and I spent many mornings driving down a desolate street to get to the Child and Adolescent Orthopedic Center on the outskirts of town. There, the technicians would take x-rays of my back. The doctor would then go over the x-rays and measure the curvature of my back with a ruler, tracing the progress.

She told me that I had scoliosis—my back was crooked. Then she told me I would have to wear a plastic brace around my waist, ending just below my chest, for years.

Nobody gave me a choice in my treatment options. My doctor never explained whether the brace was likely to work, how long I would have to use it, whether my back would end up perfectly straight, and whether the scoliosis might prevent me from having children someday. These questions swirled inside my thirteen-year-old head, but I never voiced them.

No doctor or technician ever x-rayed my well-being or measured it with a ruler. I never told anyone that I was certain my back looked like a giant lizard's, or that I could not bring myself to look at it in the mirror. Under the brace, I wore a long tank top that kept the cold contraption from my skin but did nothing to prevent the harsh material from rubbing against my pelvic bones, leaving bruises that would linger long after I stopped wearing it altogether.

My loving, doting father was a bank teller with a high school diploma who had the utmost deference for physicians. It never occurred to him to question the authority of a doctor. My father couldn't be my advocate or my voice. And my mother, too upset by my suffering to address it, delegated the treatment to him entirely.

This was before the internet. To find medical information, I would have had to go to the university library, a place I only discovered later in life. There I would have had to look for a book or journal article on "alternatives to back brace in adolescent idiopathic scoliosis," as if I knew these terms.

After a few x-rays and ruler sessions, I asked my doctor if I should swim. I had heard it was good for the back. She insisted that the brace was all I needed. Regardless, I wanted to play an active role in my care and to befriend my second-rate body. My parents, forever eager to help, bought me a swimming pool membership. After months of regular swimming, I ventured a peek in the locker-room mirror. My back took me by surprise: it looked kind of okay.

I had a happy ending. By the time I turned sixteen the brace was gone. I swam regularly and stayed away from orthopedic specialists' offices. I had left that episode behind me—or so I thought.

TWENTY YEARS LATER, I WAS STILL SWIMMING. I WAS STILL LOOKING AT people's backs, admiring how straight and symmetrical they were. I was now an organizational psychologist and a married mother of three. I had recently lost my loving, doting father to prostate cancer, Parkinson's disease, and pneumonia. Yearning for change, I went back to graduate school, studying for a PhD in social psychology and researching what is called the confirmation bias, where you embrace the first idea you hear and tend to stick with it even in the face of opposing evidence. I studied it in expert and lay judgment; Jerome Groopman described it perfectly in his book *How Doctors Think*.[1]

Then medical decision-making snuck up on me: my department chair told me that the director of the genetic-counseling program was looking for someone to teach a course on the psychological aspects of medical decision-making to genetic-counseling students, and he thought I was the right person for the task. The gig was an honor, but the task was daunting. I read everything I could on the subject, but I felt as if I was taking swimming lessons online. I had to get my feet wet. I asked to sit in on a few genetic-counseling sessions.

The first couple I observed arrived at the genetic counselor's office just minutes before I did. They, too, were out of breath from rushing through the hospital's corridors in search of the counselor's office. Both were deaf, and the woman was pregnant. They had come to ask whether their deafness might be passed on to their baby, and if so, whether it would be through the husband or the wife. The couple didn't mind either way which parent was the source, but the husband's family wanted to know. They brought along a sign-language interpreter and their hearing two-year-old son.

The counselor had charts of their paternal and maternal genetic heritages, complete with little icons for male and female, arrows, boxes, and markings. She explained the genetic bases for their deafness, walking them through the facts of genetics. I dug into memories from my ninth-grade biology class and recalled that humans have twenty-three pairs of chromosomes and who-knows-how-many genes. The interpreter seemed to be doing similar mental digging, which she signed to the couple. The child was getting fidgety, and the room was more crowded now that chromosomes and genes had joined us.

The worried parents looked at the interpreter, then at the counselor, then back at the interpreter.

"So, from the husband's side or the wife's?" the interpreter tried.

The counselor tied together the biology and the family history. The bottom line: if the baby was deaf, it would be because of the husband. Perhaps this wasn't what the husband's family wanted to hear, but at least now they had an answer.

During this one-hour session, the couple received more information than I ever did from my doctor. Yet despite the genetic counselor's considerable knowledge and patience, the couple left the office trailing a cloud of questions. I wondered what they understood out of everything they had been told, what hadn't been lost in that double translation. The number of chromosomes in a human body? The difference between dominant and recessive? Their baby's probable chances of hearing? Even if they'd had perfect hearing and hadn't needed an interpreter, would they have been able to accurately repeat every-thing the counselor had so diligently explained?

Many, maybe most, patients leave a health expert's office still confused. Our well-meaning but stressed healthcare systems cannot always serve us the information we need, let alone verify that we understand it and integrate it into our decision processes.

After I taught the course, my students told me that the insights they gained were missing from their other courses—they had learned how to meticulously calculate genetic risk, but no one had taught them how their clients processed the information.

Since then, I have taught this and have put this knowledge to use in many contexts, always hearing how this was the missing link. You had to understand how people made health choices in order to get them to adhere to their medi-cation or figure out what their fitness tracker or glucometers were saying and what to do about it.

THE YEAR AFTER THAT FIRST GENETIC-COUNSELING SESSION AND THE course I taught, I started my postdoctoral research at Princeton University, studying happiness. I worked with Daniel Kahneman, the Nobel laureate who revealed the ways we think, both the fast and the slow, and who created the foundation for behavioral economics.[2] I found that low points influence our feelings more than peaks do and that our thoughts about financial security matter to our well-being as much as our income.[3] Still, I was increasingly drawn to studying medical decision-making, both then and later while teaching consumer behavior at the Wharton School, University of Pennsylvania.

I remembered how powerless I had once felt. I had a voice now, which I vowed to dedicate to helping people at the moments when they might have lost theirs. I vowed to study health choices, the kinds of choices that have an impact on us, sometimes irreversibly. I'm an optimist, and yet I was gradually realizing how unfair it was to expect us all to speak up and to manage our medical choices on our own. I have learned that even now, when information is so readily available and the digital health industry is booming, it's still hard to make good choices.

The challenges we face today when making these choices are many: dealing with an imperfect health system, being freaked out and mentally overloaded, getting too much incomplete information from too many unreliable sources, and then having to make sense of it all and choose. I will show you all the insider tips and psychological tricks to do just that, to the degree possible.

AFTER FINISHING MY POSTDOCTORAL WORK AT PRINCETON, AND WITH some overlap with teaching at Wharton, I became a business professor in Israel, and later also a visiting researcher at Cambridge University. I consult for companies, from start-ups to corporations, on behavioral economics and on the psychological drivers of patient and prescriber behavior. I have spoken about these issues internationally, to entrepreneurs, doctors, and health management organization directors. When my mother attended my talk at a medical conference where I spoke about adherence to medication, she complained that I speak too fast. You bet I speak too fast! I have a voice now and so much to say.

THEN, WHEN I FELT ON TOP OF MY PROFESSIONAL GAME, MY BACK GAVE out. I was in excruciating pain. Reluctantly, I consulted an orthopedic specialist. He said I hadn't ruptured or herniated a disk and sent me home to rest and "drink a cup of tea." Just like my thirteen-year-old self, I said nothing. I was too sore to speak. I spent several days in anguish before calling him again to beg for help.

The doctor's advice escalated from tea to a morphine patch, which he assured me had no side effects. In hindsight, I should have known that "no side effects" made no sense. I was now a scientist studying medical decision-making. I knew where the university library was, and I didn't even need to go there because I could access everything online. Still, I was too sore to look up whether the patch would work, what the risks were, and what the alternatives were; too miserable to think about how odd it was that the doctor had gone from offering me no painkillers whatsoever to offering a heavy-duty opiate; too desperate to read the brochure (in minuscule print) I received with the patch. Just as with the child me, nobody explained anything or asked about my preferences. I was being treated not as a person but as a back to be fixed. In my normal state, I could wrap my head around the medication, then voice my reservations. In my condition, with zero input from my physician, that was mission impossible.

My husband placed the patch on my shoulder along with a kiss. It was supposed to stay on my shoulder for a week. I didn't last twenty-four hours.

The next morning, I sat on the couch, intending to get up and drive to work—we were having a New Year's celebration that day, and my promotion was being announced. A blink of an eye passed, and I was still on the couch, except my watch indicated three hours had gone by. I had never been so listless. No college shindig for me. My mother called, and when she heard the lethargy in my voice, she alerted my husband. Before he got home, my mind recovered for a moment from the daze. I realized this was the morphine's doing and asked a merciful neighbor to tear the patch from my shoulder. The mental fog subsided, but the pain returned.

I, who did so much research on how to present medical information and was certifiably poised to make informed health choices, failed to exercise any real judgment, to ask the right questions—or even to read the brochure! This was painfully disillusioning.

In theory, the world had come a long way from the era of doctor-chosen treatment. We can self-diagnose (or misdiagnose) with a quick Google search, we can order an online-touted cure-all with a wave of our credit card, and we can voice our objections in the doctor's office when something doesn't feel right. But in reality, we still rely heavily on our doctors and healthcare systems. And they, in turn, require a wake-up call and a serious lesson on truly involving their patients. This book provides both.

Making better health and medical choices is neither intuitive nor easy, especially in the face of a life-threatening decision, medical jargon, and confusing probabilities. Expecting us to handle these flawlessly is unrealistic and ignores issues of cultural background, a whole slew of cognitive barriers, lack of professional training in how to convey medical information, time constraints, and health-system deficiencies.

The good news is that there is still plenty you can do once you understand what you are up against. Reading this book will give you the tools to do so. In the chapters that follow, I offer psychological hacks and nudges that will compensate for some of the flaws in the system. I apply research from behavioral economics, medicine, psychology, sociology, and more to develop a model that guides you toward making better health choices.

IN THE FIRST PART OF THE BOOK, YOU WILL GAIN A DEEP UNDERSTANDING of the societal, legal, and commercial forces that require us to play a more active role in our healthcare. You'll see what happens when health choices go wrong, and what psychological processes—like the tendencies to save cognitive effort or to succumb to the hope-and-fear appeal—prevent us from properly sorting them out on our own.

In the second part, you'll get a profound sense of the unique barriers to making good health choices. I will offer some practical, science-based advice about what you and your physician can do to overcome these barriers. I will discuss shared decision-making, as well as the emotionally fraught and complicated choices surrounding end-of-life care.

In the third and final part of the book, I will explore the promise of digital health solutions, wellness programs, and innovative means of providing care, especially when this promise is boosted by psychological insights. And I will address the fact that some challenges are burdens to be faced by the medical system itself and are grounded in the financial incentives that inform medicine. I will suggest how health organizations can truly empower patients to make better health choices.

THIS BOOK CAN BENEFIT ANYONE WHO RUNS A HOSPITAL OR IS A DOCTOR, anyone who has ever cared for a patient or cared about a patient, anyone who ever was, is, or will be a patient, and anyone who wants to lead with their health choices. This book is for all of us. Read on, because your life depends on it.

PART I

HOW DID WE END UP HERE?

CHAPTER 1

OH, THE CHOICE YOU NOW HAVE

In a scene in *When Harry Met Sally*, the titular characters are eating at a diner. Harry orders a "number 3" and Sally orders the chef salad with the dressing on the side and an apple pie à la mode. Barely pausing for breath, she specifies that she wants the pie heated and the ice cream on the side, that she wants strawberry ice cream or whipped cream if they don't have strawberry ice cream, and what to do if either the ice cream or real whipped cream is unavailable. The waitress writes down Sally's order, makes a disgruntled sound, gives Sally a judgmental look, sticks her pencil behind her ear, and leaves. Then Harry stares at Sally in silence for five straight seconds (an eternity on-screen) until she asks, "What?!"

The audience found it hilarious, as did I. But now I see Sally as a tragicomic figure, trying to assert herself to an exasperated professional, surrounded by unsupportive peers. Harry silently pleads with Sally to be quiet, to accept the options on the menu without remark. The uniformed waitress, towering above Sally, wants the same thing from her: that she know her place and not make too many demands.

NOT SO LONG AGO, IT WAS ASSUMED THAT MEDICAL PATIENTS ALSO needed to know their place and say little: accept what was offered without attempting to influence it. We call this the paternalistic model of care.

Paternalism involves giving people—employees, citizens, or patients—what the person in charge believes is beneficial for them and allowing them no other choice. In the medical context, this meant that doctors dominated the decision-making process—examining, diagnosing, and determining a course of treatment—without their patients' active participation. This ancient model relates to medicine's historical association with the divine: disease was initially considered a divine punishment.[1] The first doctor in Greek mythology was Asclepius, son of Apollo, the god of healing and medicine. Who can argue with the son of a god? In the middle ages, sickness remained a punishment from God, and cure came by praying for forgiveness. Doctors were then usually priests or other religious scholars.[2] Their authority was derived from their professional knowledge and was backed by powerful religious institutions. "Patient empowerment" would have been utterly meaningless, because the whole point of seeking a cure was to reaffirm the authority of God. More-secular healers, midwives, and nurses sought cures with charms and herbs instead of prayers. Because they threatened the absolute power of the church, they were persecuted and vilified as "witches."[3]

BY THE NINETEENTH CENTURY, THE DEITY HAD LARGELY BEEN REMOVED from the equation, but not much else had really changed. An 1847 ethical code of the American Medical Association stated, "The obedience of a patient to the prescriptions of his physician should be prompt and implicit. He should never permit his own crude opinions as to their fitness, to influence his attention to them."[4]

But the place of the client in medicine is rapidly changing. Patients are now expected to be active participants in their care and are more likely to speak their mind, whether or not they're invited to do so. Now they have more power and more opportunities to make medical choices. This seems obviously desirable because we consider choice to be highly positive and because our medical conditions, circumstances, and personalities warrant tailored treatments beyond a standard "number 3." But how good are people at handling all this choice, considering what is at stake—their breasts, prostates, hearts, and lives? For some people, choice is, and always was, highly desirable. Some people feel they have achieved command of these choices. And some, especially in critical times, feel that this choice is thrust upon them.

In either case, the unfortunate truth is that the choices people make about their health can easily go awry. Throughout this book, I'll discuss the cognitive mechanisms that hamper patients' judgment and the environmental factors that make it uniquely hard for them to make choices. After decades of research, I've found people are not fully capable of making good medical choices in the ways they're currently offered.

And yet choose we must.

THIS BOOK IS ALL ABOUT THE GAP BETWEEN THE THEORY AND PRACTICE, not just in choice or in informed consent, but in general. It is about the gap between the power we as patients now have to make health choices and our restricted ability to act upon this power. I'll point to places where the gap exists and suggest ways to narrow it, while acknowledging that we lack the power to close it completely.

In order to understand why the current model of choice-based care doesn't yet meet the psychological needs of patients, we need to consider how and why it developed at all. Like any paradigm shift, this shift in power did not happen overnight or in a vacuum. Several developments, although not directly related, made patient involvement in decision-making possible and socially acceptable: the burgeoning consumer culture, the legal push for more-active patient involvement, the internet of things, and the financial considerations surrounding decisions regarding health.

But first, let's talk about coffee.

THE PATIENT'S PLACE . . . AND STARBUCKS

It would be an overstatement to say that the first driver of change was a coffee chain. The change in the patient role was partly driven by the consumer culture that now assigns power of choice to the people. But a coffee chain can show us something about how the notion of the consumer has changed, illustrating the new consumer role and the larger trend toward choice in everything from baby onesies to caskets.

In 1982, Starbucks operated 4 Seattle cafés. By the time Harry met Sally in 1989, it had 55 branches worldwide. In 1994, when Amazon started selling books, Starbucks had 425 branches. And by 2012, when the dating site Tinder began offering an endless array of potential romantic partners, Starbucks had over 18,000 branches. As of this writing, more than 30,000 branches are in operation.

Starbucks was the pioneer of personalized coffee, reinventing the way we consume java. This model compels customers to have preferences about nearly every aspect of the product (size, flavor, steamed or cold milk, whole or skim or almond milk, number of shots of caffeine, and so on). At Starbucks, customers don't just buy coffee. They are in some sense collaborating with the barista.

This is key. At Starbucks, you are not just tolerated when you speak; you are required to actively state what you want. It's no coincidence that they ask for your name when you place your order, so they can announce "tall green tea latte for Talya." Similarly, Nike By You allows you to customize your own sneakers. MAC Cosmetics offers you to customize your makeup palette. And while most of us say we like this level of agency, it can easily lead to choice overload, suboptimal use of information, even paralysis and an inability to choose.[5] Most of us stick with our "usual" beverage at Starbucks rather than sample the entire range. Most of us prefer to buy prefabricated shoes and eye-shadow palettes rather than be overwhelmed by choice.

However, as much as we feel overwhelmed by choices, we have come to expect ample choices, not only in our coffee but in almost all our consumer products and services. This extends to our medical care, as well, where the stakes are so much higher and where our experience is so much more limited. We drink endless cups of latte during our lifetime, but we have knee surgery once or twice. To choose well, we need to know what our options are and what they entail. We need to be well versed in the risks and benefits and their probabilities. We need information, and in theory it is available to us.

THE PATIENT'S PLACE . . . AND INFORMED CONSENT

A second, more direct driver of change in medicine was the legal concept of informed consent, the idea that before a patient could be enrolled in a medical study, the procedure, the aims of the research (or treatment), the anticipated benefits and potential risks of the study, and the discomfort it might entail had to be explained. The patient would then have to explicitly agree to those terms.

The importance of informed consent in medical situations cannot be overstated: without our autonomous consent, nothing separates us from lab animals. "Informed" implies that you have information. Without it, every effort at choice and control is moot. Imagine that Starbucks didn't have to tell you what is in the drink you ordered or even make what you asked for in the first place. You could only hope you would get what you ordered. Your coffee might come carbonated and with a slice of lemon. Or your wishes might be disregarded altogether, and you might end up with a Japanese seasonal favorite made from cherry petals, condensed milk, and white bean paste. In the medical context, you could wake up from gastrointestinal surgery, surprised to discover you now had screws in your knee.

For most of history, this was the case. The requirement that patients be asked for informed consent arose in response to public outcry over several atrocious medical studies in the late nineteenth and throughout the twentieth centuries. In one study, University of Breslau researcher Dr. Albert Neisser injected an experimental syphilis vaccination into unsuspecting patients, causing some of them to develop the disease. Subsequently, in 1900 the Prussian minister for religious, educational, and medical affairs issued a directive to all hospitals and clinics demanding informed and unambiguous consent.[6]

The international consensus around informed consent also traces back to the brutal and torturous experiments Nazi doctors conducted on helpless prisoners during World War II. The outcry against war crimes and abuse disguised as research led, in 1947, to the Nuremberg Code outlining permissible medical experimentation.

In 1964, the World Medical Association convened in Finland and crafted the Declaration of Helsinki, an international agreement on the ethical principles guiding medical research involving human subjects. Nowadays "participants" replaces "subjects," a word banned for being too passive and demeaning.[7]

The Declaration of Helsinki cited the International Code of Medical Ethics that the World Medical Association adopted in 1949: "A physician shall act in the patient's best interest when providing medical care." Then it elaborated on how to conduct research, ultimately mentioning informed consent.[8]

These guiding principles for medical research were later expanded to include informed consent in medical care at-large, not just in experiments. In 1982 in the United States, Ronald Reagan's President's Commission for the Study of Ethical Problems in Medicine and Biomedical and Behavioral Research stated, "Although the informed consent doctrine has substantial foundations in law, it is essentially an ethical imperative." In one short sentence, the commission intertwined the two distinctly different foundations of informed consent: law and ethics.

Ruth Faden, who founded the Johns Hopkins Berman Institute of Bioethics, and Tom Beauchamp, professor of philosophy at Georgetown University, authoritatively disentangled law and philosophy in *A History and Theory of Informed Consent*, a work widely known to doctors and bioethicists.[9]

The law approaches informed consent from a pragmatic perspective: physicians have a duty to obtain consent, and they are liable if they fail to fulfill this duty. The focus is on physicians and on financial compensation should medical outcomes go awry during a procedure or treatment that a patient has not consented to. Philosophy approaches informed consent by focusing on patients or participants. The priority is to respect their autonomy and their right to govern their own choice. This distinction means that patients will receive consent forms and sign them—a pragmatic step that can be easily handled and even enforced. But this does not capture the essence of informed consent. It doesn't mean very much unless patients understand what they are signing and have time to contemplate before putting pen to paper.

Twenty-four-year-old Stefanie can describe what informed consent looks like in practice.

Stefanie was fasting before a scheduled gynecological procedure. She'd been lying in the hospital bed for a while, wearing a robe and covered with an itchy blanket. At almost six p.m., someone roused her from her restless anticipation and shoved a piece of paper in front of her to sign.

She needed to sign the form, not read or discuss it. So much for deliberation. Asking a question was out of the question. When she ventured a meek "Who are you?" to the person who handed her the form, he responded, "I'm the anesthesiologist," in a flat tone that implied he'd been up since five in the morning. So much for speaking her concerns. Stefanie was hungry, tired, scared, and understandably reluctant to argue for her ethical right to information with the man about to put her under. Her mother, who had accompanied her to the hospital, was also wary of upsetting the anesthesiologist and possibly getting bumped from the surgery schedule.

Stefanie signed the form and gave her supposedly informed consent to the procedure. Supposedly, the law mandating informed consent had been obeyed, but the spirit of the law had not been met. In Stefanie's case, we see the abyss between the legal perspective and the philosophical or ethical perspective on informed consent, a gap Stephanie was powerless to cross.

THE PATIENT'S PLACE . . . AND DOLLARS

Money makes the world go round, and it is the third driver of our increasing role in healthcare. The biggest decisions and biggest spending come from high deductible medical insurance plans that turned us all into not just patients but healthcare consumers. High-deductible plans make medical care more of a fee-for-service industry, attaching a dollar sign to our health-related decisions, informed or otherwise. With these plans, you are essentially betting that you won't need to use your healthcare very much, paying a relatively small constant monthly premium while agreeing to pay handsomely for treatment if you need it. The appeal of such plans is that their monthly premiums are usually lower than with other insurance structures. However, when you incur health expenses, you pay more for them yourself (that's your deductible) before the insurance coverage kicks in.

This gives being an informed patient a monetary value. In casinos, on average, the house wins; gamblers, on average, lose. In medical insurance we're betting on our health as well as on our wallet. Yet with high-deductible plans, our betting capabilities can only carry us so far, and the house (aka the insurer) still wants to win. The Commonwealth Fund found that the average per person deductible more than doubled between 2003 and 2013, and employers increasingly offer only high-deductible plans.[10]

According to NYU historian Beatrix Hoffman, high-deductible plans did not bring down medical costs, nor did they curb spending for the American consumer, who had to pay large sums when battling a health condition or illness. In addition, out-of-network expenses don't count toward meeting the deductible and reaching the limit after which the insurer picks up the tab.[11] So the consumer pays out of pocket.

Behavioral economics can help us understand what this means and how it plays out. Prospect theory, developed by Nobel Prize winner Daniel Kahneman along with Amos Tversky, forms the foundation of behavioral economics.[12] The theory posits that our feelings toward and evaluations of what we receive, own, or lose aren't rational. That is, these feelings and evaluations aren't based on mathematics. One of the tenets of prospect theory is that losses loom larger than gains. Losing something, or even paying for something so our wealth is diminished, causes us some emotional pain. This pain is greater than the joy we experience when we gain. Every single payment hurts.

There are more financial considerations around health. High-deductible insurance plans have relatively low premiums, because you're supposed to cover many expenses with a Health Savings Account (HSA). These accounts allow health consumers to set money aside, tax-free, in order to pay for qualified medical expenses, from copayments to contact lenses, over-the-counter medication, compression socks, and condoms. Consumers have to estimate their health consumption ahead of time, betting on it versus anything else on which they would like to spend disposable income. But not every health expense is covered through HSAs, thereby further complicating the health consumer's life.[13]

Here is a bigger complication, marred by loss aversion. As the name "Health Savings Account" implies, whatever money isn't spent is saved for future health expenses. This can lead to hoarding money for unknowable future health needs rather than spending it on real, immediate ones. A guiding principle of prospect theory is that we are prone to favor the status quo. We like to keep things as they are, because any change implies losing something. A health expense is considered a loss: it reduces the amount of money in our savings account. And we are averse to losses. But with an HSA, we need to decide whether to keep our health savings in the event we need it for some big expense later or squander it, painfully, on Advil.

Fear of losing might be why, according to the Centers for Disease Control (CDC), in 2017 only 19 percent of adults with employment-based coverage enrolled in high-deductible health plans with a Health Savings Account.[14] Most eligible Americans preferred not to guess how much they would spend on their health each year. Instead, they paid for their physical therapy, contact lenses, and contraceptives from income they had already paid tax on—a decision any accountant would frown on. I'm not sure if the house won, but the consumers certainly lost.

Despite all this, those who get to make decisions over their health insurance at all are among the lucky ones. In 2018, 27.5 million Americans were uninsured.[15] Uninsured patients pay for every medical expense out of pocket, and those who don't have deep pockets can be driven to "consume" healthcare only if it's cheap or in case of an emergency.

THE PATIENT'S PLACE . . . AND THE INTERNET

The fourth force that has driven our involvement in our medical care is the internet. Patient involvement and a doctor-patient dialogue require that the patient be informed. But this is only feasible when patients can inform themselves and don't have to rely on their doctors as their sole source of knowledge. And what handier information source than the internet? The internet isn't a perfect source of knowledge (more about this in the next chapter), but its success is indisputable. In 1999, twenty-four out of every hundred people in developed countries such as the United States had access to the internet, and in 2017, it was eighty-one out of every hundred. In 2019, the Pew Research Center estimated that 90 percent of Americans use the internet and, at least in theory, have access to updated and valid medical information that can guide their health choices and their conversations with their physicians.[16]

The rise of personal biometric devices in recent years has given patients even more information to sort through. In January 2020, one in every five Americans had a smartwatch or fitness-tracker watch that could trace their heart rate, along with their sweat rate, brain activity, and other indicators that in the past could not be measured on your own. Home-use glucose trackers have been around since the 1980s. They allow people living with diabetes to monitor their blood sugar levels without having to go to a laboratory and wait for results. In theory, this is an unparalleled treasure trove, uniquely you-focused—but perhaps not in practice, as there is still little evidence that wearable devices provide a benefit for health outcomes.[17]

THOUGH THESE DRIVERS OF CHANGE WERE DISTINCT FROM ONE ANOTHER, they all propelled us in the same direction. The consumer climate prioritized choice. Informed consent provided the legal impetus for giving us knowledge and choice (and sanctions when we were denied them). High-deductible plans, Health Savings Accounts, and other ways of investing money in our health gave us financial incentives to be involved. The information highway gave us knowledge that could guide our care.

More than ever, we are invited to decide—and don't we have a knack for making the wrong decisions.

OH, THE MESSES YOU'LL MAKE
(OF YOUR MEDICAL DECISIONS)

Your health decisions and choices are up to you—they depend on your preferences, experiences, culture, and values. However, you don't always know what choices will work best for you. And your choices can also hurt others. The push to carry out COVID-19 vaccinations (or any other vaccinations, for that matter) is so strong because vaccinating not only protects the one vaccinated but also helps the community break virus transmission chains, thereby protecting those who cannot vaccinate for medical reasons.[18]

Some decisions are big, such as whether you enroll in cardiac rehabilitation following your heart attack. But seemingly small health and medical decisions can also accumulate and lead to a big impact overall. When you light a cigarette, you expose yourself to the risks of tobacco smoking: ask sixteen million Americans living with smoking-related diseases. When you stay on the couch or in the gaming chair instead of getting enough exercise, you, like 80 percent of American adults and children, expose yourself to the risks of obesity, heart disease, stroke, type 2 diabetes, and several types of cancer.[19] And we all know what can happen when you decide not to use a condom.

FEW OF US ACTIVELY CHOOSE TO HAVE COMPLICATIONS OF UNCONTROLLED diabetes, to fall deep into the pit of depression, or to become addicted to opiates. Sadly, these are just a few examples of events resulting from common "small" decisions people make with their medications. This is why improving the way we make medical decisions is so important.

Lipids are part of your "bad" cholesterol. They're fat-like molecules that cir-
culate in the blood, forming triglycerides. As many as 39 percent of the adult
population globally suffers from high lipids. Take Frederick, for example.
Frederick takes statins, lipid-lowering medications, such as atorvastatin (Lipi-
tor). High lipids can lead to big trouble. But until they do, they don't cause any
noticeable harmful symptoms.[20] This leads Frederick to doubt he was sick to
begin with or to question whether the medication is helping him. Why, then,
should he keep on taking his statins? Based on his intuitive thinking, he is
absolutely right. If nothing feels wrong, surely there isn't a problem. In fact,
it's a miracle Frederick started taking statins in the first place—a quarter of
patients don't fill their initial statin prescriptions.[21]

Medically, though, Frederick is absolutely wrong.[22] Doctors Lisa Rosenbaum and William Shrank encountered so many patients like Frederick
throughout the course of their careers that they wrote about it in the *New England Journal of Medicine*. Medications like statins aren't intended to heal patients. They are intended to reduce a patient's chances of becoming sick—in
this case, of experiencing a heart attack or a stroke.[23] And yet a study involving
over eighteen thousand people who were prescribed lipid-lowering medication like Frederick's, from thirty-nine countries, found that within a year, 14
percent of them had quit their statins, and that after seven years, fewer than
half were still taking them.[24]

DIABETES AFFECTS 463 MILLION PEOPLE GLOBALLY. IN THE LAST TWENTY
years, the number of American adults diagnosed with diabetes has more
than doubled.[25] And patients' decision-making around diabetes is not
promising.

One-tenth of people receiving an initial type 2 diabetes diagnosis don't
fill their new prescriptions.[26] They schlep to the doctor's office, pay a co-pay,
see their doctor, discuss how a new medication might help them, get a prescription, then go home without stopping at the pharmacy on the way.

They may want to manage their diabetes through exercise and nutrition instead. Still, they could call on their doctor's expertise to understand whether
this is plausible given their current blood sugar levels, how to monitor the
blood sugar level during a trial period of lifestyle change, and when to revisit

their regimen to avoid the complications—glaucoma, kidney disease, or loss of sensation in limbs—that arise from unmanaged diabetes.[27]

More than half of those who are prescribed diabetes medication quit taking it after one year. Dolores, Frederick's wife, is one of them. This explains why she always feels hungry and tired and why her cuts and wounds heal slowly. In the long run, Dolores and others like her face faster progression of disease, greater spending, and higher mortality rates.[28]

OR CONSIDER ANOTHER AILMENT, DEPRESSION. DEPRESSION AFFECTS 264 million people globally. It is considered the most disabling condition worldwide. It causes people to suffer and to function poorly at work, at school, and at home.

Eileen had been suffering from depression for a long time. Finally, she and her doctor found the right medication and dosage. The antidepressants kicked in! Then Eileen erroneously thought that she no longer needed the medication since she no longer felt depressed, even though that meant the medication was working and that she should keep taking it. What Eileen didn't know was that because her body was already accustomed to the medication, if she were to go cold turkey, she would probably experience withdrawal symptoms similar to flu symptoms, or much worse—insomnia, anxiety, and suicidal thoughts— everything Eileen took the medication to avoid in the first place. She found this out the hard way, and she is not alone. Unfortunately, half of all patients prescribed antidepressants decide to stop taking them prematurely.[29]

FREDERICK, DOLORES, AND EILEEN ARE CHARACTERS I CREATED BASED ON many patients' experiences. Across medical conditions and populations, five out of ten people don't take their medication as directed.[30] Yes, that is half of us. Of course, patients sometimes forget. Once, in Finland on a business trip, I was sitting in a park, admiring the birch trees and writing about nonadherence to medication, when I suddenly realized I had forgotten to take the pill I take each morning. I had left it in my travel toiletries kit. Forgetfulness is common, but while problematic, it doesn't involve a deliberate decision-making process.

Ditching meds altogether or skipping doses are decisions that need to be made responsibly. Each year, 125,000 Americans die because they do not take their medication as prescribed.[31] Adverse drug events—such as lowering blood sugar too far, to the point where a person experiences dizziness, blurry vision, palpitations, and anxiety—cause 770,000 injuries or deaths and cost up to $5.6 billion each year in the United States.[32] We need to be able to make good decisions about which medication to take and for how long, and then adhere to what was decided.

ON OPIOIDS AND ALTOIDS

Opioids are a specific kind of medication, and we know they are beneficial in dealing with extreme pain. You are probably well aware of the extreme risks they carry.

In 2017, out of every one hundred Americans, seventeen had an opioid prescription filled. In fact, among those seventeen, the average patient received more than three opioid prescriptions, each lasting eighteen days. This is bad news. Opioids become more likely to cause addiction or death with prolonged use. In 2017, 2 million Americans misused prescription opioids for the first time. A similarly large group, 2.1 million, had an opioid use disorder causing them clinical distress or impairment. That year, forty-six people died each day from overdoses involving prescription opioids. In light of this, the US Department of Health and Human Services declared the "opioid epidemic" a public emergency.[33]

To help address opioid addiction, the *Lancet* set a special commission to explore opioid use. The commission estimated that the US population received thirty times more opioid pain relief medication than it required.[34] That is a frightening quantity of opioids, and its consequences are equally frightening. In 2019, Oklahoma became the first state to sue a drug manufacturer— Johnson & Johnson—for its share in the opioid crisis that cost the lives of around six thousand Oklahomans.[35] The state was awarded $572.1 million to fund addiction treatment and prevention.

I came across an enraged letter to the *Journal of the American Pharmacists Association* by Kansas City anesthesiologist and critical care professor Brigid C. Flynn. Dr. Flynn cited a conversation she had overheard at a busy airport between a woman who was rummaging through her overstuffed bag and a man who asked what she kept there. The woman triumphantly pulled out a prescription bottle and said, "You never know when you'll need a Vicodin!" as though it were the occasional Altoid.[36] The man said, "Vicodin! And they aren't even prescribed to you!" at which the fellow travelers shared a laugh. Not Dr. Flynn.

Given how dangerous opioids are, people need to be mindful in deciding when and how to take them and should bring up their concerns to gung ho prescribers. Making sensible opioid-related decisions is crucial, because even small doses of opioids can lead to addiction. One real problem is that many patients are simply unaware of this.

SOMEONE TO WATCH OVER ME

We rely on the notion that medical professionals will watch over their patients. What we often don't recognize is that doctors, hospitals, and insurers have other interests aside from their patients'. Opioids present a strong example of this. They are medications that can only be purchased (legally) with a doctor's prescription. In theory, doctors make the best, safest choices for their patients when it comes to opioids. In theory, when they don't, pharmacists notice and alert patients. We need their help because most of us don't know medications and doses, and, well, we are in pain.

However, as the Netflix documentary series *The Pharmacist* demonstrated, pharmacies are businesses, and they will keep selling medication even when they are aware that it jeopardizes their patients' health. This explains why one pharmacy chain did not question why a branch in a town with a population of 2,831 was ordering 3,271 bottles of oxycodone a month as long as the money was rolling in.[37] To be fair, like our doctors, most pharmacists are dedicated to helping their clients. It does not require malice or greed for pharmacy employees to skirt or ignore proper work procedures. They do so because of stress and what they feel are unrealistic expectations for medication delivery time. These feelings lead pharmacy employees to make mistakes while filling prescriptions or to ignore certain safety procedures. Without harboring any ill intent, they unknowingly contribute to the opioid epidemic. But still, they do contribute to it, and the chains and private pharmacy owners don't make them stop, thereby leaving us powerless.

IT TAKES ELEVEN YEARS TO BECOME A DOCTOR AND ANOTHER FIVE TO eight years to become a surgeon.[38] All so they can work tirelessly to promote their patients' health and save their lives. The notion that these professionals "work tirelessly" is no exaggeration: on average, doctors work 59.6 hours a week. From residency to retirement, they'll spend thirty-six years working, almost 1.5 times more than most other Americans.[39]

However, we cannot always count on our doctors to make the right decisions for us. An extreme example is a physician from the Mount Carmel Health System in Ohio. This physician was prescribing lethal doses of fentanyl. Fentanyl is fifty to one hundred times as potent as morphine. It's considered to be one of the most powerful opioids available.[40] In July 2019, the doctor was charged with murder after twenty-five of his patients died with fentanyl dosage levels of 500 micrograms and above.[41] The lawyer who represented seventeen of the victims' families said that one of the victims, Melissa Penix, an eighty-two-year-old lady with pneumonia, received 2,000 micrograms—enough to kill an elephant. The lawyer could not find a motive for the doctor's actions. The doctor's own attorney said he aimed at delivering "compassionate very-end-of-life-care."[42] Indeed, some of his patients, Penix among them, died within minutes of being administered the medication.

But this doctor, vile as the accusations against him are, isn't the story. An entire medical system failed to safeguard against hazardous prescribing, and as a result people died. That system ignored a pharmacist who declined to fill the 2,000 microgram fentanyl order and was bypassed (not for the first time) by the doctor. When the pharmacist expressed his concerns to his supervisor, he did not receive a response.[43] A month after the doctor was charged with twenty-five killings over a four-year period, the CEO of Mount Carmel Health System in Ohio resigned, and twenty-three employees were terminated.

DOCTORS DO ENTER THEIR PROFESSION WITH A SENSE OF DEDICATION AND a commitment to have patients' best interests at heart and to base their actions on clinical evidence, not dollar signs or fear of a lawsuit. Regrettably, they do not always hit their target. In 2010, the Institute of Medicine (IOM) suggested that "unnecessary services" are the largest contributor to waste in our healthcare system, accounting for approximately $210 billion of the estimated $750 billion in excess spending each year.[44] Again, this spending is for services performed or ordered by individual doctors, but such egregious sums cannot go unnoticed by hospital systems and clinic managers. It would be naive to think they were highly motivated to trim the unnecessary services that were bringing in additional profit.

Heather Lyu of Harvard Medical School asked two thousand physicians, "In your specialty, what percentage of overall care do you think is *unnecessary?*"[45] The answer was around 20 percent of overall medical care, including 25 percent of tests, 22 percent of prescription medications, and 11 percent of procedures. All the more reason to probe doctors for the reasons behind their choices. I'll show you how to do just that later in this book.

For the majority of doctors (85 percent), the most common reason for overtreatment was fear of being sued for malpractice. This ties in with the third most common reason for overtreatment: patient pressure or request, mentioned by 59 percent of the doctors. Doctors dislike conflict, and who can blame them—they are strapped for time and have the threat of being sued hanging over their heads. Then there are patients who regularly press for tests, medications, or procedures that conflict with their physicians' views.

The second most common reason for overtreatment was profit: 71 percent of physicians estimated that doctors were more likely to perform unnecessary procedures when they profited from them, tainting these encounters a sickly dollar green. "Fee for service" means that doctors are paid per number of tests, procedures, treatments, and so on they administer. Most respondents believed that de-emphasizing fee-for-service physician compensation would reduce healthcare utilization and costs. On the bright side, Lyu also showed that 38 percent of clinicians believed that value-based compensation would significantly improve the quality of care, and 36 percent believed that it would significantly lower costs.

Fee-for-value payment models, on the other hand, pay doctors based on health outcomes: "Providers are rewarded for helping patients improve their health, reduce the effects and incidence of chronic disease, and live healthier lives in an evidence-based way." The transition from a fee-for-service payment model for hospitals and clinicians is a paradigmatic shift in the health system, and a slow one at that. Fee-for-service models still bring in 75 percent of health organizations' revenue.[46]

According to Dr. Daniel Sands of Harvard Medical School, at least some fee for service is here to stay, which is a plus. If healthcare organizations are only paid for patients' health outcomes, they are motivated to avoid the sickest and most complex patients, as well as patients who do not (or cannot) adhere to care plans. As long as a fee-for-service paradigm exists and as long as doctors view medical affairs through different lenses than patients do, we should take care to invest our own judgment to monitor what is being offered and done to us.

More than ever before, we have wide options, greater power, and an increased capacity to be good stewards of our own health. And yet we see that the trend toward consumer choice in healthcare comes with a caveat. The stakes of medical choices can literally be life and death. It matters that we have all the help we can get in making them. We're not in Starbucks anymore, Toto.

Even with a new, more desirable payment structure, there's no real guarantee patients will be able to get the advice they need. Doctors struggle under time constraints, strenuous conditions, financial requirements, lawsuit threats, the desire to do good, and the fear of making mistakes. Clinics and hospital systems, as well as pharmacists, have their bottom lines in mind—not just patients' best interests.

None of this is to suggest that we shouldn't seek help from doctors. Of course we should, and of course we should listen very carefully to what they have to say. But now more than ever it is important that we prepare ourselves to make our own medical decisions. Even if our healthcare professionals have our best interests in mind, we are still the only ones who can combine our feelings and preferences with the appropriate medical information in order to reach the decision that is right for us.

All things considered and all obstacles acknowledged, we are incredibly lucky. Our health and medical decisions are intrinsically ours. We are the only ones who know what feels right to us, and we also must live with our choices. We are lucky to be living at a time when we are openly invited to partake in medical decisions. Admittedly, it's hard, but it's also unprecedented and empowering. In theory.

In the next chapter we'll learn why in reality this is so hard.

TAKEAWAYS

The takeaways for this chapter are inspired by Superman and Wonder Woman pajamas: wearing them does not grant you their superpowers, such as the ability to fly. And if you think they do, let's hope you don't live on the tenth floor.

As health consumers are given more choice and as more information is readily available, patients need to make sure that their decisions—on their health habits, medication, procedures—are the right ones for them. And this is hard. We all have our own powers, regardless of what pajamas we wear. We should be proud of our powers, use them, and know their limitations.

FOR PATIENTS:

1. You are a health consumer, and you have a right to be involved in decisions surrounding your health.
2. Make sure that whatever you ask of your doctor is medically sound.
3. Your healthcare providers aim to do good, most of the time.
4. As any superhero would tell us, if you want to win, you can only rely on yourself.

FOR HEALTHCARE PROFESSIONALS:

1. Patients are health consumers, and they have a right to be involved in decisions surrounding their health. This is here to stay.
2. Even when it is obvious to you why a prescription is necessary, explain to the patient why you are writing it, especially if the patient's condition is asymptomatic. Make sure he or she understands why it's a bad idea not to adhere to the treatment plan and then experience the consequences.
3. To the degree that it is possible, prescribe medications, tests, and procedures based on your better professional judgment, not on patient pressure, fear of lawsuit, or financial considerations.
4. You came into medicine in order to heal people and do good in the world. No one should ever make you forget that.

FOR HEALTHCARE SYSTEMS:

1. Patients are health consumers, and they have a right to be involved in decisions surrounding their health. This is here to stay. Create the necessary mechanisms to enable this involvement to occur.

2. Doctors are under tremendous pressure, between work demands and patients' wishes. Supervise them to make sure their judgment is medically justified. Opioid prescribing is an obvious example.

3. By creating guidelines for prescribing medication, tests, and procedures, you'll be helping doctors withstand patient pressure for non-evidence-based prescribing.

4. Many health institutions are for-profit enterprises. Regardless, when advertising, provide complete, accurate information that will allow patients to choose well. Don't be misleading. Otherwise, even if you're not breaking the law, you are not playing fair.

CHAPTER 2

DELIVER ME FROM THINKING

In June 2019 alone, there were nearly seventy-six million visits to WebMD.[1] Googling "How to lower blood pressure" got over six million results, and "How to lose weight fast" got over twenty-four million. Never before have we had so much information at our fingertips. So why do we still seem to know so little about the treatments available to us?

In practice, access to medical information often has little to do with whether we make good choices about our health. In this chapter, I'll outline the basic psychological processes through which we form judgments and make choices: bounded rationality, being a cognitive miser, and System 1 thinking. They all mean that, in spite of our sophistication, our thinking is shaped to deal with evolutionary problems and to come up with quick and dirty answers. We must understand our human limitations, and we cannot ignore them and simply ask people—both doctors and patients—to "think harder." Without knowing these processes exist, it is impossible to understand the unique issues that suffuse all medical decision-making.

From these basic limitations stems an entire catalog of heuristics and biases, but the main principles of how they operate can be explained by looking at just a few: the framing effect, the routes to persuasion, the affect heuristic (particularly relevant when dealing with our health), and the confirmation bias.

But first, let's talk about sandwiches, and the thought processes at our disposal for choosing among them.

THINK ONE AND THINK TWO

It's lunchtime and you're hungry. The cafeteria offers a bacon, egg, and cheese croissant; a veggie wrap; a ham and Swiss panini; a club sandwich; and a grilled cheese sandwich. You just want to grab a sandwich and get back to work. This does not involve deep thinking. If I asked you why you chose the one you did, you would probably shrug or say "I felt like it." This isn't just how we think about sandwiches. This is how we think, period.

We are, by default, reluctant to use our brain power because we all have limited time, knowledge, attention, and mental capabilities.[2] Herbert Simon outlined these limitations when he introduced the idea of "bounded rationality." It was a bold departure from the prevailing concept that decision-makers had to adhere to "axioms" of rationality—rules based on mathematical reasoning. If people strayed from the axioms, they existed in a rationality-free no-man's-land, which neither economists nor other scientists cared to model. Instead, Simon postulated that people are rational (that is, they adhere to logical rules, ones that make sense and are clear to them) but not in a perfectly mathematical way. People seek to arrive at answers and make rational decisions within these limitations, while curbing the cost of thinking. Simon paved the way to examining our imperfect decision processes instead of dismissing them for not being rational. He won the Nobel Prize in Economics in 1978 for providing people with a stamp of approval to make decisions that are based on a far-from-perfect use of their gray cells.

Other frameworks overlap with Simon's. Psychologists Susan Fiske and Shelley Taylor claim that people are "cognitive misers"—that is, we treat our brain power as a valuable resource and spend as little of it as possible.[3] My students have heard me tell them a thousand times, "You're lazy." Before they run to the dean to complain, I say "I'm lazy too." We all are: our minds are wired to be thought-lazy no matter how smart we are. We turn to cognitive miserliness by using mental shortcuts instead of thoroughly reviewing evidence. If the lettuce in the club sandwich appears tired, we reach for the grilled cheese sandwich without giving it another thought.

As Daniel Kahneman most recently conceptualized it, we think fast and slow.[4] Kahneman suggests that, although we are often unaware of it, we use two different kinds of thought processes when making decisions: System 1 and System 2. System 1 is fast and effortless. We use it when we count to ten, open a beer bottle, or decide that we dislike a man just by the sound of his voice. System 1 helps us proceed with life without giving it too much thought—a useful thing when maximum speed of processing is more important than accuracy. Many of the little choices we make throughout our days are best handled by System 1. Courtesy of System 1, we often apply heuristics—mental shortcuts that we use as rules of thumb when we wish to avoid wrinkling our forehead.

System 2 is a deliberate, effortful, and slower way of thinking. Using System 2 processes, you could spend an hour in front of the sandwich counter comparing the dietary qualities of club versus grilled cheese. You would be maximizing accuracy and reaching a judgment based on a logical—as opposed to emotional—analysis of all the evidence. You would also be hungry and tired. We use System 2 when we calculate a 15 percent tip on a $137.60 check (although we probably use System 1 to decide how much to tip), when we follow a complicated recipe for the first time, and when we compare the grilled cheese with the club based on calories, sodium, carbohydrates, and protein.

System 1 is so named because it's the first one to be implemented, not because it is better. We alternate between the two systems. They coexist because the benefits they provide and the circumstances in which they are used are very different. What is good for a quick response when survival is at risk works less well for reading scientific medical narratives. And yet, bounded rationality, being a cognitive miser, and System 1 are our go-to thinking strategies. The choice to apply them isn't conscious. It just happens, and it is therefore perhaps more influential than if we had deliberately planned to adopt them. Since this is how we think, we don't always mull over information, even when we are capable of understanding it (and as we will later see, we can't always understand it). That our minds are effort-saving rather than accuracy-driven makes it easy to manipulate us and give us incomplete information, even when our health is concerned.

JUST AS WE SEEK EASY PROCESSING AND QUICK ANSWERS, SO, TOO, DO OUR overworked doctors. For a few years, I led a series of tech-exposure events within Health 2.0, a New York City group composed of entrepreneurs, technology bigshots, physicians, and health administrators. At that time, the group had about four thousand members; it now has more than seven thousand. We found that interoperability—the ability to connect seamlessly within and between systems, such as health records and devices—can be a stumbling block for doctors, who do not have the time, mental space, or wherewithal to learn how to use every application and technology out there. It is just too hard. To help doctors make better, smarter, easier decisions that improve our health, solutions from behavioral economics and smart information technology (IT) must minimize cognitive effort.

"NONSTANDARD," REBELLIOUS, OR USELESS CANCER TESTING

Even when accuracy is crucial, and we would like to make ourselves slower thinkers and deliberate on the evidence, it can be difficult or impossible. We do not have the ability to critically evaluate the information we're given because of our relative ignorance. The world's greatest authority on abstract expressionism or international taxation is probably at sea when aiming to determine the worth of the personalized cancer treatment a cancer center is promoting.

Here is a striking example of why I have so little faith in our ability to evaluate cancer treatments: researchers at the Dana-Farber Cancer Institute in Boston examined the reliability of the communication of cancer center websites. To do this, they put together a panel of fourteen faculty and staff members, each an expert in one or more specialty areas.[5] The panel identified cancer-related websites that offered personalized cancer medicine: one or more tests, products, or services that could be used to tailor care based on genomic or tumor-derived data. Then the researchers classified the tests that were offered as "standard" or "nonstandard."

"Standard" meant that thirteen of the fourteen professionals who reviewed the evidence agreed the test was useful. Testing could yield improved health outcomes by helping with drug selection or dosing; informing prevention, early detection, or treatment strategies; establishing a definitive diagnosis;

or helping assess a prognosis. For example, mutations in the BRCA1 gene indicate that the carrier is at considerable risk of developing breast and ovarian cancer. This information might lead a woman to decide to have her breasts removed as a preventative measure against the disease.

If testing results weren't medically actionable, they could be useful for personal decision-making. People with one copy of the APOE4 gene variant are at an increased risk for early-onset Alzheimer's disease. Two copies of this variant imply an even higher risk. Medically, there is nothing to do about it. Regardless, the result might lead you to write a will and to discuss what care you'd like to receive in case you develop Alzheimer's.

"Nonstandard" may have a hip, rebellious sound to it, but it actually refers to tests that lack evidence of clinical utility. Nonstandard tests say something that means nothing. They have not been proven to prevent or improve adverse health outcomes (such as mortality). The results of these tests cannot be used to decide which treatment to choose. They indicate the presence of gene variants, but as any genetic counselor knows, our genes offer many VUSs, variants of unknown significance. In the cancer context, some nonstandard tests can, for example, detect gene mutations that haven't been proven to help with risk assessment for breast or pancreatic cancer. In prenatal testing, counselors give women the option not to know about a VUS in the baby because it is meaningless and learning about it can cause unhelpful anxiety. Over time, these genes may be found to contribute to diagnosis or treatment decisions. But when the Dana-Farber panel reviewed them, the variants detected by nonstandard tests were found to be useless.

Most (over 80 percent) of the tumor testing that websites offered was nonstandard. In other words, most of the available options were medically useless. Even though "marketing may be detrimental if it endorses products of unproven benefit," websites were more likely to market nonstandard tests than standard tests.[6] Most tests advertised won't help clients make good decisions; they will make them poorer. The cost of the testing offered by the commercial websites reviewed ranged from $99 to $13,000—big ticket items, and in many cases, a total waste of money.

It took a medical village to evaluate all aspects of state-of-the-art testing—this is a massive System 2 effort. Ability is required. And where does this leave you? No better off. Fourteen experts are not the kind of team you can summon to your living room when you are pondering a test for a tumor and trying to distinguish the valid from the invalid, standard from nonstandard.

The websites reviewed belonged to commercial companies, academic institutions, physicians, research institutes, and similar organizations. Of the commercial sites, fewer than a third prompted patients to discuss the personalized cancer products with their physician.

ALL THE RISKS YOU CANNOT SEE

Assuming we are willing to spend the cognitive effort to appraise our options, we need an opportunity to do so. For sandwiches, we want to be able to see them and to read about their nutritional value. In pharma ads that tell us about medication, we also want to see all the relevant information, but we are unlikely to. While these ads are running through a medication's side effects and risks, they show distracting images, soothing footage of nature and happy families. The images hinder viewers' processing of the verbal information (which is far less soothing) by creating a mismatch between them. This is cognitively demanding, and our minds resolve to the easy solution: we focus our attention on the blooming daisies and the sweet children. We treat the long (potentially alarming) list of side effects and risks as background noise. These ads teeter on the line of what was once considered the fair balance of information presentation—a condition for allowing pharma advertising. Some even call it deception.[7]

This is why I went to such great lengths to discuss bounded rationality, being a cognitive miser, and System 1 thinking. We shouldn't just blame viewers for not trying hard enough to process the perils of medication. Viewers are being duped, falling prey to advertisers who are all too familiar with how we think.

Discrepancies, and sometimes gaping holes, in the way information is presented to us are prevalent on numerous medical platforms. When it comes to cancer treatments, a complete set of evidence would give us the opportunity to learn about their risks, not just their benefits. Yet the researchers from Dana-Farber found that although most websites of cancer centers contained information about the benefits of personalized cancer medicine, fewer than a third discussed its limitations.[8] It's an appalling discrepancy. We cannot weigh limitations when we don't know what they are.

We should not be surprised, since these websites deliver marketing communication. They aim to sell, not to fully inform.

Cancer treatments can have some unpleasant side effects that patients need to be aware of and consider before choosing a treatment. Anemia, bleeding, delirium, fertility, and sexual issues—the list on the National Cancer Institute's website goes on and on. Another study, conducted by the University of Pittsburgh, looked at cancer center advertisements in top US consumer magazines and on television.[9] They found that a measly 2 percent of these avenues mentioned risks.

But don't enraged patients and their family members call the centers, demanding to learn about the missing pieces? Don't they question the quality of the information they received and therefore also the quality of the treatments? The answer to both these questions is no. In fact, advertisers count on patients not noticing the holes and gaps in the information they provide. Brilliant though we might be, our minds' automatic mode of operation is to accept things at face value instead of identifying potential pitfalls and risks.

In addition, our brains are such magnificent instruments that we don't need to worry about lacking information or be concerned when we make decisions based on too little evidence. This doesn't mean we actually have valid information, just that we feel we do. Our "associative memory" (the core of System 1) continually constructs a coherent interpretation of what is happening in our world at any instance.[10] We feel that we have a complete picture, even if we've only seen snippets.

Kahneman and Tversky, the same researchers who brought prospect theory to the world, also conceived the heuristics and biases paradigm.[11] As I mentioned, heuristics are mental shortcuts that help us reach quick conclusions. They are congruent with what Kahneman later defined as System 1. They also save cognitive effort and are driven by bounded—not full-fledged—rationality. The biases occur when some cues appear and sway our conclusions and choices in a specific direction. Framing is a very effective bias: people accept information in the way it was framed for them.[12] Playing around with what is presented to us and reversing the framing requires us to use our gray matter. Instead, we stick with what we've got, the way we got it.

During my time teaching consumer behavior at Wharton, and in many other instances, I've seen even the brightest individuals fall prey to framing bias. I taught my students about framing, then told them about a lethal disease for which there was a solution that would save one-third of the patients. They voted in favor of this solution. Then, I showed another solution—it would kill two-thirds of the patients. They voted against it, even though it was the flip side of the solution they had just voted for. Their System 1 quickly evaluated the framing: "save" is good, whereas "kill" is bad. Framing is why when we only talk about the third of patients who are saved, no one ever asks, "But what about the others?"

THE PERSUASIVE POWER OF FLOWERS

If you manufacture and produce club sandwiches, you want cafeteria patrons to choose them over grilled cheese, with as little mental effort as possible. In the same vein, if you are the director of a cancer center, you want prospective patients to choose your center over others. To do this, you need to persuade them that yours is the best, and you need to have them expend as little mental effort as possible, because the way we are persuaded is closely tied up with the way we think in general. Our cognitive mechanisms—and cognitive limitations—close in on us from every direction.

Enter psychologists Richard Petty and John Cacioppo, who studied persuasion.[13] They claimed that people were persuaded through two different methods of processing information—the central route and the peripheral route. They called their theory "The Elaboration Likelihood Model" and gauged the likelihood that a person will elaborate on a message, using the central route to persuasion.

The central route is akin to Kahneman's System 2. It is elaborate and logical. In this route, a person is persuaded by the arguments at the heart of the matter. In choosing a sandwich, these arguments could involve the glycemic value of the bread and whether there's any saturated fat in the filling. In choosing a cancer center, a person might weigh whether the center has been approved by the Commission on Cancer of the American College of Surgeons and whether it has participated in clinical trials and worked in accordance with evidence-based guidelines.[14]

Petty and Cacioppo explained that evaluating the arguments via the central route is not easy because appraising arguments requires three things: motivation, opportunity, and ability. Motivation is self-explanatory, and when it comes to cancer treatments, we can assume your motivation for choosing what's best is high. Opportunity means you had the time to delve deep into the arguments for and against, and that all the information you needed to review was available to you. Ability means you had the knowledge and skills to look at that information, assess it, compare between alternatives, and establish your choice based on this evaluation. This isn't easy to come by; try deciphering a diagram of a radiation machine emitting x-rays, a table of survival rates, or any other central-route evidence. According to Petty and Cacioppo, we need all three conditions to process information through the central route. When you lack them, you use the peripheral route and wrinkle your forehead no more.

The peripheral route is akin to Kahneman's System 1—it is quick and effortless and does not attempt to get to the bottom of issues. Petty and Cacioppo named it the peripheral route because when we utilize it we are persuaded not by the arguments at the heart of the matter but by the elements surrounding them. In fact, "a simple cue in the persuasion context affects attitudes in the absence of argument processing."[15] Some examples of such cues are the quantity of arguments we've been given (try "there are a ton of reasons to choose this medication," regardless of the quality of those reasons), the attractiveness of the person delivering the message, fast-paced talk, and emotion.

Instead of looking at diagrams and tables indicating success rates for patients, we use cues. Show me a radiation machine that's decorated with flowers, a handsome doctor with a reassuring smile, or a beautiful young woman high-fiving her toned boyfriend as they leave the cancer center behind them. These would be peripheral indicators that this cancer center offers the best treatment. The flowers, smiles, and high-fives help us save cognitive effort and tell us that this center is awesome. They bring us hope and create persuasion. They also evoke the affect heuristic,[16] which leads us to choosing and liking things because they have an emotional appeal.

EMOTIONAL CUES—THE HOPE-AND-FEAR APPEAL

We don't have a panel of fourteen experts sitting in our living room, and companies know that. They know we can do our own research in order to determine quality of testing, treatment, care, or anything else they expect us to buy from them. They also know this research will be hard: the information might be buried in medical journals, drowned in jargon. Companies—and cancer centers—make it easy for us to use System 1 rather than System 2.

Often, ads rely on the affect heuristic: "Using an overall, readily available affective impression can be far easier—more efficient—than weighing the pros and cons or retrieving from memory many relevant examples, especially when the required judgment or decision is complex or mental resources are limited."[17] Tell me a sandwich is "Like Mom Used to Make" and I'll choose it, because it offers a quick, emotionally positive answer to the question of what to eat.

The affect heuristic—a peripheral mean of persuasion—is one of advertisers' preferred tools. To examine how it works, researchers from the University of Pittsburgh, in the study mentioned above, scrutinized 409 ads placed by 102 cancer centers in top US consumer magazines and on television.[18]

The vast majority of the ads used emotional appeals. Hope was the most often used—around two-thirds of the ads evoked hope with messages such as "Our advanced care adds another dimension to cancer care. Hope."[19] Hope is wonderful—unless it maneuvers you in the wrong direction and proves to be false.

Fear came in second, with wording like "When David was diagnosed with cancer in his chest, he felt like he was losing everything."[20] This is textbook fear-based persuasion: first the fear-inducing image, then the solution that will alleviate the fear suggested by a seemingly reliable source. Using the solution—going to the center that posted the ad—increases your sense of self-efficacy.[21] Fear appeared in a third of the ads.

Hope and fear are purely System 1. They are emotional. They also tell a story, and stories are far more compelling than statistics. People love them, remember them, repeat them to their friends, and take them at face value. That's human nature. Kahneman and Tversky found that people will only use statistics if they have to, if there's no easy (System 1) way of reaching a conclusion. Otherwise, give people a good story and they'll believe it—ignoring any evidence that the story is not entirely plausible.[22]

Accordingly, nearly half the advertisements included patient testimonials, usually focused on survival or cure. Testimonials that evoke either hope or fear provide plenty of personal, gushy details and brave smiles. They are memorable and easy to process. Everyone loves a good testimonial—myself included. What I don't love, however, is the fact that the testimonials never describe the results a typical patient might expect.

Cancer centers often advertise a miraculous recovery and neglect to mention that miracles are rare. Only 15 percent of the ads included a disclaimer such as "Most patients do not experience these results."[23] Without the disclaimer, anyone reading the ad can hope to also have the outstandingly good outcomes because that is what is presented to them. We are bombarded with beguiling narratives that are too good to be true and often cannot really be true for most of us. We are not in control of the narratives we're fed, and we don't even notice when they deviate from the truth.

THE CONFIRMATION BIAS—KEEPING A CLOSED MIND

We have now covered multiple psychological mechanisms, and we must become familiar with another one—the one that keeps our minds closed. The confirmation bias guarantees that once an idea gets into our heads, whether it's a good idea or not and whether it got there through the central or the peripheral route, it will stay there. It's our human tendency to stick with our preliminary hypothesis or the first idea we had (sketchy as it may be) and to look for information that supports what we're already thinking and discredit evidence that does not support our thoughts or convictions.

In my PhD dissertation I examined the confirmation bias in the context of evaluating job candidates, but the bias appears everywhere.[24] It is one of the reasons why it's so hard to convince your friends to switch their dim-witted political views to yours—or you to switch yours to theirs, for that matter. It's a powerful mechanism that also applies to medicine. Suppose you were persuaded by a hope-appeal ad for your pancreatic cancer. When you hear that the test the ad is offering doesn't meet the National Comprehensive Cancer Network guidelines, your first reaction is to belittle this contradictory evidence or dismiss it altogether. The bias will get you to say things like "What do these national guidelines even know?"

Sticking with an initial belief is the easiest thing to do cognitively—much easier than thoroughly weighing the pros and cons, evidence and counterevidence. Even if you want to learn more about the test, you look for proof that the test is good, not for some nonsense (as you perceive it) to show that it's basically junk. In order to capture your attention and persuade you, the nonstandard test doesn't have to be better than any other test. It just needs to get to you first, ideally with some System 1 emotional cues and peripheral means of persuasion. Confirmation bias will make sure that once it gets in your mind, it stays there.

WE NEED ALL THE HELP WE CAN GET

Although we are constantly provided with opportunities to make our own medical decisions, we are often ill-prepared to make them. The psychological mechanisms I've highlighted here, as well as the commercial forces that take advantage of them, are just a handful of the obstacles making it difficult to gain critical, valid knowledge of the medical issues we face.

Given what we now know of our thinking, are we really capable of handling all that extra responsibility? No, of course not! In the following chapters, you will see why it is unfair to ask patients to navigate a healthcare system that is still not set up to help them make better judgments.

In theory, when patients' knowledge is incomplete and online sources are dubious or unapproachable, or when patients understand but still have concerns, they can consult with their doctors. In practice, the doctor-patient relationship can be another barrier to an instructive two-way dialogue. This relationship is the focus of the next chapter.

TAKEAWAYS

The takeaways for this chapter are inspired by the Greek philosopher Socrates. He proposed that men (and I add "and women") must strive to discover the truth. Freedom, he thought, was freedom from false beliefs and self-deceit. He did not have cancer treatments in mind. The only concoction we know he consumed was the poison administered to kill him, and he had no false beliefs about it. Still, he was spot on.

As more and more choice is provided to health consumers and as more and more information is readily available, patients can at least aim to discover the truth. They need to make sure that their decisions—around their health habits, medication, procedures, the works—are based on valid, complete evidence. Many psychological and commercial mechanisms conspire against patients, encouraging partial (and sometimes flat-out false) beliefs.

FOR PATIENTS:

1. Be aware that you are a cognitive miser, and your mind is programmed to save on effort rather than maximize accuracy.
2. When viewing medical information, especially ads and commercials, activate your System 2, of slow, elaborate thinking. Your health deserves this.
3. If there are benefits, always ask how many of the people who receive this treatment will enjoy them.
4. If there are risks, always ask how many of the people who receive this treatment will suffer from them.
5. Be aware that what you don't see in ads and commercials or what your doctor neglects to mention (for example, risks and side effects) may very well still exist.
6. When an idea seems convincing, ask yourself, Am I being persuaded through the central route, by issues related to the core of the argument, or am I being persuaded by peripheral issues, such as the attractiveness of the presenter? Ideally, the answer is "the former."
7. Hope is important. But so is realism. Otherwise, hope can turn to hype. In the context of disease, this can be hyperdepressing.

FOR HEALTHCARE PROFESSIONALS:

1. Your patients are human; therefore they are prone to using mental shortcuts. Be sure to give them succinct, yet accurate, information.
2. When providing information about medication and treatments you propose, always tell your patient how many of the people who receive this treatment will enjoy the benefits.
3. When providing information about medication and treatments you propose, always tell your patient how many of the people who receive this treatment will suffer from side effects and other risks the medication or treatment carries.

4. Fear and hope are powerful, persuasive currencies. Use them with fairness and caution. Providing hope is magnificent; misleading your patients is malicious.

FOR HEALTHCARE SYSTEMS:

1. Patients have a right to be involved in decisions surrounding their health. They are also human and are therefore prone to using mental shortcuts. Make sure the persuasive materials you give them allow for careful scrutiny of the facts.

2. Fear and hope are powerful, persuasive currencies. Use them with fairness and caution, as persuading and selling cannot be your only goals. Even from a standpoint of institutional reputation, providing hope is magnificent; misleading your patients is malicious.

PART II

WHY IS IT SO HARD?

CHAPTER 3

"WHAT KIND OF A DOCTOR IS THIS?"

HEALING STARTS WITH YOUR RELATIONSHIP WITH YOUR DOCTOR

When thirty-five thousand people from thirty-five countries were asked what profession they respected the most, they said "doctor." When 1,001 Americans were asked about their trust in doctors, more than 900 of them reported it as high.[1] People worldwide sit glued to their TV screens, watching doctors' and health teams' heroic efforts on *ER*, *House*, *Grey's Anatomy*, *M*A*S*H** (the final episode had 125 million viewers!), *Scrubs*, and the indefatigable *General Hospital* (which started in 1963 and is still running after a short break due to COVID-19).

On TV, a doctor who is a brilliant misanthrope is tolerated. In real life, we expect our doctors to be personable. We want to feel that we have a relationship with them. Our lives depend on having good, caring doctors. And, as we'll see, we also depend on having a health system that cares about our doctors caring.

Doctor-patient relationships may seem like icing on the cake, a side benefit to healing. But the truth is that relationships play an essential role in good healthcare. When they turn sour or when they are never even allowed to develop, they form a barrier to being properly treated and, no less important, to feeling cared for. This relationship influences whether we persist with the life-saving treatment we're given, how we evaluate our doctors, and whether we sue them. This is an academic finding. It's also an intuitive truth we all feel, especially in critical situations. The doctor-patient relationship directly affects health outcomes. Doctors need to be instructed in how to nurture it, and medical institutions must sustain it.

In the first part of this chapter, I show that a respectful and communicative relationship is crucially important to patients. When they write thank-you letters, they gush about their doctors' personality and demeanor. Conversely, patients who feel dehumanized drive complaints and lawsuits. All these factors suggest that people judge doctors less by the outcomes of their treatment and more by their attitudes. Doctor-rating platforms follow a similar course.

We'll then see how impersonal relationships between patients and doctors actually hurt outcomes. Sometimes that's because doctors don't listen to patients' symptoms and accounts. And sometimes, it's because patients internalize their doctors' criticism or lack of care, almost like rejected children, and, accordingly, don't take care of themselves. We need our doctors to care, or to care enough, *so we'll be good enough patients*. We don't expect superheroes; we expect capable individuals, doing their best under challenging circumstances. I'll suggest institutional changes that can be made to promote a humane relationship between doctors and patients.

Finally, we'll see what happens when doctors feel humanized by patients and systems and the dire consequences—such as medical errors, burnout, and physician suicide—when they don't.

But first, let's talk about going to buy sneakers.

"WHAT KIND OF A DOCTOR IS THIS?"

One summer evening more than ten years ago, I was waiting for my mother outside the residential community where she lived to take her shopping. She had finally built up the confidence to join the gym and needed a pair of sneakers, the first she would ever own. But fate intervened when the building's sliding doors closed on her, throwing my tiny mother to the ground. She ended up with a broken hip and a broken arm.

That night at the hospital, Mom's arm was already in a cast, but her hip still needed surgery. Her insurance allowed her to choose the surgeon (and paid 90 percent of the charges). Who should be the surgeon?

We were obviously motivated to choose the best surgeon for her. But how should we do that? We didn't have the opportunity to examine a list of surgeons, let alone data on their success rates, the average age and physical condition of their patients, or any other validated information that would allow us to gauge the surgeon's skills and track record. I doubt such statistics are readily available anywhere. After the incredibly stressful evening we had just experienced, we also lacked the mental resources and the ability to make any educated judgments. No slow and elaborate information processing for us.

Instead, we resorted to one of the means of persuasion outlined by persuasion researcher Robert Cialdini: seeking authority.[2] In this means of persuasion, we rely on signals—such as diplomas on the wall, a uniform, or a warm recommendation—that a professional is credible and knowledgeable. The emergency department nurse was an authority on broken bones. We asked him for advice, and he recommended two surgeons, whom I immediately contacted.

The first, Dr. L., came to see my mother right away. He explained the procedure with his gaze fixed on his hiking boots, a great match to his shapeless old khakis. His monotonous tone suggested to me that he had performed the procedure—and explained it—several thousand times before. I assumed he would be more proficient with the knife than he was at connecting with his patients and gaining their trust. To my mom his manner suggested he was indifferent. After he left, she expressed her doubts. "What kind of a doctor is this?" she asked. She was tiny and broken but still insistent on feeling that her would-be surgeon cared about her. "I don't want him," was her verdict. Who could blame her? She wanted to be operated on by a good surgeon, one who cared about her. She used the latter criterion to gauge the former. Unknowingly, she applied a mental shortcut called attribute substitution, a psychological process defined by Daniel Kahneman and Shane Frederick.[3]

Attribute substitution means that when forming judgments, if you don't know the answer to a particular question (e.g., How good is this doctor?), you instead respond to the questions you are able to answer (e.g., Is the doctor's office clean, and does the doctor smile at me?). Mom had no way of assessing Dr. L.'s surgical skills. His appearance and his personableness were what she could evaluate. In both departments Dr. L. was lacking, appearing disheveled and failing to look her in the eye. Based on his poor interpersonal skills, my mother decided that his bone-reconnecting abilities must also be deficient. A big thumbs-down for Dr. L.—and a big health risk for my mother, because the second doctor never showed up and forgoing hip surgery can leave the hip displaced. The patient ends up suffering increased pain and unable to move.[4]

I didn't know how good a surgeon Dr. L. was. So I tried to reassure her on the interpersonal front. "I can tell he's a very nice person, Mom. He's just shy. That's why he didn't look at you." I even believed it. My mother let Dr. L. operate on her; he did a good job. She recovered, though she never made it to the gym.

"A PHENOMENAL PERSON AND DOCTOR"

My mother was not alone in wanting a relationship with her doctor, even one who only saw her briefly. This was my impression from glancing at thank-you letters to physicians. Over the years I have seen many such letters hanging on doctors' office walls. Patients are always thanking the doctors for listening, answering questions, being patient, being available. Not so much for their care.

Being a scientist, I wanted data rather than impressions. I analyzed a hundred thank-you letters from patients and family members that medical centers had posted online.[5] By their nature, these letters are idiosyncratic, reflecting what matters to a particular person at a particular moment. And one can assume that medical centers only posted the more positive letters. But by gathering so many, I gained a priceless peek into what patients noticed, appreciated, and chose to write about. I loved the raw glimpse into their hearts.

In the letters, people were as likely to thank healthcare providers for their personality and demeanor as for their medical skills. They—we—vividly remembered and were moved by personal gestures and interactions, especially ones that provided reassurance amidst worry and pain. People gushed with tributes like "The technician was so comforting and caring and sat with me while I waited for an ultrasound. She did not have to do that, but she was sweet." Or "Dr. Timothy D. was amazing at keeping me informed &

was very considerate of my feelings/emotions during the miscarriage I was experiencing."

While patients could appreciate nuances in interactions, they offered far less detail on the intricacies of the treatment, and what they did offer was mostly from the perspective of how treatment made them feel: "They made sure my pain level was tolerable." Often, patients used general accolades like "I had two nurses that took great care of me." This broad-strokes approach was justifiable: as patients, we lack medical knowledge, so we resort to saying, "He took great care of me," instead of saying, "The way he stitched the nasty cut on my arm reduced the risk of infection by 52 percent."

The one quality of medical care that did come up often in the letters was how treatment had worked out. People mostly mentioned their treatment outcomes: recovering, being free of pain, or regaining the capabilities that had been lost due to illness.

Outcomes give the long-term perspective on medical care and are easy to detect. Here is what one parent wrote about the treatment outcomes for his baby, who had had a liver transplant: "Now Dean truly is . . . a good size and growing fast." I'm sure the grateful parent was highly appreciative of the doctor's skills in having performed the transplant. But, as a layperson, he could not perceive or describe the skill involved in the procedure. Instead, and understandably, he perceived and rejoiced in the outcome: little Dean, who used to be small and yellowish, had become "a typical toddler."

LETTERS OF COMPLAINT ARE THE MIRROR IMAGE OF THANK-YOU LETTERS, and they, too, are idiosyncratic. A review of studies exploring online patient complaints provided insights that resembled the ones I gleaned from the thank-you letters. Dissatisfied patients' complaints converged on several topics.[6] Half the patients' grievances were about interpersonal and emotional issues: their doctors did not respect their values, preferences, or expressed needs; neglected to provide information or emotional support; and failed to alleviate their fear and anxiety.[7] A quarter of the patients criticized doctors' lack of skills and knowledge and the care environment—geographically and in terms of affordability.

The complaints proved that human interaction with their doctor meant as much and perhaps more to the patients as medical outcomes: under 2 percent of the patients complained about the expected outcomes of their treatment. The rest were either satisfied with how the treatment had turned out or accepted that treatment was a bumpy process. I've also seen patients sideline poor medical outcomes if the patient and doctor had a strong relationship. One husband wrote an enthusiastic thank-you letter to his wife's doctor even though she didn't fully recover. We come to the doctor to heal, but we first and foremost want to be treated as humans.

Doctor-patient relationships that go sour sometimes lead to malpractice lawsuits, which have become expensive and prevalent, leading some physicians to leave the profession altogether.[8] Rather than blaming greedy insurance companies or belligerent patients, two Baylor University researchers summarized evidence from deposition transcripts, questionnaires to plaintiffs, and surveys of families who had filed medical malpractice claims. They found that the decision to sue was associated not so much with the administrative load that the patients had to bear, insurance hoops they needed to jump through, or even medical mistakes as with "a breakdown in the patient-physician relationship, most often manifested as unsatisfactory patient-physician communication."[9]

The depositions are a master class in how to alienate patients. Patients complained that their doctors would not listen, did not understand their perspective, or did not respect their views. Doctors were perceived as being misleading, failing to warn against impending problems, or delivering information poorly. Patients felt that they had been deserted by their doctors.

A minority of patients' letters of complaint or gratitude pertained to the outcomes of care, and so it was with malpractice claims: unfavorable medical outcomes were forgivable; unfavorable human interaction was not. As the Baylor University researchers discovered, "Nothing defuses patient anger better and faster than a sympathetic, open-minded physician who is willing to discuss not just the successful outcomes of care but the glitches and problems that arise as well."[10]

TREATMENT OUTCOMES—WHETHER THE PATIENT WILL INDEED BE healed—matter enormously but cannot be guaranteed. Dr. Glyn Elwyn of Dartmouth College explained to me that outcomes are partially stochastic: they are subject to random events and cannot be fully predicted. For example, a carefully planned and carefully executed knee surgery can lead to an infection. Therefore, Elwyn claimed, a medical decision cannot be judged by how well it played out. It can only be judged by the quality of the processes leading up to the decision, over which doctor and patient have more control.[11]

Elwyn and I created the DelibeRate scale to do precisely that.[12] Our often-cited idea was to measure patients' knowledge of their options, their feelings surrounding those options, and their sense that they can choose among them, elements that we defined as necessary for a good deliberation process. It also measures a readiness to decide, which is necessary for a good process of determining what course of action to take. For instance, DelibeRate was used to measure the quality of a decision aid by comparing patients' scores before and after using the decision aid. Elwyn later developed the CollaboRate scale, which measures another important aspect of the process: how much doctors involve patients in decision-making around their care.[13] I will discuss that topic at length later in the book.

HEALING ME SOFTLY

Does it matter if doctors look at their computer screens (or hiking shoes) or make eye contact? Health is the top priority when patients meet doctors, and if the relationship doesn't affect patients' health, maybe doctors should put their time and effort elsewhere. But separating care and health from the relationship is a false dichotomy. Research shows that the human connection does more than sprinkle some feel-good dust: having a good rapport with your doctor—including trust and a feeling that he or she cares about you—can make a tremendous difference to your health.

All patients have unique information about their own symptoms, nutrition, habits, adherence to medication, alcohol intake, and so on. Their doctors need this information to diagnose problems, find the right treatment options for patients' specific characteristics, and assess how the treatment is going. Patients must have a certain level of trust in their doctors if they are to confide about multiple sexual partners, substance abuse, embarrassing symptoms, and the like. It's the only way to coestablish the diagnosis and healing process. If a treatment isn't working, is it because the patient has been skipping doses or gone on a bender? If a treatment will take three weeks to kick in or cause muscle pains, the doctor should forewarn the patient, who can prepare and respond accordingly.

Just as in formal dancing, the teamwork necessary between doctor and patient doesn't happen without an invitation, even to the most skilled dancers. A tango is a very precise image, being inherently nonegalitarian: someone must lead. In medicine, the doctor is supposed to take the lead on the communication dance. I learned this when speaking with Dr. Tessa Manoim.

WON'T YOU LISTEN TO WHAT THE PATIENT SAID?

When I met with Manoim, who trained in South Africa to be a family doctor, she had just sneaked a swim into her busy schedule. Her hair was still wet, because blow drying it would have taken too long. All the more reason to appreciate the time this esteemed member of the medical community spent with me. Her eyes sparkled when she said, "The pleasure for me really is in the relationship. Illness is not always that interesting, but people and their lives, families, and processes are." Her patients stay with her for years, decades. She sometimes treats two, three, even four generations of the same family.

But even esteemed members of the medical community sometimes get sick. Tessa's eyes stopped sparkling when she told me of her experiences as a patient:

Recently, I was at an outpatient consultation at a big teaching hospital. Someone—I assume she was a doctor, or maybe a resident (she did not introduce herself to me), came up to me, did not look me in the eye, and just started taking a history: a very narrow and focused history leaving out critical questions. Then another doctor (who also did not introduce himself or even look at me) walked by and asked, "What's the case?" And she said, "The case is . . ."

This is everything we were taught *not* to do—the patient is not "the case"; they are not their illness. The illness is the illness, but it is not the person. She did not address *me* in any way, she addressed (and even that only partially) some of my symptoms.

I could see that she was then going to "present the case" in a way that was inaccurate and incomplete. I could have helped her, but there was no opening to do that. She had not once looked me in the eye or made any interpersonal contact at all. Really, it starts with rudimentary good manners . . . but it is so much more than that.

When the professor came in, he came up to me, shook my hand, looked me in the eye and said—"How do you feel?" And I said, "I'm feeling dehumanized.

I am not my diagnosis. It is critical that these students at the beginning of their careers be taught how to interact with patients."

Later, when Manoim reviewed my notes and approved them, she added, "All physicians have to take notes and type during a consultation. It is critical for accurate and complete note taking. But this does not preclude eye contact and interpersonal contact."

When doctors become patients, they have the same knowledge and social standing as the people treating them. So, theoretically speaking, doctors should be the most empowered patients. Manoim was more senior than the person who examined her. And yet, as she put it, "I'm already in a compromised position: she's the doctor, she's got the computer, and she's asking the questions." The late Dr. Paul Kalanithi described a similar experience in his memoir *When Breath Becomes Air*.[14] He said that once you sit on the other side of the table, the balance changes drastically.

Manoim said that her mistreatment as a person also led to a misunderstanding of her condition. Since she was not invited to share her medical history, her circumstances, her concerns, or how her symptoms had played out, her doctor was making choices based on partial data.

IF WE ARE A PERSON, NOT A TUMOR OR A RUPTURED DISK, THEN WE HAVE something to contribute to the conversation. Our doctors should invite us to speak and should listen to us when we do so. The health systems they work in and, even before that, the medical schools where they are trained should ingrain this in them, but sadly the schools often don't.

Dr. Victor Montori of the Mayo Clinic in Minnesota and his team examined doctor-patient encounters.[15] They asked, first, whether doctors elicited patients' concerns and, second, whether, having encouraged patients to speak, the doctors cut them off. If it weren't for decades of research showing otherwise, you would expect the first answer to be "Of course!" and the second to be "Never!"

In only one-third of the medical encounters that Montori and his colleagues examined did doctors elicit patients' concerns, a practice that could have helped the doctors understand the main reasons for the consultation.[16] Uninterrupted, patients took from 2 to 108 seconds to state their concern. The latter number, 108, is sacred in Hinduism, Buddhism, and Sikhism. In yoga there is a special practice of doing 108 sun salutations in a row. In visits to the doctor, however, 108 is not sacred. Doctors don't wait that long (if under two minutes is long) to hear their patients' concerns. In two-thirds of those fortunate encounters where clinicians asked patients about their concerns, the clinicians interrupted after about 11 seconds.

In over one hundred doctor-patient encounters that Montori witnessed, only thirteen patients were invited to state their concerns and were not interrupted. The others had no room to voice their doubts about the medication or about the follow-up visit they had just been invited to or anything else that, if left undisclosed, might later interfere with their treatment.

CARE ABOUT ME, SO I WILL TAKE CARE OF MYSELF

We await our physicians' invitation for us to speak, their advice and approval, their acknowledgment of us as people. According to the Berman Institute of Bioethics at Johns Hopkins University, HIV patients who believed that their doctor knew them as persons were more likely to adhere to an antiretroviral medication that prevents HIV from developing into AIDS.[17] Regardless of age, stress level, gender, or sexual orientation, feeling that they were known as persons made a tremendous difference.

When we feel our doctors' disapproval, the effect can be detrimental. Dr. Deborah Jones of the University of Miami, her colleagues, and I discovered this when speaking with approximately fifty women living with HIV in South Florida.[18] We asked what the most important factors were in deciding to become pregnant, and these women listed the following: whether their partner wanted a baby, whether their family supported the idea, and whether their doctor supported the idea.

The women said that when they felt—or feared—that their doctor disapproved of their decision to become pregnant, they simply didn't talk to him or her about their desire for a child. That was tragic, because doctors can prescribe medication to reduce the risk of losing a pregnancy or delivering a baby preterm, at low birth weight, with birth defects, or with HIV.

Women (and their partners) who discuss pregnancy plans with an HIV healthcare provider are more likely to engage in behaviors that lead to optimal fetal health and pregnancy outcomes.[19] This is crucial in such pregnancies, in which adverse effects loom over infants: abnormalities in liver function tests, anemia, low birth weight, preterm birth, children who are small for gestational age, birth defects, and thrombocytopenia. Understandably, given this list, admissions to neonatal intensive care units can also be significantly higher for infants born to HIV-infected women. Mothers who consult with their doctors and adhere to their own medication regime are also more likely to give their infants all their necessary prescribed HIV medications.[20]

The tragic consequences of poor doctor-patient relations extend beyond women and their babies. Dr. Manya Magnus from the Milken Institute School of Public Health at George Washington University interviewed nearly five hundred HIV patients in a statewide public hospital system in Louisiana.[21] If treated, people living with HIV can have a life expectancy that is close to normal. But if untreated, they can develop AIDS, and they have a substantially shorter life expectancy. In spite of these gloomy prospects and in spite of the emphasis that medical systems place on treating HIV as soon as possible and without breaks, almost a third of the patients reported taking a break from treatment or postponing the start of treatment by over a year.

These dangerous breaks in patients' treatment were associated with interpersonal challenges: they felt that their healthcare provider failed to listen carefully most or all of the time, that there was stigma around their condition, and that their provider disliked caring for people with HIV. Again, the lack of a supportive doctor-patient relationship has dire consequences: in this case, breaks in treatment leading to overall poorer health outcomes.

I chose several HIV-related examples because the consequences of not treating HIV properly are severe and irreversible. And yet patients will probably stop optimally caring for themselves if they feel their doctors are not equally prioritizing their care. Just as an unsupportive relationship with one's doctor can hurt, a trusting relationship (ideally also imbued with some personal care and interest on the doctor's side) can help.

THE SEVERE EFFECTS OF FLAWED RELATIONSHIPS WITH ONE'S DOCTOR extend to multiple medical conditions in addition to HIV. Diabetes is one of them. Left untreated, diabetes can lead to serious complications such as foot ulcers, eye damage, heart disease, chronic kidney failure, and stroke. A study of almost ten thousand diabetes patients from Northern California also showed how much patients craved some TLC, peppered with shared decision-making (SDM). Patients who gave healthcare providers lower ratings on involving them in decisions, understanding their problems with treatment, and eliciting confidence and trust were more likely to have poor adherence to their diabetes medication.[22]

And so, having a doctor you trust, who involves you in decisions and listens to your concerns about treatment (about side effects and the difficulty of following the prescribed regimen), who communicates clearly and candidly, can be a matter of excusing or suing, a matter of feeling embraced or dehumanized, a matter of life and death.

FOR WEEKS, THE ACCOUNTS OF COMPROMISED HEALTH STAYED ON MY mind, and here is where my thoughts took me: a patient is, or can be, a weakened adult and therefore bears a similarity to a child, perhaps even an infant, in relying on emotion, which is already a dominant, primal human channel.[23] This explained the emotional insistence in thank-you letters, complaints, and lawsuits.

I needed to take my thinking one step further to understand patients' self-harm: a doctor, a revered authority figure, perhaps bears a similarity to a parent, and children desperately need their parents' approval. Therapist Hal Shorey explained that in a case of parental alienation syndrome, a child would prefer to believe there was something wrong with her that caused her parent to hate her (but she can change it!) than to believe that she was fine, but her parent hated her nonetheless.[24] If a child believed there was something wrong with her, she could also believe she deserved to be mistreated or even to die. This might be why HIV patients, diabetes patients, or any other patients impaired their own health. Taking this interpretation to an extreme, nonadherence to life-saving medication could be viewed as a form of death wish due to "parental" rejection, where the doctor takes on a symbolic parental role.

FIRST-RATE DOCTORS

One cannot choose a doctor based on thank-you letters, letters of complaint, or lawsuits—these form a biased selection of the responses that doctors receive, and outsiders are unlikely to be privy to them anyway. When seeking a good doctor, the capable patient may do what could be conceived as the responsible thing and look for rating platforms to provide objective, consistent evaluations, not unlike the ones used for evaluating hotels and sneakers—evaluations that would encompass the interaction and the medical aspects of what the doctor has to offer.

Rating systems of doctors, however, lean toward the interpersonal, often leaving out the professional. I discovered this at a consulting job: the company that hired me intended to ask patients to rate their doctors. The scale that the company developed was made up solely of assessments of the availability of appointments, office cleanliness, and other aspects of the visit experience, including how amiable the doctor was; there was nothing about the quality of the medical treatment. I maintained that when patients saw a rating, they expected it to also inform them of the doctor's medical abilities, along with his or her demeanor and the procedural aspects of the visit.

I was worried, for example, that patients might pass on a doctor whose rating was 3.5 on a scale of 1 to 5—where 1 was unsatisfactory and 5 was great—not realizing that she was an expert in her field and therefore heavily booked (which led to her low grades on availability) and that it was hard to find parking near her office (which further lowered her score).

Was this the standard of doctor ratings? I did some research and found that the short answer was yes. Even established doctor-rating platforms—such as DrScore, Healthgrades, and RateMDs, online doctor-rating platforms—focused on features of the doctor's work that patients could easily judge for themselves.

DrScore, for example, asked, "On a scale of '0' to '10,' where 0 is the worst possible care and 10 is the best possible care, how would you rate (enter name of doctor, MD)?" It was unclear what went into "care" and how we would know what the worst—or best—possible care might be. Patients may not feel equipped, indeed may not be equipped, to rate "care" reliably. It was much easier to rate, instead, how long they had to wait and whether they liked the office decor, factors that can influence but should not determine our choice of physician.

Healthgrades inquired about the trustworthiness of the doctor, how well the doctor explained the condition, how well he or she answered questions, and whether time with the doctor was well spent. It also inquired about the "office and staff performance": scheduling, office environment, and staff friendliness. These two distinct factors were then combined to calculate the doctor's score.

Healthgrades added a separate dimension, biographical data about doctors—how long they have been in practice, their education and training, licensing, certification, and hospital affiliations. I learned, for example, that as of 2019, Dudley Brown Jr., MD, had been practicing for sixteen years, and Antonella Leary, MD, for twelve.[25] This is an objective, if incomplete, measure of experience (missing, for example, how many patients the doctors treated, and with what conditions) that does not accurately predict treatment quality. Still, the bio presented alongside the doctors' ratings might help patients decide whom they want to see.

RateMDs attempted to add the factor of medical quality. It asked about the doctor's knowledge—though how could a patient gauge? It inquired about the doctor's helpfulness, which lacked a clear definition—did "helpfulness" mean that the doctor was willing to help or that he or she had solved the patient's problem? If the definition was open to interpretation, different people would understand it differently, thereby reducing the reliability of the score.

Psychometrics is the science of creating tests and designing measurements; it was part of my training in psychology. Having psychometric education under my belt, I knew that the scales I just described lacked content validity: they didn't fully cover all the aspects of what being a good doctor includes. The existing scales only focused on the aspects that the patient could easily evaluate. They didn't include the doctors' diagnostic acumen, skill with the scalpel, or ability to find the right dosage of the right drug. Granted, these are less tangible to patients. But without them, you don't get the whole picture. This was easy for consumers to miss—doctor ratings may look like the ones on Tripadvisor or Amazon, which tell you all you need to know about a hotel or sneakers. But because doctors' medical capabilities aren't fully reflected in their ratings, these ratings are in fact misleadingly partial.

I opened this chapter with my mother's question—"What kind of a doctor is this?"—one you should always ask before letting anyone prescribe your psychiatric medication, diagnose your cancer, or fix your hip joint. It's really two questions: what is the quality of the doctor's work, and what is he or she like as a human being? Both of these questions are vitally important.

HOW CAN GOOD DOCTOR-PATIENT RELATIONSHIPS BE ENSURED?

Now that we know what hangs on a doctor-patient relationship, how do we foster a discussion that respectfully invites patients' input and treats each one as a person, not just a problem to be solved or a symptom to be rid of? The answer starts with knowing what good relationships look like. From there, it makes them into a standard, defines actionable rules for this relationship, and verifies that these rules are implemented.

Dr. Sam Brown, director of the Center for Humanizing Critical Care at the nonprofit organization Intermountain Healthcare, created the Dinner Party Rule—a short set of directions designed to help doctors treat patients with respect.[26] The idea is that doctors should regard patients as the hosts of a dinner party, thereby treating them with the common courtesy that is not necessarily common in critical care settings. The Dinner Party Rule entails the following:

> *Knock—or ask permission—before entering a patient's space.* This way you offer the patient some control over personal space and privacy.
>
> *First address patients as Mr. or Mrs. Last Name, and then ask what they want to be called.* This allows the patient control but also lets the doctor know something about the patient as a person: Is it Mr. McNulty, Thomas, or Tom? Only the patient can determine.
>
> *Treat coma patients as if they are listening.* Doctors should address coma patients as they would any other patient, asking permission to touch, explaining what they are doing and why.

I admit that the last item gave me the shivers. But if doctors treated coma patients cordially, they were bound to do the same to noncomatose patients. Amazingly, one in four patients in vegetative state has a brain electromagnetic response to the sound of his or her own first name, a response significantly different from responses to other names.[27] We cannot demand that our doctors harbor warm feelings toward us. What we can and should demand is that they respect us. If we know the Dinner Party Rule, then we also know when it's being violated and we can demand that it—and our dignity—be maintained.

Sir David Spiegelhalter is the director of the Winton Centre for Risk and Evidence Communication at Cambridge University, where I am a visiting researcher. We were sitting in Cambridge's Centre for Mathematical Sciences—a symbol of rationality, with its office pavilions arranged in a parabola—when Sir David Spiegelhalter told me that one of the things he hated the most about being a cancer patient was being addressed as "Love" or "Dear" (perils of being an English patient). He found it patronizing and infantilizing. That one of the smartest, most unassuming men I know, who had to endure cancer treatments, so resented the way he was addressed further emphasizes the importance of the Dinner Party Rule. It has to be applied to all patients, from the comatose to the wide awake.

Doctors and the institutions they work for need to ensure the implementation of this rule and other relationship etiquettes, such as giving patients room to express their concerns—which Dr. Tessa Manoim and Dr. Victor Montori found did not happen satisfactorily. All it takes is asking, What brings you here today?, and listening until the end. How can this happen within the confines of short doctor visits, where a considerable part of the interaction is spent with the doctor tapping away at a computer?

IN ORDER TO ADDRESS THIS ISSUE, AN UNEXPECTED ALLY COMES TO OUR aid—the online doctor-rating platforms that I was criticizing earlier. What the ratings lacked in comprehensive measurement capabilities, they more than made up for by being simple, public, and ridiculously easy to compare across doctors and medical centers. Doctors and hospital directors may not care if you hate being called "Dear," but they do care about online ratings, which guide future patients—driving new revenue in the door or keeping it out. Money talks, ratings scream, and these very ratings can be harnessed in the patients' favor.

The United States has standardized, publicly available ratings of patient satisfaction, which allow for comparisons across hospitals, locally, regionally, and nationally. The Centers for Medicare and Medicaid (CMS) sample all patients and reach out to them forty-eight hours after discharge, to learn about their recent hospital experience.[28] The survey is the Hospital Consumer Assessment of Healthcare Providers and Systems (HCAHPS)—a mouthful but also true, as the survey measures the patient experience comprehensively.

HCAHPS looks at staff responsiveness and nurse and doctor communication in general as well as at discharge and medication information—everything that is often sorely missing. It also asks how clean and how quiet the hospital was. Hospitals can gain or lose a small percentage of their yearly Medicare payments (half a million dollars or more) based on how high or low their ratings are.[29] That incentive is on top of driving patients into or away from the hospital.

In 2016, University of Utah Health Care presided over four hospitals and ten community clinics in the Salt Lake City metropolitan area. Federal patient satisfaction scores placed the Utah health system in the thirty-fourth percentile nationally. Patients complained about delays in the scheduling of appointments, poor communication, and lack of professionalism, among other things.

In response, Utah launched an Exceptional Patient Experience Initiative, aimed at increasing patient satisfaction.[30] This was a catalyst for a cultural overhaul that required painstaking efforts and genuine introspection. The initiative identified several factors that affected the health system's ability to provide good care: (1) lack of good decision-making processes, (2) lack of accountability, (3) the wrong attitude, (4) lack of patient focus, and (5) mission conflict (referring to misalignment among the visions of various hospital and faculty group practice teams).

Here is how they got there.

Utah patients filled out detailed feedback forms that provided a road map for how to conduct a successful encounter. All patients filled it out, so it did not just arrive from patients who felt strongly about the care they had received, for better or worse. They rated the ease of getting the clinic on the phone, the courtesy of registration staff, nurses, and doctors: anything that had ever aggravated a patient visiting a health facility.

Doctors were also rated on their explanations of problems, conditions, or medications, their concern for patients' questions and worries, their efforts to include patients in decision-making, their instructions for follow-up care, their use of clear language, and the time they spent with the patient. These could be summed into a checklist that was more actionable than the vague expectation that they should deliver "good care." Doctor ratings were made public, which increased positive competitiveness. Coaching was offered to low performers, meaning that the health system didn't just identify a difficulty but also allocated the resources to administer the solution.

The Utah health system encouraged innovation, which came in various forms. The cardiology unit rearranged its scheduling system and operating hours to reduce wait times. The neuropsychiatric institute developed the "Hi, Goodbye, Manage Up" card. "Hi" meant establishing a personal connection as the shift or consultation began: the healthcare provider introduced him- or herself and got to know the patient. The shift ended "with a sincere goodbye." "Manage Up" meant the doctor transferred some of the trust established with the patient to the next practitioner, introducing the colleague and the patient and assuring the patient "that she or he is in good hands."

IS IT DISCONCERTING THAT HUMAN INTERACTION IS GOVERNED BY A "HI, Goodbye, Manage Up" card? Not as disconcerting as being treated by someone who doesn't know who you are and doesn't seem to care. In any case, medicine already uses guidelines and checklists, like the nineteen-item list Dr. Atul Gawande and his colleagues developed for surgical safety (e.g., "Before skin incision, confirm the patient's identity, surgical site, and procedure").[31] The guidelines, checklists, rules, and cards for making medical interactions more humane, on the other hand, are by and large still waiting to be written and to be widely adopted.

Utah took seven years to overhaul the hospitals' protocols, and it did not shy from addressing system-level practices. Everyone, veteran and rookie alike, had to commit to the initiative. They revised the process of interviewing new staff members and developed values-based recruitment. The human resources department was involved, not just customer relations. And employee satisfaction also went up.

The initiative mantra was "Medical care can only be great if the patient thinks it is," which resonated with people's intuitive judgments and profoundly respected their experience. The patient experience is all-encompassing. So is their caregivers' experience. I'll never forget the security guard who pointed me to the parking at the facility where I went to get my mother a wheelchair following her surgery. He smiled at me encouragingly. After endless hours at the hospital, I needed that. Whenever I returned there, they smiled. It wasn't a fortunate encounter; it was how they insisted on welcoming their guests.

At the end of Utah's long journey, they had transformed what used to be a second-rate experience into something exemplary. When the peer-reviewed academic publication regarding the initiative came out, half the University of Utah Health Care providers ranked in the top 10 percent compared to their peers nationally, and 26 percent ranked in the top 1 percent.

The initiative came with a mild decrease in the cost of care, which at the same time increased in other medical centers. Patient volumes were up, as was revenue. Malpractice litigation declined, as did insurance premiums. In terms of patient outcomes, the University Hospital Consortium ranked the Utah system number 1 in quality in the nation from among more than 118 academic medical centers. Since 2014, the consortium has included mortality, safety, effectiveness, efficiency, equity, and more in their ratings. And Utah has been ranking in the top 10 ever since.

The Exceptional Patient Experience Initiative also led to an increase in employee satisfaction. This is a logical outcome—employees should be happier when working in more-welcoming conditions, receiving training for performance in the interactional aspects of their job, and treating patients who are less aggravated to begin with. What was good for the patient was good for the doctor. This takes us to the next piece of the doctor-patient relationships puzzle.

WHEN DOCTORS FEEL DEHUMANIZED

Any healthy relationship involves reciprocity. We may treat our doctor as a son of God, as a parent, as an equal, or as a service provider. We look up to the doctors, praise or complain about them, sue them, and rate them and post it online. But we mustn't forget that doctors are human too.

Doctors, nurses, and other health professionals work tirelessly for their patients' health, sometimes at the cost of their own. By September 16, 2020, 1,718 American healthcare workers had lost their lives to COVID-19, and some contended that the numbers were even higher. Two weeks earlier, Amnesty International estimated that there had been 7,000 COVID-19–related deaths of healthcare workers globally: 649 in the UK, 164 in Iran, 159 in Egypt, 188 in Italy, and 1 in Sweden.[32] In March 2020, in the midst of the COVID-19 crisis, people worldwide, many in lockdown, stood on their balconies and at their windows, applauding their doctors' and health teams' heroic efforts.[33]

A recent article in the *New England Journal of Medicine* commented on the increased mental burden that COVID-19 has placed on physicians who treat patients that die, who are afraid of being infected themselves, and who are no less afraid of infecting their loved ones. The authors noted that during this period, "Although meant to be appreciative, messages depicting clinicians as heroes imply an expectation of personal sacrifice at all costs."[34]

Burnout is a state of physical and mental exhaustion caused by prolonged exposure to stress and to overwhelming, constant demands.[35] Dr. Maria Panagioti at the University of Manchester, England, looked at dozens of studies on burnout and found that when doctors felt they were depersonalized—treated as instruments rather than humans by their employers and patients—they were at a greater risk of burnout.[36] This put them at risk of heart disease, shorter life expectancy, problematic alcohol use, broken relationships,[37] stress, depression, thoughts of suicide, and actual suicide.[38]

According to Medscape, a company that provides information on medication, regulation, medical conferences, and other medical news items, half of US doctors disclosed having signs of burnout. *Mayo Clinic Proceedings* published similar findings, gathered from 6,600 physicians in active practice.[39] Over half of them reported signs of burnout, and about a third reported excessive fatigue—a harsh reality for doctors.

Physician burnout is also detrimental for patients' care and safety. Burned out doctors show less empathy toward patients and are more likely to make medical errors.[40] About 10 percent of all the doctors in the Mayo study reported having made a major medical error in the prior three months, more if they were burned out. What may seem like a low percentage translates to 691 doctors in such a large sample. If you were to extrapolate those findings to the entire US physician population, you would be looking at major medical errors performed over the prior three months by more than 50,000 specialists[41] and 23,000 other physicians in active care.[42] Physicians who reported that they had made a major medical error (or is it *several* major medical errors?—a scary thought) were more likely to have symptoms of burnout and fatigue and to have recently contemplated suicide.

KNITTING CLASSES FOR PHYSICIANS

Hospitals are finally starting to deal with burnout, some because of their good hearts, and some because the growing evidence of the association between health professionals' well-being and patient and organizational outcomes demands it.[43] I will not be a cynic. I will refrain from making a snide remark about how professionals' well-being should be important in and of itself, not just as an instrument for improving their performance. Whatever moves hospitals to take care of their physicians and nurses is better than not taking care of them, even if the motivation is improving organizational outcomes, not bringing back doctors' joy.

Some medical specialties require more effort at finding joy, or at least less misery, than others. Those treating pediatric cancer patients deserve all the support they can get. But do they actually get it? Debriefing sessions following a patient death were the most common form of staff support at the UK's children's cancer treatment centers.[44] They provided an opportunity for the staff to discuss the death of their patients and to process their emotions surrounding it. Even if they only lasted ten minutes, those attending found the sessions helpful and educational. Medical residents appreciated when the sessions offered leadership by attending physicians.[45]

The teams taking care of the children in the UK cancer treatment centers were composed of several professions; doctors—the ones whose burnout puts themselves and their patients at risk—were the least likely to have access to support. This was a personal choice.

Other choices were institutional. Cancer treatment centers could choose to put few resources into creating support plans, or they could choose to create good ones. They could choose to advertise the programs widely or to make them inaccessible. Most centers chose to do the minimum: they did not create the support interventions with input from clinical psychologists or psychiatrists. Nor did they offer their teams the ongoing support of resilience building over time, instead offering just the crisis-driven sessions after the death of a patient. Very few of the centers actively raised awareness of the support their hospital's occupational health department offered.

Things weren't any better for doctors on COVID-19 wards. They deserved trigger-based outreach (that is, support offered after a specific event), especially if the triggering event was the death of a patient who had also been a colleague.[46] They deserved ways to express their well-being needs safely, even anonymously. More than that, they deserved to have the system drop the pretense that doctors only needed personal resilience. They deserved to have organizational support strategies, along with personal accountability by hospital managers to allocate resources for support and to reduce the impossible burden.

Increasing patient satisfaction in Utah required extensive effort, commitment, and resources over time. Reducing physician burnout and increasing their satisfaction merit no less.

At a national health conference, a VP of performance improvement for a hospital network said that it had recently run its first employee satisfaction survey and realized how burned out its physicians are. She told the audience that one physician said, "I've been working for this hospital for the past twenty years. No one has ever thanked me for doing a good job." Doctors, like patients, crave to be seen as human beings. And it is their employers' responsibility to make sure they are thus treated.

The hospital network now sends doctors' spouses thank-you letters on birthdays, realizing how crucial spousal support is to the doctors' well-being. The network became keen on making doctors "rediscover joy in the practice of medicine"—which was, of course, associated with the expectation that they would perform at a higher level.

After the panel, as I was waiting to speak with the VP, a doctor approached her and talked about his isolation and his ways of breaking out of it. He included me in the conversation and recounted excitedly that he had met another doctor from his hospital at their kids' softball practice. They knew each other's name from various forms they had both signed when dealing with mutual patients. After years of working for the same employer, they had finally met, outside the hospital. Clearly, this doctor had felt siloed. His hospital system was working on it, he said. He became quite emotional when telling us about the knitting group for doctors he had joined. It provided a hobby as well as a refuge from illness and loneliness.

A REVIEW THAT EXPLORED THE CAUSES OF BURNOUT SUGGESTED THAT burnout could be reduced by improving clarity in work roles, organizational communication, feedback, and openness, by developing a shared vision, and by "improving workplace social support through enhancing peer to peer or supervisory support." Amen to those. The main cure to burnout was "decreasing job demands by having more people do the same tasks, giving more time per person to do the same tasks or reducing the number of tasks per person."[47]

Hospitals are businesses, and for the most part, profitable ones, operating at a profit margin of 8 percent.[48] This means that they can afford to reexamine their task-assignment and workforce policies. Plus, the University of Utah Health Care system has managed to improve patient and employee satisfaction and quality and safety of care while reducing costs.

A sense of being connected to one another, of being acknowledged as human beings, can make a huge difference for both doctors and patients. A formal connection, when a patient is connected to a specific doctor rather than to a clinic, is already beneficial. A study of over 150,000 patients showed that patients who "belonged" with a specific doctor were more likely to receive care consistent with guidelines, such as getting routine mammograms and having balanced blood sugar levels.[49]

Mary Catherine Beach, professor of medicine at the Johns Hopkins University School of Medicine, interviewed primary care physicians and discovered that while they liked "their" patients in general, they had a few favorites—mainly people whom the doctors had taken care of (and cared for) over a long period of time. One of the doctors said about such a patient, "He treasures me, just like I treasure him."[50] This kind of relationship is an emotional win-win for doctor and patient, and a triple win when you consider that the patient's health may hang in the balance. No! A quadruple win, because doctors who experience less burnout can also work more and better withstand the health system burden. We cannot formalize a rule that will make people treasure one another. But we can ensure that they are not anonymous to one another, that they have enough time together, and that they are treated cordially. That's a good start.

Patients and doctors depend on the health systems to allocate more time to appointments, to create visions and develop communication practices, and to bring in more professionals to shoulder the workload. Knitting classes are nice. But there isn't enough yarn in the world to knit a blanket that decreases the job demands of nurses and doctors, which is what they need. Before they break down, the health team needs their employers to develop effective interventions, advertise them, and make them readily available.

There are two parties in this relationship. One is vulnerable in the patient role—uncertain of what the doctor will find and maybe in pain. The other is vulnerable in the doctor role—frightfully overworked and too often socially isolated, afraid of making medical errors, and afraid of being sued for them. What strange symmetry—one of us can sue the other, one of us has the power to cut the other up. Both of us want to be acknowledged as people. And the system under whose auspice we meet rarely gives us enough time to do so leisurely, or even to speak for 108 seconds uninterrupted. This does not bode well for doctor-patient relationships, for doctors' burnout rates, or for our health. Thankfully, we can take action to make this better.

Our challenges as patients don't end here. Even when we have great rapport with our physicians and endless motivation to follow their orders, we don't always understand what they are saying. And we don't always understand what the internet has to say about our condition, as we'll see in the next chapter.

TAKEAWAYS

The takeaways for patients reading this chapter are influenced by Byron Katie, a new-age priestess whom *Time* magazine crowned "a spiritual innovator for the 21st Century." Byron's teaching calls for "loving what is."[51] She suggests we take an open-eyed look at reality, reevaluating our emotional response to it. All too often our response is determined by our interpretation, governed by our assumptions of what reality should be like. "Loving what is" involves relieving our agony by challenging our assumptions of how things should be. Katie suggests playing around with potential reversals to assumptions that cause us distress over our reality.

FOR PATIENTS:

1. You deserve to be humanized, treated as a person. A doctor who does not make you feel this way is hurting both your emotions and your health.
2. When you look at doctors' online ratings, make sure you look at what goes into them. Don't disqualify a doctor or choose one based on ratings that do not reflect his or her medical ability.
3. You too can benefit from Byron Katie's reversals. "The doctor should take an interest in me and see me as a person" is an assumption that can hurt us, even if we're justified in wanting it. Potential reversals would be "*I* should take an interest in the doctor and see her as a person," or

a realistic "The doctor shouldn't take an interest in me and see me as a person," since doctors are so overworked. The conclusion can be that *I* must drive my doctor's interest, and if possible, I must demand this from my health system.

4. Another reversal could be "*I* should take an interest in me and see me as a person." This final reversal was born when internists who invited me to speak at their department told me they were crushed and frustrated when their patients allowed their situation to deteriorate. When you take good care of your health, you make your doctor happy.

5. At the end of the day, though trust and care from your physicians are necessary, they can never suffice. You need to take charge of your health—no one else can do it for you. Your life depends on it.

FOR HEALTHCARE PROFESSIONALS:

1. Pay as much attention to your interactions with the patients and the bonds you form with them as you do to the medical care you provide them.

2. Follow one of the routines I described above (the Dinner Party Rule, "Hi, Goodbye, Manage Up"), both of them, or a routine you create for yourself—anything to streamline patient interactions and make sure that patients feel humanized.

3. You can also hugely benefit from a good reversal. "My patient should take an interest in me and see me as a person" is beyond your control. Why not try "*I* should take an interest in me and see me as a person"? This is golden, especially in a culture that values performance over well-being and pushes physicians to do more and earn more while paying little attention to their well-being.

FOR HEALTHCARE SYSTEMS:

1. Provide the time, attention, and other resources for the delicate doctor-patient tango to occur without stepping on anyone's toes.

2. Disseminate established relationship-building and patient-satisfaction-enhancing tools such as the Dinner Party Rule and "Hi, Goodbye, Manage Up," or create your own, and train your staff in using them. Either way, commit to their ongoing implementation.

3. If possible, assign patients to specific doctors, so they become "their" patients.

4. Consider following the example of the University of Utah Health Care network and examine practices and protocols with patient experience and satisfaction in mind.

5. Support your physicians. Appreciate their efforts. Acknowledge their challenges and help them deal with those before a crisis arises.

6. Relationships, patient satisfaction, and an environment that is nurturing for physicians are not peripheral to the business of health; they are enmeshed with it, front and center.

CHAPTER 4

SAVING FACE OR SAVING YOUR SKIN

THE CASE FOR HEALTH LITERACY

It is paramount that you understand the state of your health and what options you have. You cannot make informed decisions if you have only a vague or misguided understanding of the terms your health professionals use or if you misunderstand the information that they give you. Enter health literacy.

According to the World Health Organization, health literacy involves "cognitive and social skills which determine the motivation and ability of individuals to gain access to, understand, and use information in ways which promote and maintain good health."[1] When motivation comes up, it becomes tempting to "solve" health literacy issues just by asking people to do a better job of reading the materials they receive. This won't do. Health literacy affects people of different educational backgrounds, age ranges, and linguistic proficiencies. "Try harder" is a fake solution.

High health literacy is an asset that significantly contributes to one's health. It helps people understand and follow the necessary steps for the preventive care that keeps them healthy (all that flossing, exercising, and rubbing on sunscreen).

Low health literacy is a health risk.[2] It goes hand in hand with poor health status, higher mortality rates,[3] reduced quality of life, and lower self-efficacy— your belief in your ability to perform the behaviors necessary to attain certain goals.[4] Indeed, low health literacy makes it harder to engage in necessary self-care during radiation therapy, and people with low health literacy are more likely to experience graft failure after an organ transplant.[5]

Low health literacy is also costly. The United States spends an additional $600 billion annually on treating individuals whose health has been mismanaged due to misunderstanding. Midsize community hospitals spend an additional $1.8 million covering the costs associated with low health literacy. In fact, the health literacy level of a city's population is one of the key indicators of a healthy city.[6]

Health literacy measures people's capabilities, but it is often determined by the quality of the information patients receive, not just their preexisting knowledge. This is a problem that medical institutions need to help solve. Ignoring it is like judging someone's dancing without taking into account the cracks in the floor.

We will cover all aspects of health literacy.

But first, let's talk java.

GOURMET COFFEE WITH A SHOT OF ANTI-TNF

Our doctors speak at least two languages: English and Medicalese. Medicalese sounds like English but is sprinkled with terms from ancient and classical languages that can sound foreign to even the most educated person. To doctors, the language of medicine is clear and familiar. To you, it might as well be Greek. Not just to you, but also to policy makers, journalists, and insurers—all those who are supposed to convey information so that you can understand it and can act upon it.[7]

It's Greek to me too.

I was once consulting for a pharmaceutical company that wanted to increase patient adherence to rheumatoid arthritis medication. We were in a sleek conference room, sipping the latest in gourmet coffee. I was feeling confident and competent. Then the marketing and product teams started throwing strange terms at one another—like code words to a secret club to which they all belonged. Someone said, "anti-TNF." Someone else retorted, "subcutaneous." From across the room I heard, "biologic" and "biosimilar." These words sounded familiar, but that only made matters worse, because then I thought I understood them.

This presented a dilemma. On the one hand, I had been hired because of my academic credentials, industry experience, and unique insights. I should have been commanding authority, not standing at the club door, embarrassingly ignorant of the secret code. On the other hand, I could not do my work unless I knew what my clients were talking about. To find my way out of the predicament, I said, ever so humbly, "My PhD is in psychology, not medicine, so I don't quite understand. Would you mind explaining?"

I needed to ask. Patients also need to ask when they don't understand something their doctor is saying. I used my academic credentials to avoid what I feared would be professional humiliation and thus saved face. Crucially, such credentials are something patients often don't have. Creating an environment in which we feel safe to ask questions is the first step in improving our health literacy.

WOULD YOU GET AN A IN HEALTH LITERACY?

Ninety million American adults are estimated to have low health literacy.[8] Functional literacy is the ability to use reading, writing, and computational skills well enough to meet the needs of everyday life.[9] With health, this includes our ability to read and understand information, to follow treatment instructions and regimens, to provide our doctors with information about our symptoms and medical history, and to inquire about the treatments they offer.

Health literacy falls on a spectrum; people don't just have "high" or "low" health literacy, and not every one of us can perform every health task. Here is how well we perform with functional health literacy:

- Only 12 percent of the US adult population has the highest proficiency level of health literacy. They can, for example, use a table to calculate their share of health insurance costs for a year.
- About half the population has an intermediate level of health literacy. Though unable to use the insurance table described for the first group, they can still read the instructions on a prescription label and determine when to take a medication.

- About a quarter—21 percent—of the population has a basic level of health literacy. Though they cannot read instructions on a prescription label and determine when to take their medication, they can read a pamphlet and give two reasons why a person with no symptoms should be tested for a disease.
- At the lowest, below-basic level of health literacy is 14 percent of the population, who cannot perform any of the tasks above. Still, they can read a set of short instructions and identify what they are allowed to drink before a medical test.[10]

Regardless of your health literacy level, you can get sick, need plenty of meds, face exorbitant out-of-pocket fees, or have debilitating chronic health conditions. You need to figure out whether to get tested for colon cancer if you're over fifty and whether it's okay to have a few beers if you're on an antidepressant.

You can get sick at any age. Functional health literacy decreases with age, and does so faster than other aspects of cognitive ability. This has consequences: seniors with inadequate health literacy are 50 percent more likely to die than are those with adequate health literacy, even after accounting for education and socioeconomic status.[11]

HEALTH LITERACY ALSO INVOLVES SOCIAL SKILLS AND ADVANCED COGNItive skills to critically analyze information. The skills are interconnected, yet different. For instance, interventions have increased the functional health literacy levels of immigrants, but not necessarily their social or critical-thinking health literacy levels.[12] People still needed help asking questions and reviewing materials critically, even when they could read the materials. If patient involvement is dough, the social and critical-thinking aspects of health literacy are the yeast that make it rise.

You probably know why people don't ask questions. I had to muster up the courage to ask for explanations in my meeting with the pharmaceutical company. (TNF stands for "tumor necrosis factor," a substance in the body that causes inflammation.) Patients have it harder. Patients might be paying customers, but that does not erase the power and knowledge imbalance between them and their healthcare providers. On top of the pain and fear that come with illness, "patients with limited health literacy might not feel empowered to speak up or ask questions; they might be self-conscious, embarrassed, or deferential."[13]

Low-literacy adults ask fewer questions than do patients of higher literacy levels. They are also less likely to request additional services or seek new information. In hand-surgery clinics, for example, patients of adequate health literacy asked significantly more questions about their therapeutic regimen and had longer visits than patients of limited health literacy.[14] With the help of interventions that build their skills and confidence—for example, when physicians encourage patients to ask questions—patients can participate effectively in their care, achieving better health outcomes and better care experiences at lower costs.[15] Only a third of the hand surgeons asked patients if they had questions, but when they did, about 80 percent of their patients actively participated.[16]

KEEP YOUR HEALTH ABOVE WATER

Nancy is a retired school principal. Her doctor called to say Nancy's routine blood work had come back suggesting there was a problem with her kidneys. At her appointment, her doctor said that her creatinine levels were elevated. He explained that creatinine is waste that muscles dispose of through the kidneys after they produce energy. Nancy nodded in distress as questions were racing in her head. Was she developing kidney disease? Would she need dialysis?

Then the doctor took the communication up (or is it down?) a notch. He said the elevated creatinine levels might be because Nancy was dehydrated. Nancy's sharp mind snapped into action. Now that she understood what he was talking about, she could turn things around.

She reminded her doctor that a few years earlier she had fallen and hit her head. At the hospital they had found that the sodium content of her blood was severely diluted, which caused dizziness.[17] She had been drinking too much water. The hospital staff told Nancy not to exceed four cups of liquid a day, an instruction she has followed religiously since. Her doctor hadn't been informed, and this instruction, which over time may have caused her kidney malfunction, wasn't registered in Nancy's medical record.

"What if I started drinking six cups of liquid a day?" Nancy asked, proposing to try it for a month and see if her creatinine levels improved: an easy fix, unlocked by the shift from speaking in Medicalese about creatinine levels to discussing water.

Nancy was fortunate to have had this annotated dialogue with her doctor. Too often the tango with our physicians gets tangled up by time constraints and emotional turmoil, and we are left to figure out Medicalese on our own.

Doctors' time is restricted by health insurance reimbursement policies that allot fifteen minutes per visit—a number established in 1992 by Medicare based on a formula that took into account factors such as liability insurance costs and practice expenses.[18] Once this time slot was set, the number caught on as a benchmark for visit lengths. Since then, the population has aged, so people suffer from more medical conditions. In 2010, the CDC reported that one-third of elderly patients had three or more chronic medical conditions and that four out of every ten patients take three or more medications.[19] This gives them and their doctors a lot to talk about—certainly, more than fifteen minutes' worth.

BLAME IT ON THE GOOGLE

Thanks to the internet, there's endless information available at our fingertips. Our phones, tablets, and computers connect us to a wealth of knowledge: hospital websites, patient forums, national disease associations, academic journals giving access to cutting-edge research. With this abundance of resources, you might think that understanding medical terms is a no-brainer. You might think that people can just Google "TNF" or "creatinine" and that there is thus no excuse for not knowing what anything means. After all, everything health and medicine related exists on Wikipedia.

This is only partially true and only partially fair. While there is undoubtedly plenty of health information out there, being "out there" is not enough. Even when medical information is directed at the layman, it is often written at a level that is beyond comprehension. Enter readability. Health literacy measures the reading level of the person looking at texts, and readability measures the literacy level of the texts. Instead of judging patients, we are now judging the medical information itself.

Here's what one explanation looks like on Wikipedia, the obvious place for quick, reliable, and approachable information—just the tough balance

Wikipedia is supposed to strike: "A breast implant is a prosthesis used to change the size, shape, and contour of a woman's breast. In reconstructive plastic surgery, breast implants can be placed to restore a natural looking breast mound for post-mastectomy breast reconstruction patients or to correct congenital defects and deformities of the chest wall."

Between "breast mound," "contour," and "congenital," the readability level of this sentence is through the roof. It's a good thing most people already have an idea of what breast augmentation is, because it requires somewhere between undergraduate and graduate school reading level in order to comprehend this text.[20] I don't expect Wikipedia to resort to talking about "boob jobs," but the language used to describe this procedure and others could be simpler.

Wikipedia entries on epilepsy, a common disease, have an eleventh-grade readability level, and an analysis of what ninety-six websites wrote on common medical procedures such as anesthesia found that they were at a 13.5 grade reading level.[21]

Want to know about cardiopulmonary resuscitation (CPR)? Scrolling down the Wikipedia entry for "Cardiopulmonary Resuscitation" to the section entitled "Medical Use" eventually gets to "Effectiveness" and to a table of survival rates and ROSC, "return of spontaneous circulation." To understand ROSC requires another click, which leads to this: "Return of spontaneous circulation (ROSC) is resumption of sustained perfusing cardiac activity associated with significant respiratory effort after cardiac arrest." The clicking goes on and on.[22]

Try reading that when you are in distress. Psychologists identify the ego as the part of our psyche that gives us the energy that governs how we function and handle ourselves. Ego depletion happens when we overuse the limited mental resources that fuel self-control and elaborate thought processes. Distress also leads to depletion.[23] And, when we are depleted, our cognitive processing abilities are impaired.[24]

EVEN WIKIPEDIA ENTRIES ARE HARD TO READ, WHICH UNDERSCORES the importance of creating and serving information at a level people can comprehend. To expect or demand that patients understand health information regardless of its level is to pretend that everyone has high health literacy, absolving systems from helping patients, all patients, understand.

Detroit's Henry Ford Health System is providing such help. At a digital health conference, one of their officials announced that they were modifying their materials to bring them to a fifth-grade level.[25] Some attendees commented that the change was insulting. I find it effective. Given our memory constraints, when you give people the gist of what they need to know in an approachable manner, you ensure that it isn't lost amid more information. And you minimize the risk of misunderstanding. It's a good starting point for designing communications.

Clearly, simplification is not an unalloyed good; plenty of information is lost when material is presented at a simplified level. By no means is that the only level we should offer patients. Some patients will struggle with the fifth-grade level, some will feel it's just right, and others will want more.

My colleagues Ben Goldacre, Odette Wegwarth, Ben Bowen, Ingrid Mühlhauser, Richard Smith, David Spiegelhalter, and I wrote about handling the differences in patient health literacy.[26] We recommended a stratified approach: giving everyone accessible health information but also making it possible for anyone who so desired to drill down all the way to the academic papers the information was based on.

This is precisely what pharmaceutical companies do. I saw firsthand that when a new medication goes on the market (in fact, some time before that), they make available the relevant scientific publications about it, but they also hire people like me to brief sales reps on its advantages or to moderate advisory boards where the merits of the new drug are explained to opinion leaders. This is wise, given time and motivation constraints.

YOU NEED MOTIVATION TO GOOGLE MEDICAL TERMS. INFORMATION about birth control, migraines, or irritable bowel syndrome does not just land on your phone. You must pursue it actively. But people don't always look for information. According to one estimation tool, every month the term "advance directive" has fifty thousand searches; "Beyoncé" has more than a million.[27] It is much more fun to learn about Beyoncé than to think about death. But, with no offense meant to Beyoncé, advance directives can affect your life much more than can the multiple Grammy winner.

If only there was a means of mass education that could teach us medical information. Something highly accessible that we would have plenty of motivation to follow...

Wait! There is—it's called television. The problem is that TV shows and movies are designed to entertain, not to convey scientific facts. When TV suggests that every waitress in New York lives in a cute, spacious apartment with her hip roommate, it's inaccurate but harmless. When TV reduces your motivation to learn about medical events and procedures because you already "learned" about them from TV, there is cause for alarm.

LEARNING THE WRONG THINGS FROM WATCHING GEORGE CLOONEY

Given how popular hospital shows are and given that for many of us, they are the only experience of emergency medicine short of actually being in an emergency room (ER), we should examine how closely these shows follow reality.

Researchers went over 269 episodes of *Grey's Anatomy* and matched each fictional trauma that was portrayed on the show with actual patients who had incurred such a trauma. As expected, TV events unfolded faster and more dramatically than events in real life: most TV patients (71 percent) went straight from the emergency department to the operating room, whereas only 25 percent do so in real life. TV patients were more likely to die, and while half of severely wounded TV patients were hospitalized for less than a week, only 20 percent of real-life patients were so lucky. The researchers worried that the television portrayal of rapid recovery after major injury would "cultivate false expectations among patients and their families."[28]

The fascination with medicine on TV continues. Susan Diem, an internist, and her colleagues watched every episode of *ER* and *Chicago Hope* during the 1994–1995 viewing season and fifty consecutive episodes of *Rescue 911* broadcast over a three-month period in 1995.[29] (Why doesn't my own research involve curling up on the sofa in front of George Clooney, who was on *ER* that season?)

Diem examined how television depicted medicine, specifically CPR. This emergency procedure involves chest compressions performed when a person's heart has stopped beating, preserving brain function until an electric shock can be applied to the heart to restart it. You've seen that on TV: the doctor yells "Clear!" and applies a powerful shock to the patient's chest. Of course, Diem did more than curl up on the sofa and watch. First, she counted: CPR appeared eleven times in *Chicago Hope*, eighteen in *Rescue 911*, and as many as thirty-one times in twenty-five episodes of *ER*. Television was giving us a course in CPR, the only course in CPR most of us would ever get. But how accurate was this televised education?

For the sake of science, I sacrificed an afternoon and looked up resuscitation scenes from *ER*. The first to come up was season 7, episode 11, where John Truman Carter III, a slim medical student in his twenties, lay on an ER table, his chest bare. His heart stops beating so, by the book, he receives ventilation via his mouth and his heart is manually compressed. But we have seen enough television to know that more is required. A young doctor in a gray T-shirt shows up, grabs the defibrillator, and yells, "Clear!" This happens repeatedly, the doctor relentless in his defibrillation attempts. Within a few seconds, Carter comes to. His eyes still shut, he smiles coyly. "Of course. You saved me," he tells the doctor.

They look more like frat boys after a successful prank than a physician and the patient he has brought back from the dead. It seems as if within an hour, Carter will bounce off the table, and the two will head to the nearest keg party.

This is typical of television, where 65 percent of cardiac arrests occur in children, teenagers, or young adults. This is not, however, the typical profile of patients who require CPR in real life. Compared with real-life resuscitated patients, television patients requiring CPR were usually younger, had fewer background illnesses, and tended to suffer more exotic afflictions—they had nearly drowned, had been shot, or had been struck by lightning.

The reality is not as pretty as it looks on TV. The chances that the rescuer will break ribs, break the sternum, or rupture the liver or the spleen during the procedure, or that the patient will develop an infection following CPR, are high. The odds of surviving after CPR are low, as the medical staff cannot necessarily address the cause of the cardiac arrest. CPR's dire aftermath is *not* what you see on television.

Diem found that on *Rescue 911*, every single CPR case was a success. Ten were described as miracles. We should not be surprised—it's showbiz. In real life, however, most CPR patients are older and are already hospitalized. They have a 40 percent chance of short-term survival following CPR, as opposed to the 75 percent portrayed on TV. Their long-term survival rate—the patients' chance of being discharged from the hospital after CPR—is half of the 67 percent that's shown on television. Most real patients receiving CPR, those who were hospitalized to begin with, would remain in their pajamas and hospital beds long after the doctor yelled, "Clear."

As Diem and her colleagues revealed, it was hard to infer anything about real life from television. The TV–real life gap is all the more alarming given that television is one of people's main information sources about hospitals and medicine.

Television programs are important storytelling mechanisms.[30] And we all love a good story—so much, that people worldwide spend, on average, 167 minutes (nearly three hours) a day watching TV.[31] Americans dedicate four and a half hours a day to television and streaming services, and seniors watch for more than seven hours a day. The stories we watch seep into our minds, just like the fairy tales we hear over and over again that "teach" us that women need to be rescued by princes.

WE ALL KNOW THAT TELEVISION SHOWS LIKE *ER* AND ITS CONTEMPORARies are a touched-up presentation of reality. Even *Rescue 911*, which offers dramatic reenactments of real rescues by emergency services, chooses what to leave out. And yet Susan Diem and her coauthors are concerned that the public does not distinguish fact from fiction. It's the very realism of these television programs that makes them attractive.

Watching quasi-scientific shows can "teach" you about the world. Heavy viewers of crime shows think that crime and violence happen frequently.[32] Heavy viewers of medical dramas underestimate how serious cancer and cardiovascular disease are. They are fatalistic about having to take care of such issues, because so many people die of illness on TV.[33] Half the studies that examined TV viewers' postviewing knowledge found that people learned correct health information.[34] The other half had negative or mixed outcomes.

Seeing is believing. What the psychology of persuasion calls the "sleeper effect" is at play here. Even if we get a signal that a message isn't credible, over time we increasingly ignore that signal and remember the message without questioning it.[35] In the health context, the sleeper effect means that when we watch ads or TV or read antivax Facebook posts, we receive messages that may not be credible, but over time, we will accept those messages as valid.[36]

The portrayal of a miraculous end to a dangerous and painful procedure caters to our intuitive, quick, and emotional way of thinking, our System 1 thinking. The fact-checking, deliberative way of thinking, our System 2, is often left out of the picture. And when we fear for our life or the life of a loved one, it's easy to resort to what was so vivid on TV, letting it guide our decision-making. After all, a miraculous resuscitation on TV is more convincing than dry statistics, which we don't have access to and may not be able to understand even if we did.

I would venture to guess that many of us don't separate what we "know" about CPR from where we learned it. If we don't question this "knowledge" or seek more validated information, then the next logical step is to opt for CPR in real life, expecting its outcomes to be the same as seen on TV.

Some researchers actually asked, in relation to CPR on television, "Are we miseducating the public?"[37] The answer was yes. They surveyed people on the practice of CPR (how deeply one needed to compress and at what rate). Those who reported watching medical dramas regularly had poorer knowledge than those who only watched them occasionally.

CPR is not the only medical subject where TV is misleading. A review of almost twenty papers explored what people learn from television about cancer screening, sexually transmitted infections, heart disease, and more. After watching TV, a third of viewers knew more and were more likely to engage in desirable health behaviors. A few acquired inaccurate knowledge and faulty health practices. And for more than half the views, the effect was mixed.[38] As researcher Beth Hoffman told me, television viewing is associated with real-world outcomes.

To test whether people really base their decisions on fictional characters and overly optimistic depictions of resuscitation, we would have to design an experiment that manipulates how CPR is portrayed on TV. We would then record their resuscitation decisions and learn how television influenced their perceptions and choices. That is impractical. It's equally impractical to expect television to fully reflect reality.

A more practical proposal is to use TV, an easy, accessible, and visual medium, to convey critical information to the public, regardless of health literacy level. Rather than using TV to provide inaccurate albeit sticky facts, we can use it to convey accurate data in a sticky way.

A CLIP CAN CHANGE YOUR LIFE—AND DEATH

Apart from the complex psychological issues involved in thinking about one's end of life, patients probably feel they lack the vocabulary to answer advance care questions and to make decisions. They might very well be right: popular media is inaccurate, and health information isn't always readable (and we'll also see in Chapter 7 that doctors are reluctant to discuss death and provide information about it).

An oncologist at Massachusetts General Hospital, Dr. Areej El-Jawahri, and her colleagues aimed to help patients overcome these barriers by creating a digestible three-minute video clip that accurately described CPR and intubation and their risks. Watching the short clip doesn't require impossible levels of health literacy or of motivation. The researchers hypothesized that patients who watched the video clip would be more willing to communicate their preferences to physicians and would choose differently from patients who didn't have access to such information.[39]

I found their idea so innovative that I told my son about it. A young, healthy student, he could not fathom why anyone would choose to refuse life-saving techniques such as CPR and intubation. For him, as for many of us, choosing death over life was counterintuitive. And he had not watched the video clip and didn't know what the risks were.

El-Jawahri found elderly hospitalized patients whose doctors estimated they had less than a year to live. Seventy-five such patients watched the video clip on CPR and intubation and were then asked to state their CPR and intubation preferences for their advance care orders. This was the intervention group. The control group was another seventy-five similarly ill patients who received the usual care—no video clip and no questions on advance directives.

The three-minute video clip had an indisputable effect: the patients who saw it knew far more about CPR and intubation than their control group counterparts. This knowledge affected the patients' decisions. Over 50 percent of the patients who watched the video clip subsequently documented advance orders to withhold CPR and intubation, compared with less than 20 percent of the control group. But the real success of the intervention was that these patients had an *opinion* and *controlled their own fate*.[40] A video clip had made the difference in terminal patients' decision to knowingly accept their fate when their condition deteriorated, or to subject themselves to resuscitation, with its built-in complications and risks.

Patients should, of course, choose as they see fit. I am not advocating for one choice over another. What I am advocating is making choices based on scientifically validated and understandable information. The video clip experiment proved that, given easily digestible materials, patients can be involved even in the most emotionally taxing decisions. Hospitals and clinicians must make a conscious effort to cater to patients' health literacy levels. Once they do, the playing field is leveled, and patients become truly empowered to partake in decisions about their lives and deaths.

NOT BEYOND REPAIR

So far we've been talking about medical procedures that many people will have at least a passing familiarity with. But no matter how many episodes of *Grey's Anatomy* you may have watched, many medical situations will be unfamiliar to you. You may not know what they're called or how to spell them. How then, can you make a choice about them?

When I interviewed Dr. Tessa Manoim about her medical practice, the circumstances seemed less than ideal. We were at a swimming pool cafeteria, buzzing with people walking by. Her sweet daughter was at the next table playing a game, but the child's patience would soon run out. I later realized that this situation was far better than the environments in which many patients will have to act. I had motivation galore. I was pain-free and anxiety-free, and I wrote down everything Tessa said.

I didn't ask her to spell any of the medical terms she used because our time was limited, but also because I did not want to appear ignorant. What foolish bravado! I messed up every medical term she used except "bronchitis." I misspelled "paresthesia" and "myasthenia gravis." Fortunately, I had something written down, jumbled up but close enough that I could figure out what she had meant and search for the correct term. What would a patient do in my place? Go home thinking they had a problem related to prosthetics, or something that sounds like "forsythia"?

Patients don't always show up for a doctor's visit with a recorder, laptop, notebook, or notepad (they should!). And they might jumble things up even worse than I did. We need solutions we can apply without technology or funding—ideally, solutions we can put into action during the clinical encounter. And while we're making a wish list, let's ask for solutions that also take away the embarrassment of not knowing what the doctor is talking about.

Both parties, patient and doctor, need such tools to guide them through the communication dance.

According to a recent systematic review, most healthcare professionals reported that they did not know enough about the concept of health literacy and the difficulties it poses to patients but that they had a positive attitude toward learning about it.[41] This may have been a discouraging case of the blind leading the blind had the means for improvement not been so simple.

The review proposed that providers give patients reading materials and aids and use everyday language to make sure that patients understood them. It also suggested that providers ask for so-called teach-backs, in which patients or family members are asked to explain—in their own words—what they understood.[42] It is both prudent and polite to use accessible terms and to invite discussion rather than guess at a patient's health literacy level. In fact, the review showed that patients are ashamed of exposing their low literacy levels and of undergoing health literacy assessments.

Reading materials, teach-backs, and simple language come from the doctors' side. Other tools are more egalitarian—every doctor and every patient can have them in the arsenal. I propose three feasible strategies for obtaining health information and ensuring its correctness.

Strategy 1: Repair

"Repair" is a mechanism for self-correcting: in conversations between doctor and patient, both parties clarify what they mean and ask the other to explain what they are talking about. Repair was described by American sociologist Emanuel Schegloff, one of the fathers of conversation analysis. Schegloff noted that "common" or "shared" knowledge often isn't really common, shared, or understood similarly by different people. The desirable state in which people agree on meaning is called "intersubjectivity": two or more people align their subjective concepts or are "coshaping an appreciated grasp of the world."[43]

Intersubjectivity is needed so that your myasthenia gravis doesn't turn into my forsythia.

Dr. Rosemarie McCabe of Queen Mary University of London listened to more than a hundred recorded consultations between schizophrenic patients and their psychiatrist and looked for repairs.[44] She found that Repair was easy to implement, even for these patients, who are known for having communication failures.[45] Repair helped solve misunderstandings and minimize comprehension gaps. Patients could self-repair by giving clarifications, such as "I saw you three, no two months ago." Or they could other-repair by asking their doctor for clarifications—for example,

> Doctor: Yep well that is a possible side effect
> Patient: Side effect? [request for clarification]
> Doctor: Of the haloperidol [clarification].[46]

The patient expressed uncertainty about what the doctor was referring to, so the doctor clarified that she was talking about a side effect of haloperidol, a pharmaceutical commonly used to treat schizophrenia.

These simple acts of repair led to better health outcomes. Patients who repaired by actively verifying and echoing back their understanding of what the doctor was saying were more likely to continue taking their medication six months after their appointment than were those patients who didn't. Greater adherence led to better control over the disease.

The good news is that we can all do conversational repair just by listening closely to our doctors and asking for clarifications whenever we are not certain of what is being said. The less good news is that these patients' tendency to clarify and repair was probably facilitated by their psychiatrists' openness and approachability.

McCabe phrased it perfectly: "The effectiveness of medical treatment depends on the quality of the patient-clinician relationship." Such a relationship depends "on the extent to which the patient and clinician build a shared understanding of illness and treatment." She concluded that to get there, we should "investigate how patient clarification can be encouraged among patients *and facilitated by psychiatrists' communication*" (emphasis added).[47]

I emphasized that last bit because doctor-patient relations are inherently asymmetrical. Patients can be motivated, and they can attempt to apply their social skills. But they need a partner open to answering their questions, making the health information accessible, and helping them to repair.

Strategy 2: Ask Me 3

The second strategy to combat low health literacy assigns roles to both doctors and patients, who now share the responsibility to create shared knowledge. "Ask Me 3" is an intervention that was developed by the National Patient Safety Foundation.[48] Ask Me 3 can help you learn more about your health by prompting you to ask your doctor three questions:

What is my main problem?
What do I need to do?
Why is it important for me to do this?

This set of questions is brilliant in several ways.

First, Ask Me 3 provides an anchor—in this case, the number three. Behavioral economics defines an anchor as a number, however irrelevant it may seem, that your mind latches onto and is thus influenced by.[49] If you're told to ask three questions (or to buy ten apples, for that matter), you're more likely to do it than if you're told to ask as many (or buy as many) as you would like.

Second, Ask Me 3 provides you with a motivation. If you ask yourself, Why am I asking the doctor questions?, you can answer, Because Ask Me 3 says I should.

Third, Ask Me 3 solves the social skills dilemma—the fear of appearing argumentative or dumb—by creating a new social norm. It establishes that your role as a patient is to ask questions and that your doctor's role is to listen and provide answers.

The fourth reason is closely related to the third, but it relates to your doctor. A doctor who wears an Ask Me 3 pin or hangs an Ask Me 3 poster in the waiting room is showing openness to being asked questions by patients and a commitment to answering them.

Research shows that patients trained in using Ask Me 3 reported "no longer fearing questions would be construed as criticism" and furthermore reported that using Ask Me 3 allayed "fears that information is being withheld."[50] Other researchers have found that Ask Me 3 increased patients' empowerment levels.[51]

Strategy 3: Ask Me About What Matters

Here is another set of questions that takes you to the expert patient level and allows for greater involvement while encouraging critical thinking. I developed these questions—Ask Me About What Matters—to help build your critical ability, an often-neglected part of health literacy. Whenever a doctor proposes a medication, test, or procedure—anything you need to make a decision about—ask three questions:

What are the benefits?
What are the risks?
What are the alternatives?

Without being argumentative or contrarian, these questions allow you to get information that may not be aligned with the course of action your doctor is suggesting for you. In other words, they may reveal important information you might not otherwise have uncovered.

Whenever I need to choose a course of action, and especially when I don't know the subject matter very well, I apply Ask Me About What Matters. It helped me deal with a blinking light on my car's dashboard. My mechanic explained that the light was connected to the fuel consumption display, a neat feature that tells me how many miles per gallon I was averaging. Fixing the light while leaving the fuel consumption indicator intact would cost $400. Was it worth it? I used Ask Me About What Matters to probe further.

The risk was $400. The benefits were clear. "What are the alternatives?" I asked. I could see that the mechanic didn't want to tell me about alternatives, but he also didn't want to withhold information or flat-out lie. "I can just disconnect it. This way it'll stop blinking, but you won't know what your fuel consumption is."

I could live with that outcome. And it would cost a mere $50. As you can imagine, that's the option I chose. But as you can also imagine, I would have agreed to the more expensive remedy if I hadn't had the Ask Me About What Matters in my arsenal.

Ask Me About What Matters can greatly improve your doctor visits (and as a bonus, your garage visits too) by allowing you to take an active role. I deliberately use the word "allowing" because we too often feel—or are told—it is not our place to ask.

THE DOCTOR WHO COULDN'T CURE THE ZUMBA DISEASE

So far we have discussed the health literacy of patients. It stands to reason that we need to discuss the other players in the interaction—the doctors. Doctors understand and have access to health information. What they often don't have is knowledge about specific patients. Sometimes they lack the motivation or social skills to find it.

A review of patients who searched online for health information prior to visiting their doctor reads like a "he said, she said" account of a mediocre date night.[52] At first glance, searches seemed to indicate patient anxiety, which isn't surprising, considering that what one finds out about a condition might be alarming. But searches "more often led to patient reassurance, clinical understanding, and empowerment." Patients also felt that searching could have a positive impact on their relationship with their clinician, depending on how the clinicians responded when patients started probing about what they'd read online.

Clinicians, on the other hand, felt that the effect of online searches on their relationships with their patients was neutral. They "commonly raised concerns about the accuracy of online content." Given what we've seen about shady online information, doctors' concerns may be justified. Still, not all online health information is shady, and there's a glaring discrepancy between doctors' and patients' views of online information.

One burly neurologist made me doubt that doctors are open to knowledge their patients find online or elsewhere. I met him when seeking a cure for the Zumba disease.

My twenty-one-year-old daughter said she had a numbness in her left arm and left leg whenever she did Zumba. "You have the Zumba disease," I laughed. "And here is the cure: don't go to Zumba anymore." I tried to make light of it. After all, I did not want to admit that something might be wrong with my beautiful child.

The numbness wasn't easy to ignore, and not just because Zumba made her happy and she did it twice a week. She apparently felt a heaviness in her left arm and leg about once every day or two, even when she didn't do Zumba. She would lie in bed and feel the heaviness on her left side.

She was worried, not buying into my cockamamie Zumba disease joke. We found out just how worried she was when she came home one day from happy hour with her friends. She lay on the sofa in drunken bliss, lifting her left arm minimally, saying in a Southern drawl that came from nowhere, "Can't feel my arm! Can't feel it! I don't wanna be paralyzed!"

I Googled numbness of limbs.

The internet suggested that an orthopedic problem might be at the root of the numbness—perhaps Zumba was creating pressure on her nerves. It was plausible that her body, and the way she used it, weren't completely symmetrical. This would cause pressure on one side, hence one-sided numbness. My daughter went to an orthopedic surgeon, who found nothing wrong with her neck or spine, nothing to indicate any pressure to nerves.

The numbness persisted. Maybe if her nerves were unduly numb, she needed to see a nerve doctor, a neurologist. She scheduled an appointment.

"He told me to do a test where I'd be electrified," she told us when she came back. They would send low voltage through her extremities to see if there was any issue with the nerve conductance. We asked if it would hurt. "He said it doesn't hurt, it's just unpleasant. But he's a really big guy," she said, doubting whether her pain threshold and her doctor's were the same. "He told me to come back even if they found nothing."

I went with her to the electrifying exam, where they strapped down my daughter's arms and legs and ran a low voltage current through her. The good thing was that they didn't find anything wrong with her. The bad thing was that the numbness continued, along with the worry and the fear of the unknown.

Eager for a solution, she Googled numbness and came up with a surprising conclusion: her symptoms might be gluten related. She was also suffering from occasional stomach aches and tightness. Could she have found the culprit?

Her recent bloodwork did not suggest celiac disease, an autoimmune disorder that is managed by avoiding gluten. However, an estimated eighteen million Americans live with gluten sensitivity but do not have celiac disease.[53] There was only one way to find out. She loved pastries, but she took a deep breath and decided to go gluten-free for at least a month. For ten days, she did not consume any gluten, and no arm or leg sleepiness occurred. Then it came back, but only during Zumba. I cracked my Zumba disease joke again, and we laughed with relief. Surely the condition of her nerves wasn't so bad if the symptoms almost disappeared by avoiding bread and croissants.

She went to the neurologist follow-up. This time, I came with her. The doctor looked at the electrifying exam results. His eyes on his computer screen, he asked how she was doing.

She started to tell him, saying, "I read on the internet," but he cut her off. His gaze focused on her now, he said "It's either me or the internet."

"But—" she started.

He cut her off again. "It's either me or the internet," he said slowly, enunciating every word.

Was there a better way of handling the internet-doctor rivalry without catching the patient in the crossfire? Definitely.

Did it matter that the patient was female? Probably. Implicit bias is people's (including doctors') tendency to act on cultural stereotypes about social groups (characterized by age, sex, or race, for example). This bias occurs subconsciously and can be at odds with a person's explicit beliefs.[54] Furthermore, since doctors constantly read scientific material, they tend to believe that their judgments are impartial. Implicit bias leads to differences not only in communication but also in treatment. Such bias explains why Black patients receive less analgesia in emergency departments,[55] and why, according to one study, Hispanic patients were seven times less likely to receive opioids in emergency departments than non-Hispanic patients with similar injuries.[56]

Women don't escape these biases. Male patients are perceived as being reluctant to report pain, so when they report it, they receive pain medication. Women, on the other hand, are described as exaggerating pain or being "hysterical" or "emotional." They wait longer for pain medication, and their concerns are often dismissed as stress related.[57] Disparities in doctors' perception lead to disparities in treatment and in overall health outcomes.

The neurologist invited my daughter to the examination table where he found her reflexes intact. "How has the numbness been?" he asked.

I tensed up. Would he cut her off again? Should I chime in, mention that I'm a psychologist who studies medical decision-making? I even outranked him academically. Should I force him to listen to her? Shame him for not doing so? But she was the patient, not me. And even though she was my baby, she was a twenty-one-year-old whom I did not want to disempower by intervening or distress by creating a conflict with her healthcare provider. Not yet.

"That's what I've been trying to tell you," my daughter persisted. "I read that it could be gluten related. So, I stopped eating gluten, and it's been much better." She reported the diminished frequency of the numbness.

I was so proud of her.

Standing up to a health professional, or indeed, to anyone who is refusing to listen, especially a person in a position of authority, requires assertiveness. But that's not all it takes, and it would be wrong to assume that personal traits are the only things standing between patients and their ability to state their case to professionals. What my daughter had at her disposal was what French sociologist Pierre Bourdieu called "embodied cultural capital."[58] Her embodied cultural capital represents the long-lasting dispositions of her mind and body, her habitus, the way she carries herself in the world, thanks to where she came from.

Her burly doctor shook his head. "That can't be it," was his verdict. Has he had enough of patients self-diagnosing, coming up with ludicrous remedies or reaching conclusions about which medication they should get? Probably. Did he experience them as undermining his professional competence? Possibly.

Shutting up a patient, as he did twice, and then dismissing her evidence, both academic and empirical (from her own hands and legs), are acts of "symbolic violence," another term coined by Bourdieu.[59] Such violence is intended to maintain the power differences and the hierarchy between whoever is applying the violence and whomever it's being inflicted upon.

Washing his hands after the exam, he may have had a moment to collect his thoughts. Or maybe he had a Post-it above the sink reminding him to be respectful to his patients. This time, he explained. "Gluten has metabolic effects. I don't see how a metabolic effect would only manifest in one side of the body."

And yet it does, I thought. It does!

He suggested an MRI, saying he did not think they would find anything there. Then he lifted his hands in despair and said, "Maybe it's psychological."

My daughter paled. What did that mean, precisely?

The neurologist asked whether my daughter might be experiencing stress. She was, except her main source of stress was the numbness. Of course, he didn't have anything to offer if the problem had been stress related or "psychological" and therefore conveniently beyond the realm of his responsibility. This seemed like blaming the victim.

Why would the doctor prefer the "psychological" dead end to the metabolic explanation that already proved to be working? I'll tell you why. My daughter's gluten hypothesis challenged the neurologist's status and the power imbalance between them. It also challenged his preconceptions. He didn't deal with croissants; he dealt with reflexes, electrification, and MRIs. To test her hypothesis, he would need the motivation to find new information. Does this sound familiar? Of course it does. This is what we expect patients to do. Their doctors should not be above it.

When we got home, I went on the internet. There I searched Google Scholar—a repository of academic literature from all disciplines—for "asymmetrical numbness gluten-related." I should have done this prior to the doctor's appointment. Within minutes I found a paper published less than a year earlier. It discussed nonceliac gluten sensitivity, which cannot be detected by a blood test.[60] It has "systemic manifestations"—effects throughout the body. "In most cases they are characterized by vague symptoms such as 'foggy mind,' headache, fatigue, joint and muscle pain, leg or arm numbness." Leg or arm numbness! Here was sound scientific evidence of the connection between gluten and numbness. Burly, surly neurologist be damned.

The gluten paper, written by Italian researchers, was published in the *World Journal of Gastroenterology*, a journal I'm sure the neurologist doesn't read. But that is all the more reason my daughter's information should have been a learning opportunity for him. When my daughter raised the gluten hypothesis at her appointment, her doctor forcefully rejected the opportunity to learn about it.

EVIDENCE-BASED MEDICINE IS CONSIDERED BEST PRACTICE. YET HOW CAN medicine be evidence-based if the doctors don't know what the most recent evidence suggests? Surely if a motivated, clever patient conducts a search and comes up with an answer where before there were only questions, the information can help point the doctor in the right direction. This partnership between doctor and patient at least merits examination. Internet-savvy patients with a healthy curiosity might be a nuisance, but they are also here to stay. They are a force to be reckoned with, a resource to be utilized, respected, and learned from. The next Zumba patient to walk into the neurologist's office would have benefited.

My daughter persevered; she found and administered her own cure. She is still off gluten, still goes to Zumba, and, thankfully, experiences no numbness. Other patients may have found a possible solution that would have needed medication, and thus the neurologist's prescription, which he might not have wanted to write. These patients could not have handled a prescription, and administered a cure, on their own.

This chapter aims to demonstrate the importance, for both patients and doctors, of improving health literacy, knowledge, and motivation to understand medical terms. This is true both for existing medical knowledge and, even more, for new, evolving knowledge. Consider, for example, the novel COVID-19 and the concepts it required us to learn.

If you think words are baffling, you're right. But if you think words—medical terms—are the only thing that's baffling about decisions regarding your health, you're wrong. Patients also need to understand the probabilities associated with the risks and benefits of treatment. And doctors also need to explain them. (If we're being honest, they first need to understand them too.) As we'll see in the next chapter, probabilities, those innocent little numbers, can get very thorny.

TAKEAWAYS

The takeaways for this chapter are inspired by the *Ethics of the Fathers*, sayings of Jewish sages who lived from 300 BCE to 200 CE, and specifically by a quotation from Hillel: "The bashful cannot learn, and the strict cannot teach."[61]

Rabbi Ovadiah of Bartenura interpreted "bashful" as referring to one who is embarrassed to ask, fearing to be mocked. He claimed that teaching involved being kind and pleasant when explaining. The twelfth-century physician and philosopher Maimonides interpreted "strict" as also angry. If Rabbi Ovadiah or Maimonides were alive today, I'm sure neither would abide by the motto "It's either me or the internet."

Patients need to understand information in order to follow treatment regimens. Before they can understand, they must have suitable materials.

Patients also need to provide their doctors with information so that their diagnoses and treatments are based on as much personalized knowledge as possible. They can only impart information if they are properly invited and listened to.

FOR PATIENTS:

1. Use every tool in your arsenal to learn about your symptoms or medical condition.
2. Use Repair, other-repair to ask for clarification of what the doctor said and self-repair to clarify and correct what you said.
3. Use Ask Me 3. Ask your doctor these questions:

    What is my main problem?

    What do I need to do?

    Why is it important for me to do this?
4. Use Ask Me About What Matters. Whenever your doctor proposes medication, a test, or a procedure—anything you need to make a decision about—ask these questions:

    What are the benefits?

    What are the risks?

    What are the alternatives?
5. Asking these questions doesn't hurt your doctor or undermine his or her expertise. You have every right to know as much as possible about your condition and to make informed choices. Furthermore, it gives your physician the opportunity to showcase and share knowledge beyond a scripted answer. It can improve the bond between you and your doctor.
6. Don't be bashful. Admit when you don't know. Never stop learning.

FOR HEALTHCARE PROFESSIONALS:

1. Speak clearly and allow your patients to drill down to the scientific terms if they want.
2. Provide your patients with opportunities to ask questions, to clarify, and repair.
3. Write down or print out relevant medical terms for your patients. Help them so that they don't have to rely on memory. Have them write down what they think they heard.

4. Use plain, actionable language, not Medicalese. Remember the difference between elevated creatinine levels and being dehydrated. Most patients will only know how to act upon the latter.

5. Don't be strict, judgmental, or angry when your patients don't understand or when they want to know more.

6. Never stop teaching.

7. The patients visit you not only to receive information but also to give it. Your patients are the gateway to firsthand, personalized information about their sensations, concerns, and symptoms. Listen to what your patients tell you and invite them to share.

8. Do not be offended when your patients bring the internet to the examination room. It's legitimate for them to actively seek information about their condition. Plus, your patients probably have more time than you do to dedicate to this inquiry. Respect their research and see what you can learn from it.

9. Don't be arrogant. Admit when you don't know.

10. Never stop learning.

FOR HEALTHCARE SYSTEMS:

1. Make it a habit to create accessible information. Tailor materials to the reading level of a fifth-grader.

2. When creating materials, also provide the option to drill down for higher-level terms so that patients can feel up to par with their doctor's knowledge when explaining what they have learned.

3. Give doctors the flexibility and resources to extend appointments beyond fifteen minutes.

4. Create institutional invitations, norms, and training around tools like Repair, Ask Me 3, and Ask Me About What Matters.

5. No patient should be made to feel too embarrassed to ask.

CHAPTER 5

THE PROBLEM WITH PERCENTAGES
AND PROBABILITIES

M edicine is a realm of probabilities: Will the treatment work? Will the bad genes cause cancer? Break your arm, you'll need a cast. That's a certainty—about one of the only certainties medicine ever presents. The rest is probability.

The winter of 2020 saw the outbreak of the COVID-19 pandemic. From my perspective as a decision scientist, COVID-19 emphasized how pivotal understanding probabilities is for making good medical decisions.

The pandemic started out small, lulling some into indifference. But catastrophe was impending—by February 5, China had reported 563 deaths from COVID-19, a mere 0.0000469 percent of its population, and yet disastrous.[1]

I was interviewed on the radio that day about the novel virus. Standing in a quiet corner of the University Arms Hotel in Cambridge, I told the reporter things like, "People returning from China should be tested," and "You have to impose quarantine on anyone who has corona." Calling for swift, aggressive action against a threat the West had yet to experience, I sounded to myself like a biblical prophet, foreseeing hail and brimstone while the hotel bar was hopping.

In early April 2020, *Reader's Digest* asked a group of scientists, myself included, how COVID-19 differed from other epidemics throughout history. I spoke about countries already taking precautions before the disease reached pandemic proportions, responding to the probability of deaths that could happen but hadn't occurred yet. I explained that many world leaders had ignored the virus when it was in its infancy and could have been more easily contained because death from the novel virus posed a small probability threat, and people ignore those. Most people treat probabilities as binaries, as all or nothing.[2] The low-likelihood probabilities, then, are dismissed as zero probability.

Eventually, the probabilities became impossible to ignore. By January 2, 2021, 3 percent of those who had had COVID-19 had died from it. That was 0.0235 percent of the world's population, but we were no better equipped to understand the numbers.[3] Yet such small percentages were an awful lot of people and caused an awful lot of damage. They carried calamitous health consequences, wreaked emotional havoc, and brought the world economy to a screeching halt. COVID-19 was forcing politicians and policy makers to become amateur statisticians (and epidemiologists). The health of nations depended on it, as did their financial prosperity.

In this chapter we'll see just how poorly we—meaning you, me, your doctor, and quite a few heads of state—deal with probabilities. We are not beyond hope. In fact, we can easily process probability when it is represented in a more natural and comprehensive way. This brings probabilities to life, leads to better understanding, and gives us and our doctors the power to make informed decisions.

But first, let's talk about rain.

A 30 PERCENT CHANCE OF RAIN, AND ONLY ONE UMBRELLA

No matter how much you pay for your coffee, how big your mansion, or how dazzlingly you play your electric guitar, you cannot make it rain. And when it rains, you cannot make it stop. You cannot prevent it from getting in your shoes and turning your hair into a soaking mess. Rain is humbling. And so is calculating the probability of rain.

This is what I talked about on a rainy afternoon in Seattle at the Presidential Symposium of the Society for Behavioral Medicine.[4] The esteemed physicians and psychologists filling the hall had come to learn how to better serve their patients, and I had come to help them experience what it felt like to be in their baffled patients' shoes as they tried to process unfamiliar and intimidating probabilities.

I started by putting them at ease, saying things they would agree with—for example, that both doctors and patients must take steps in order to make patients even minimally involved with their health, doctors doing their best to explain, patients doing their best to understand. Having planted the seeds, I then wanted my audience to experience being on the receiving end of probabilities. I proceeded with a weather-appropriate example, a classic both in decision theory and on the Weather Channel: "A 30 percent chance of rain."[5] I had it on a slide, illustrated by a cloud, though I might as well have pointed to the drizzle outside the window. "A 30 percent chance of rain." Trivial, isn't it? Then it should be just as trivial to explain what it means.

I offered them the following options:

1. It will rain in 30 percent of the area.
2. It will rain for 30 percent of the time.
3. It rains on 30 percent of days like this.

Hmmm...

For a terribly clever crowd, they were suddenly terribly quiet. Why is it so hard to answer this question? I explained just that. Even though we've heard the phrase "a 30 percent chance of rain" so many times, the reference class—what the percentages relate to—is not clear and is never spelled out. Do they relate to the area, time, or days?

Probability provides abstract information about the world in general. In this case, the probability summarizes the existing knowledge about all the days with weather conditions like this and concludes that it will rain on 30 percent of them. This is the type of question probability can answer. If you chose option 3, you were right.

But life isn't a question on a PowerPoint slide. When you prepare to leave the house in the morning, you don't want to think abstractly about days or to get an answer about the world in general. You want to know whether to take an umbrella—an entire umbrella, not 30 percent of one—and whether to wear rain boots or skimpy little sandals.

The percentages that probabilities give you refer to an entire class of events, all the days with such weather conditions. But the information you want is about a single event—this specific day—so you can choose specifically about umbrella, boots, and sandals. No wonder that the more we delved into probabilities, the more frustrated my audience became.

EVERYONE AT THAT SYMPOSIUM HAD LEARNED ABOUT PROBABILITIES. They had also learned about Thomas Bayes, whose sketched portrait gazed at us from the next slide. Bayes had been dead almost 250 years when I gave the talk, but he remained immortalized by his work. The English Presbyterian minister, philosopher, and statistician was the first to use compound probability, which is known as Bayes's rule or Bayes's theorem. It forms the basis of Bayesian reasoning.

Here is an example: You are coughing. COVID-19 patients cough. Do you have COVID-19? According to Bayes's rule, to find out, you have to calculate the probability of having COVID-19, multiply it by the probability of coughing if you have COVID-19, and divide by the general probability of coughing. Thankfully, this general probability is substantially higher than that of having COVID-19.

I wrote down the formulas for Bayes's theorem on the board, in part to help my audience remember and in part to humble them with the mathematical notations:

P(A|B) is not the same as P(B|A).
P = probability.
A = what we are seeking (disease, like tuberculosis).
B = the effect (symptom, like coughing), what we observe.

And the theorem:
$$P(A|B) = \frac{P(B|A) \cdot P(A)}{P(B)}$$

I let my audience spend some time under the benevolent gaze of Reverend Bayes. Then I pounced. I gave them the following scenario:

- The probability of colon cancer is 0.3 percent.
- If a person has colon cancer, the probability of a positive test result is 50 percent.

- If a person does not have colon cancer, the probability of a positive test result is 3 percent.
- What is the probability that a person has colon cancer, if he tests positive?

I announced, "Nick just learned that he tested positive for colon cancer." I let this sink in and then I asked, "Does Nick have colon cancer? Should Nick call his wife and tell her they're going to use up all their savings and take that once-in-a-lifetime trip they had always dreamed of?" After a moment's dramatic pause, I laid on them the ultimate question: "Should Nick get a headstone?"

I borrowed this example from a paper by Ulrich Hoffrage and Gerd Gigerenzer.[6] The embellishment and dramatization (the wife, the trip, the headstone) were mine. They give a sense of the stakes involved in a question like this.

The room went silent. Into the silence I dropped this question: "What are the chances that Nick has colon cancer?"

This is the bread and butter of medical reasoning. It's what every doctor should consider when interpreting their patients' test results.

I snuck in, "The answer can easily be calculated using Bayes's theorem," which my audience had seen in the previous slide and which every member of my audience had studied at least once.

Why then were they having such a hard time? Why no answers?

Because, Reverend Bayes notwithstanding, using the theorem is difficult. To do it without pen and paper or a calculator gives even clever people a headache. I showed them the slide with the formulas; that did not help either. Again, no quick intuitive answer.

Pretending to be helpful, I placed the colon cancer numbers under Bayes's formula. But I have done this experiment in numerous classes and talks, and only once has someone ever used the formula. She was not there with us in Seattle. Let's see:
$$P(A|B) = \frac{0.5 \cdot 0.003}{0.0315}$$

A = what we are seeking (colon cancer).
B = the effect (testing positive), what we observe.
Probability of B given A (noted as P[B|A]) = 0.5.
Probability of A (noted as P[A]) = 0.003.
Probability of B (noted as P[B]) = 0.0315.

What, then, is the probability of having colon cancer if you tested positive, noted as P(A|B)?

My audience looked baffled. Poor audience. Poor Nick. If Nick hadn't been a figment of my imagination, he would be aching to know the odds of his having cancer.

I asked again, What were these odds?

Someone ventured "97 percent," which is 100 percent minus 3 percent false-positive rate. Another brave soul mumbled "47 percent," which is 50 percent of the illness being identified minus the same 3 percent false-positive rate.

I could not blame my audience for being wrong. Probabilities are not intuitive. Neither is reconciling sensitivity and specificity. Nobody's mind is wired for Bayes's rule. But everyone's mind is wired for System 1 thinking, using whatever information is available and trying to arrive at an answer. Let's freeze frame this image. We'll come back to Seattle.

A 60 PERCENT CHANCE OF BREAST CANCER, AND ONLY TWO BREASTS

A quarter million American women are diagnosed with breast cancer every year. One out of every five hundred American women is a carrier of a BRCA1 or BRCA2 gene mutation.[7]

BRCA1 and BRCA2 are world famous, practically celebrity genes. When mutated, they are associated with an elevated risk of breast and ovarian cancer.[8] These mutations led Angelina Jolie to remove her breasts and ovaries to prevent cancer from developing.[9] These are the kinds of decisions women face when they receive genetic information, which is why it's crucial that they understand it well.

My colleagues and I set out to examine what elevated risk means to women, and how they interpret the probabilities surrounding BRCA.[10] We made a conscious effort to mimic reality. We reached out to women around age forty, who resemble the target audience for health messages on breast cancer risk, according to information from the National Cancer Institute website:[11] "According to estimates of lifetime risk, about 13.2% (132 out of 1,000 individuals) of women in the general population will develop breast cancer, compared with estimates of 36 to 85% (360–850 out of 1,000) of women with an altered BRCA1 or BRCA2 gene. In other words, women with an altered BRCA1 or BRCA2 gene are 3 to 7 times more likely to develop breast cancer than women without alterations in those genes."[12]

Just like the "30 percent chance of rain" example, the National Cancer Institute's phrasing seemed obvious at first glance but was less so once converted to everyday English. To examine how women would interpret the message, we gave them four options and asked them to choose the right one:

1. Breast cancer will develop in 36 to 85 percent of women who are found to have BRCA1 and BRCA2 alterations.
2. Breast cancer will develop in all women aged 36 to 85.
3. Women who have BRCA1 and BRCA2 alterations will exhibit 36 to 85 percent of the symptoms associated with breast cancer.
4. Women who are found to have alterations in the genes called BRCA1 and BRCA2 have 36 percent to 85 percent higher chance of developing breast cancer.

Absorb this and choose the correct interpretation before reading on.

Which one did you choose?

Of our participants, just under half chose option 4, which is incorrect. Nearly all the remaining participants—almost half the total—chose the correct answer: option 1.[13] This is where you may wonder, Isn't it splitting hairs to make a difference between options 1 and 4, between breast cancer developing in a given percentage of women and women having a higher chance of developing the disease?

These are hardly trivialities. Twelve out of every hundred women in the general population will develop breast cancer, as opposed to sixty out of every hundred women with the BRCA1 mutation (leaving out BRCA2).[14] BRCA1 represents an elevated risk of 500 percent! Not 60 percent more (which would be 19.2 percent risk of developing breast cancer). For a woman considering the removal of her breasts or ovaries or grappling with having elevated risk of breast cancer, the difference between 500 percent and 60 percent is anything but trivial.

NUMERACY IS THE ABILITY TO SOLVE PROBABILITY QUESTIONS.[15] IT'S PAR-
tially a mathematical equivalent of literacy. (Numeracy looks at how well
people understand numbers, mostly probabilities, but it doesn't assess their
motivations.) We found that the chances of choosing the correct answer were
much higher for women who were younger, more educated, and belonged to
the higher numeracy level group.[16]

The results had us worried because they meant that most women who
learned they had the mutation would not be able to make an informed decision about their treatment. In order to more closely simulate a real decision,
we ran a similar study, this time advertising to women on a breast cancer
mailing list. Most of the women who responded had either been screened for
BRCA1 and BRCA2 or had previously been diagnosed with breast cancer.[17]
Of these cancer-savvy women, a little more than half correctly chose option 1,
but a sizable proportion still believed that option 4 was the right one.[18]

In this study, instead of assessing their objective numeracy, we tested their
subjective numeracy: how adept they felt they were at tasks we're all required
to perform daily—such as calculating the price of a shirt after a 40 percent
discount or reading tables and graphs in the newspaper—and how useful they
felt numeric information was in general. The Subjective Numeracy Scale is
correlated with objective numeracy, but it takes less time to complete, and
responding to it is perceived as less stressful.[19]

Once again, younger, more educated women and those of higher subjective numeracy—that sense of being at ease with numbers—were more likely
to arrive at the correct interpretation of their risk. Once again, the less educated, older women were more prone to feeling discombobulated. I feared
they would also be more vulnerable in other ways.

MICHAEL DIEFENBACH AND I REACHED OUT TO ANOTHER GROUP OF
women.[20] We asked questions that went beyond how women understood risk. We
explained that there was a test for detecting the presence of the mutated BRCA
genes and asked, "How important is it for you that the test will . . . Give me information about my BRCA1 and BRCA2 status"; 76 percent said "very important."

Then we added two trick statements about things the test cannot do. We
included "The test cannot do that" as a response option. This would have been
the right answer to these questions:

"Tell me with certainty whether I will develop breast cancer": 32 percent said "very important." (Note that the test gives probability, not
certainty.)

"Tell me what to do in case I have breast cancer": 34 percent said "very important." (Note that no test will tell you what to do. You're always the
one who has to decide.)

More than half the women we asked fell for the trick questions and chose at
least one option that the test was incapable of fulfilling. They had lower objective numeracy than the others. They were also more worried about breast
cancer screening scores than the women who didn't fall for these questions.

Lower numeracy women were also willing to pay $250 on average for the
screening, much more than the higher numeracy ones, who would only shell
out $100 for it. I can see why: women of lower numeracy were more worried
and had higher expectations that the test would give them certainty and direction. Their lack of comprehension regarding test results and what the test
could do was hurting them: they were willing to pay more, without getting
what they wanted.

In yet another study, conducted with Elissa Ozanne, Yaniv Hanoch, and
Andrew Barnes, we showed women information about breast cancer risk in a
host of formats. Lower numeracy women were more likely to prefer graphical
formats, such as bar charts, over formats that were more number heavy. Sadly,
the lower numeracy women had poorer risk comprehension in the graphical
formats they liked, compared to other formats.[21] These women also appeared
to have no intuition as to how well—or how poorly—they were grasping their
breast cancer risk.

Women may be confused over probabilities pertaining to breasts and ovaries, but the difficulty with probabilities isn't gender related. Jonathan Rolison, Yaniv Hanoch, and I examined how well men comprehend probabilistic
information about prostate cancer.[22]

To find out whether people were more confused about how genetics works
than about probabilities, we looked at two risk factors for prostate cancer:
genetics and smoking (which is linked to male cancers, including prostate
cancer).[23] For each risk factor, we created a statement about the prostate cancer risk it carried, modeled after the National Cancer Institute breast cancer

statements we had presented to women.[24] Each statement was followed by four possible interpretations. Each man received the statements and interpretations about both genetic and smoking risk. We recruited men whose average age was just over fifty-nine, for whom prostate cancer was a tangible possibility. Almost half of them had been tested for prostate cancer.[25]

Under 40 percent of the men chose option 1, the correct one, in the context of genetic risk. The results were nearly identical for the statement that referred to smoking.[26]

The title of our paper was "What Do Men Understand About Lifetime Risk Following Genetic Testing? The Effect of Context and Numeracy." I nicknamed it "What do men understand?" Not a lot, and not more than their female counterparts. We learned that the discombobulation in understanding risk wasn't because of the genetic context. It's the probability, stupid.

Now is a good time to ask, So what? So what if some lab experiments find that some people are more confused than others or cannot calculate that a gene mutation increases their risk by 400 percent? Where does this intellectual exercise get us?

In fact, people misunderstand probabilities all the time in real life, and it can have very real consequences. People, even doctors, often think in binary terms, treating the probability of benefit as high and of harm as low. Effectively, this often means that "high" becomes "certain," and "low" becomes "non-existent." Binary thinking, which essentially is very System 1, looks at benefit and ignores harm.

However, when the American Cancer Society (ACS) looked at the probability that women age forty to forty-four, who are not at a high risk for breast cancer, would benefit from mammograms, they realized it was lower than the probability of harm from screening.[27] Therefore, the ACS changed the guidelines for breast cancer screening, now recommending that women have a mammogram only from age forty-five. The younger women were spared the anxiety and discomfort of having a mammogram, the biopsies for false-positive findings, and the overdiagnoses.

Likewise, doctors used to send women aged fifty-five to seventy-four years, who *were not* at a high risk for ovarian cancer, for ovarian screening. This was before doctors realized that the screening had no benefit—it did not reduce the number of women who died of ovarian cancer—and before they realized that the screening had consequences that could cause potential harm: women received false-positive responses and sometimes had their ovaries "unnecessarily removed as part of further diagnostic work-up."[28]

Premenopausal women who are carriers of the BRCA1 or BRCA2 gene mutations (which increase the risk for both ovarian and breast cancer) are another case illustrating the value of understanding probabilities. When the women had their ovaries removed preemptively, they went into early menopause, which significantly reduced their quality of life. Hormone replacement therapy could relieve these women's sleep, mood, and sexual-functioning issues. But doctors didn't recommend the therapy because they feared it would increase these women's already elevated risk of developing breast cancer. It doesn't.[29] However, in order to realize that, you and your doctor have to use System 2 and delve into the evidence. Ideally, it's presented to you in a way that facilitates understanding.

Like a drop of rain that gets in your ear and torments you for hours, even a small misunderstanding of probabilities can have a large, dire effect. Doctors and patients alike rely on probabilities (or rather, on what we make of them) when facing such crucial health decisions as having one's ovaries removed, declining hormone replacement therapy that could hugely improve quality of life, or rushing to have one's prostate removed, when the probability of cancer is low.

There has to be better way.

BIRDS DO IT, BEES DO IT

Probabilities predate Bayes. Our ancestors had to reckon with probabilities in order to survive. When throwing a sharpened stone at an animal you wanted to hunt, you had to make sure the odds were in your favor, or you'd become the vengeful animal's lunch.[30]

We are not the only species that has to contend with probabilities to guarantee our existence. Cheetahs need to know where they are most likely to find prey. Chipmunks need to know where they are most likely to find nuts and small frogs. And mice need to know when the cat is most likely to be away. So how do these and other animals gauge probabilities? By learning about animals (and later on, about our prehistoric ancestors), we may be able to apply this learning to improve modern human comprehension.

"Eliciting probabilities from animals is difficult," said biologist Leslie Real, but he did just that—with bumblebees.[31] Real set fifty white flowers on wells filled with four milliliters of honey water. He then set up fifty yellow flowers on wells filled with varying quantities of honey water. Most of the yellow flowers (80 percent) had less nectar than the white flowers, but a minority (20 percent) had more. Across all trials, Real made sure that, collectively, the fifty white flowers had as much honey water in them as the fifty yellow flowers. So, how would the bees choose where to go?

During each foraging sequence, each busy bumblebee gathered nectar from approximately forty flowers. The bees gave thought to their flower choices. They appeared to form probability assessments based on the frequency with which they encountered various nectar states, the four milliliters in the white flowers and the varying quantities in the yellow flowers.

The bees overestimated the probability of coming across the same amount of honey water again, be it big or small, in the yellow flowers. Their future visits reflected a belief that 90 percent of the yellow flowers had less nectar than the white flowers (remember, it was actually 80 percent) and 10 percent had more nectar than the white flowers (it was actually 20 percent).[32] The bees used probabilities, but they weren't perfect statisticians. Blame it on the bee school system.

Real cautions us not to jump to simplistic conclusions and comparisons: Humans and bees do not share a recent evolutionary history or similar ecological requirements. Nevertheless, bumblebee behavior supports the idea that bees can detect probabilities and act upon them.

PSYCHOLOGIST LEDA COSMIDES AND ANTHROPOLOGIST JOHN TOOBY ARE the founders of the field of evolutionary psychology. According to the *Stanford Encyclopedia of Philosophy*, evolutionary psychology tells us that our behavior is guided by psychological mechanisms that developed through natural selection "to help our ancestors get around the world, survive and reproduce."[33]

Evolutionary psychologists apply works like Real's (his words of caution notwithstanding) to better understand how probability factors into human decision-making processes. Cosmides and Tooby asked, "If a bird brain can embody a calculus of probability, why couldn't a human brain embody one as well?"[34]

As Cole Porter wrote, "Birds do it, bees do it, even educated fleas do it." If all these animals can calculate probabilities, why can't we? (The scientific literature is silent on fleas and probability, but it's too good a song to miss.) Cosmides and Tooby say we can. But to do so, we need probabilities to be presented as natural frequencies.

Frequencies are instrumental in solving the problems our minds need to solve, in the environments where they were designed to operate. Like the bumblebees, our prehistoric ancestors encountered frequencies. However, unlike the taciturn bees, we can assume that our ancestors conveyed these frequencies to one another. Imagine returning to the cave after a long day, stretching your legs by the fire, and conferring with your cave buddies the likelihood of hunting deer in a faraway field. Here is what I believe you'd report: "I went to the field seven times, and in three of them, I hunted deer. Can you pass the deer thigh please, darling?"

With frequencies, it's easy to gauge how reliable the information is, based on the number of observations. You know whether your fellow hunter went to that field seven times or seventy. Percentages won't tell you that. Frequencies are also easy to update with additional observations: "Went to the field eight times. Three of those times, I hunted deer. Five of them, I did not."

Even if we disposed of numbers altogether, frequencies could still help us. We could still have a "big chance" or a "small chance." We could say, "Go hunt in the field" or "Try someplace else."

Cosmides and Tooby's seminal paper spans a literature review and multiple experiments, all pointing in the same direction: people are capable of high-level Bayesian reasoning.[35] But the problem needs to be presented to them in the frequency format. Cosmides and Tooby concluded, "The argument that computational procedures embodying statistical rules did not evolve . . . is empirically vacuous."[36] This is considered strong language in science.

You will be relieved to learn that "from an ecological and evolutionary perspective, *humans may turn out to be good intuitive statisticians after all.*"[37]

DO IT LIKE THEY DO ON THE DISCOVERY CHANNEL

From the bumblebees and the cavemen, we can return to my Seattle audience, racking their brains over whether Nick did in fact have colon cancer. What can we learn from their failure to understand the probabilities I gave them?

German psychologists Gerd Gigerenzer, Urlich Hoffrage, Ralph Hertwig, and their colleagues found that the problem is with the way information is given to people, not with people's statistical abilities. When information is presented in frequencies and when each reference class—which group an item belongs to, such as "the yellow flowers that offer a small amount of honey water"—is spelled out, then people, amateurs and experts alike, suddenly understand probabilities.[38]

In a frequentist presentation, you no longer ponder the probability of a single event. There is context, and thus visualization becomes easy. You'll see.

I grabbed a marker and rephrased Nick's predicament in natural frequencies on the board:

- Out of every 10,000 people, 30 will have colon cancer.
- Out of these people, 15 will test positive.
- Out of the remaining 9,970 (healthy) people, 300 will test positive.
- How many of the people who test positive have colon cancer?

The sigh of relief was palpable. Forget Bayes's theorem. Here were numbers you could immediately grasp. A fifth grader could visualize them.

Instead of having Nick float about with a diagnosis and a few probabilities attached to it, Nick was now part of a hypothetical group of 10,000 people.[39] Of the 10,000, only a small group—30—were sick. Of the sick, 15 would be diagnosed as such by the test. They belonged to the reference class of "sick people whom the test will diagnose as such." This means the same thing as "If a person has colon cancer, the probability of a positive test result is 50 percent," but it is far more vivid.

It is also more human. With a frequentist presentation, the person is the subject, not the number. We now had people in front of us, with each reference class spelled out.

The vast majority of people, 9,970, did not have colon cancer. The test would still say that 300 of them were sick. This is the frequentist translation of "If a person does not have colon cancer, the probability of a positive test result is 3 percent." But 3 percent sounds small and harmless, whereas the frequentist way of discussing false positives evoked a clear image of a nasty reference class to belong to: "the group of 300 people who will falsely receive the disheartening colon cancer diagnosis."

We could not tell what group Nick belonged to for certain. But now my educated audience in Seattle could estimate: 15 sick people were rightly diagnosed with colon cancer; 300 healthy individuals were wrongly diagnosed. Suddenly everything made sense, even though nothing had changed. Even if you were hopeless with numbers, you could still picture the 300 misdiagnosed healthy individuals and the 15 sick ones. You could just compare the groups and understand that Nick was much more likely to belong to the big group than to the small one. And you could divide 15 (those who were diagnosed with cancer and actually had it) by 315 (all those who were diagnosed with cancer) to find that Nick's chances of being ill with colon cancer were under 5 percent (4.8 percent). No need for him to dip into his life savings or get a tombstone just yet.

In Seattle, birthplace of Starbucks coffee, Bill Gates, and Jimi Hendrix, the sun was finally shining.

IT'S THE FORMAT, STUPID

If frequentist presentation is the solution to understanding probabilities easily, you might wonder why it's not yet already standard practice. No one is actively pushing for it, that's why.

Nobody is demonstrating or organizing Facebook petitions promoting frequentist presentations. Nobody is tweeting to overthrow probabilities, or spray-painting hospitals and HMO office buildings demanding frequentist presentations. Nobody even notices there is anything wrong with probabilities. We're so used to them that we consider them objective and cannot see their effects on our comprehension and risk perception. Instead, we feel we need to be better at understanding probabilities. But how?

My genetic-counseling students faced their hardest moment when they realized that the way they presented probabilities influenced what their clients understood, how they felt, and sometimes even what they did. My students, who strove to be objectively nondirective, were now weighed down with an enormous responsibility. Every word, every phrasing, matters. This is what Yaniv Hanoch, Dana Graef, Michal Sagi, and I found in a study with

Princeton University students as participants. We gave the students a "letter to an expectant mother" summarizing the results of a prenatal screening test, including an estimate of her risk of having a baby with Down syndrome.[40]

We separated the students into three groups. The first group received the information in a probabilistic format:[41] "The probability of giving birth to a baby with Down syndrome for a woman with normal results is 1:724. The probability of giving birth to a baby with Down syndrome for a woman with abnormal results [presented to the participants] is 1:181." (As Odette Wegwarth and Gerd Gigerenzer reminded me via email, this isn't exactly probabilistic format; it's odds, which require another step for the probability to be calculated.)

The second group received the information in the caveman's format of choice, the frequentist one: "One out of every 724 fetuses of women your age will be diagnosed with Down syndrome. One out of every 181 fetuses of women your age with test results identical to yours will be diagnosed with Down syndrome." The subjects of the sentences were now the fetuses, not the probabilities.

The third group received the same frequentist information as the second group, along with visual illustrations.[42] One text said, "One out of every 724 fetuses of women your age will be diagnosed with Down syndrome. The white circle in the picture represents the only fetus with Down syndrome. There are 724 circles in the picture." The image showed 723 black circles and one white circle. A second text said, "One out of every 181 fetuses of women your age with test results identical to yours will be diagnosed with Down syndrome. There are 181 circles in the picture." This image showed 180 black circles and one white circle. We weren't sure how this format would play out, or whether the visual image would help comprehension even more or complicate it.

Regardless of how we presented the statistics, the letter to the expectant mother always concluded by saying that an amniocentesis test was recommended, given the results and the elevated risk for Down syndrome. She was invited to a genetic-counseling session.[43]

We chose 1:181 as the risk assessment because it's close to 1:200. Since 1:100 equals 1 percent, which everyone would know, then everyone might also know that a number close to 1:200 would be close to half a percent. To

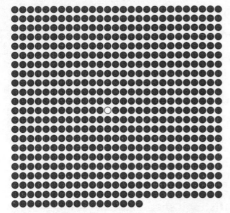

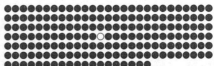

One out of every 724 fetuses of women your age will be diagnosed with Down syndrome. The white circle in the picture represents the only fetus with Down syndrome. There are 724 circles in the picture.

One out of every 181 fetuses of women your age with test results identical to yours will be diagnosed with Down syndrome. There are 181 circles in the picture.

see how format influenced comprehension, we asked, "After reading the letter, what do you think the probability is that the woman is carrying a fetus with Down syndrome?" We accepted anything under 1 percent as a right answer.

The frequentist format was associated with the highest level of understanding. Two-thirds of the participants in this format group nailed it.[44] In the visual format group, slightly more than a half the participants arrived at the correct estimation. And the 1:181 format group (the probability format, the one the women usually got), only about a third of the participants gave the right answer.

While the frequentist format was better than the probabilistic one, our participants gave them similar clarity ratings—around "medium" in both groups. The students who received the probability format did not have a sense of how much it was impeding them, nor did the students who received the frequentist format have a sense of how much it was helping them. This is one reason why they weren't petitioning for or demonstrating against any of the formats.

I believe there is another reason: people feel that numbers are never very clear to them and that it's their own fault. But it isn't. Whenever I present this research, I proudly mention that our participants were smart, motivated Princeton University students—partly because of my love for Princeton, but mostly to show that format also influences the smart and motivated.[45] Without the help of the frequentist format, even the smart and motivated were baffled by probabilities. These intelligent students, just like the rest of us, were treating the difficulty of probabilities as they would the inevitability of having rain ruin their hairdos.

And they are not alone. I was recently involved in an email exchange in an academic network where at least three Nobel laureates were subscribed. They were discussing a potential new development in detection of the coronavirus and whether the proposed test for being a virus carrier was any good. This required some guesswork for the true positive rate of carriers in the population. One of the email recipients (a distinguished mathematics professor) responded that he *finally* understood the claim the paper was making—his friend, a statistics professor, had explained it. That it took several mathematical and statistical masterminds to decipher such information is both humbling and enraging.

The fault is not in the probabilities per se, and not in ourselves, either. It's in the format in which probabilities are presented, which is—usually—stupid.

A SUBTLE BUT POWERFUL DYNAMIC

Expecting a patient to consult with a statistics professor to fully understand risk is both unfair and inefficient. Here I will present a solution that can be handmade each time with endless patience and compassion.

This solution isn't uniquely focused on probabilities—it's designed to elicit patients' questions and to explain to them what their doctors are saying. I learned about it from Yash Huilgol. I was one of his thesis advisers at Princeton. After graduating with honors, he moved to San Francisco for a fellowship at the University of California San Francisco (UCSF) Breast Cancer Center, where he conducted coaching calls for new patients prior to appointments. He would offer patients educational resources and address their concerns. Then he would sit with them in consultations, making sure the patients had discussed all the questions they had planned in advance. He would record the meetings and produce consultation summaries.

This labor-intensive yet free service Yash was delivering is the first solution. It exists at the breast cancer center, as well as on demand from other doctors at UCSF. Patients respond favorably because it comes with a healthy dose of personal attention. When I asked what his role was called, Yash said, "I've been struggling to find a word—maybe patient advocate? We aren't there for the doctor. We are helping the patient. We serve as their advocate."

This distinction is important. Dr. Jeff Belkora, who manages the Patient Support Corps at UCSF's medical center, told me that he considered the main success of the program to be "collaborating with physicians who've never seen or been exposed to this kind of program."[46] The hospital was in favor, but the program ran mainly on philanthropic support and a shoestring budget, using interns and Berkeley premed students.

I asked Jeff whether the program could be expanded to other hospitals. He said that it was being done at Dartmouth-Hitchcock Hospital but not nationally and that it would probably be a tough sell. Most institutions operate under a fee-for-service model, and there is no incentive for such a service. One of the things we know from the study of shared decision-making (which I'll get into in Chapter 8) is that informed patients make less use of defensive medicine, which would mean less revenue.

Jeff also said he sometimes heard pushback from individual doctors, such as, Informed patients might slow me down, or, If we show patients all the risks of chemotherapy and how relatively small the benefits are, how will we convince them to take chemo?

Oh boy. Such statements show a willingness to cloud patients' vision and decision-making processes by presenting probabilities either vaguely or not at all. I must have said "oh boy" out loud, because Jeff added, "It's a subtle but powerful dynamic we're discussing."

KNOWLEDGE IS POWER, SIR FRANCIS BACON SAID. IMAM ALI, IN THE SEVenth century, said it more distressingly: "Knowledge is power and it can command obedience."[47] People who lacked knowledge obeyed the people who had it. "Obey" is a strong word. When we talk about "obeying" in the medical realm, we're reminded that probabilities are associated with actions that ultimately affect the patient's life.

The solution I brought here—the service provided by Huilgol and Belkora at UCSF—is institutional. It involves intervention by a third party and the dedication of resources to promote clear, validated communication of probabilities and medical terms, all in order to solve the problem with probabilities, which patients need to understand when deciding about their health.

This solution requires the collaboration and approval of both patient and doctor. Understanding probabilities can then lead to action, especially when discussed with the doctor.

Once you've overcome the problem of probabilities, you'll be able to use the knowledge to help you in the health choices that, at some point, you will need to make. The goal of the health information you receive and need to decipher is to assist you in that process, and probabilities should be able to help guide you. Choice is inherently woven into our health journey and is the topic of the next chapter.

TAKEAWAYS

The takeaways for this chapter are influenced by the movie name *Definitely, Maybe*. How can these two terms work in tandem, almost interchangeably? The answer is that they can only work in tandem in our heads, because, as humans, we don't deal well with uncertainty, so we turn it into a certainty. And yet most medical conditions and treatments are associated with chance and probability, not certainty. Patients need to know the statistics in order to make informed choices. Compound probabilities must be presented in a way that is clearly accessible to patients and to their physicians.

FOR PATIENTS:

1. If probabilities are unclear to you, you are not alone.
2. When your doctor recommends a treatment, ask about the probabilities of benefit in terms of frequencies: "Of one thousand people like me who will receive this treatment, how many will benefit, and how?"
3. When your doctor recommends a treatment, ask about the probabilities of risk in terms of frequencies: "Out of one thousand people like me who will receive this treatment, how many will have side effects? How severe will they be? For how long?" When you hear these numbers as frequencies, you'll be better able to judge whether you want the treatment.
4. When your doctor recommends a test, ask to have the false-positive rate of the test spelled out. This dry statistical term can mean major health

scares, for it shows how many healthy people will be incorrectly identified as sick.

5. When your doctor recommends a test, ask to have the true-positive rate spelled out: "How many sick individuals will be accurately identified as such?" And the false-negative rate: "How many sick individuals will be misidentified as healthy? When you hear these numbers as frequencies, you'll be better able to judge the effectiveness of the test.

6. Asking for frequencies may still be uncommon, but it makes sense. Don't feel ashamed if "three out of every thousand people" is clearer to you than "0.3 percent." It's clearer to most people, doctors included.

FOR HEALTHCARE PROFESSIONALS:

1. Always use frequencies when you explain statistics to your patients. Say "out of one thousand people with your condition, thirty will die within a year." It's clearer than "3 percent." Or say "out of one thousand people who receive this treatment, three will have a benefit in terms of better survival." It's a lot clearer than "0.3 percent," and it's far more helpful.

2. Spell out the reference class. Are you talking about people who are sick, who test positive, or some other specification?

3. If you are unsure of what the numbers are, do the research beforehand.

4. It's your responsibility to provide the most accurate numbers and present them in the clearest manner. It's your patients' responsibility to then choose based on their interpretation of the probabilities and on their preferences.

FOR HEALTHCARE SYSTEMS:

1. Make sure your materials present probabilities as frequencies, or add the frequency presentation format instead of including only percentages. This should always be done, whether facing patients or health professionals.

2. Insist that materials spell out reference classes; for example, "Out of every 10,000 people, 30 will be sick. Of the 9,970 healthy people, the test will wrongly identify 300 as sick."

3. Don't worry about deterring patients from choosing treatments that carry only a small chance of succeeding. Your concern should be over whether patients are making an informed choice, and about improving health, obviously.

4. Teach doctors how to present probabilities as frequencies. Make sure that out of every one hundred physicians at your institute, one hundred use this transparent way of conveying information about chances.

CHAPTER 6

CHOOSING IS A PAIN

In this book, which is all about health choices, we now get to the very act of choosing. Everything we've discussed so far leads up to it: the increased ability we now have to choose, and the blunders we sometimes make doing so; our cognitive mechanisms, and their limitations; the unique challenges we encounter when dealing with our health—from the relationships with our doctors, who present our options to us, to the language in which these options are described and the probabilities surrounding them. Now, we must make a choice. It is the pinnacle of our empowerment as patients, in theory.

Choice is a part of life. We've grown so accustomed to choosing that we view it as a natural right, just like life, liberty, and the pursuit of happy hour. Choice is something we need, want, and deserve. Imagine the dairy section at the supermarket with only one kind of cheese. Outrageous! Imagine going on YouTube and finding just one power-yoga video. Inconceivable!

There are clear advantages to having the power to make your own choices, such as control and freedom. Indeed, as psychologist Barry Schwartz points out, "When people have no choice, life is almost unbearable."[1] But with choice come responsibility, cognitive overload, and the potential for regret. These afflict us and our doctors, leading to inaction, confusion, and occasionally mistakes. Having too much choice can be just as problematic as not having enough. This is the love-hate relationship that Schwartz describes as the "Paradox of Choice."

Sheena Iyengar elaborates on this idea in her book *The Art of Choosing*. In 2006 she gave a talk at the Institute for Advanced Study at Princeton that blew my mind: she questioned choice! The cornerstone of our existence! She went at it at full speed, and she had the relevant research to show why choice, whether of chocolates or pensions, wasn't always good for us. The more choice we had, she said, the more excited we were. But we were also less inclined to choose, and when we did choose, the results weren't optimal.

She and Schwartz showed that having more options could make people feel worse about what they did choose, even if they had taken the best option. Schwartz and Iyengar studied how students felt about their first jobs after college.[2] If there was something about a job the students didn't take that was better than the one they did take—even if it was insignificant, like a better coffee machine—students "deducted" this from how much they valued the job that they had. They did this even if their salary and their benefits were greater than they would have been in the job with the better coffee. So the negative emotional outcomes of choice might linger even after a choice has been made.

Schwartz and Iyengar are not alone in questioning the value of choice. In their book *Nudge: Improving Decisions About Health, Wealth, and Happiness*, Nobel Prize–winning economist Richard Thaler and legal scholar Cass Sunstein explain their objection to choice. They claim that people often consider it a nuisance and prefer to have a good default option—having someone choose for them or present them with an option that is best overall. A good default option is particularly helpful when choice is complex.[3] A "nudge" does that—it gently pushes in the right direction, simplifying choice but allowing one to choose differently.

In this chapter we will tread in increasingly larger circles: from a patient who was forced to make a choice under impossible circumstances, to patients who choose in the comfort of their physicians' office but are not sure how, to seniors who choose (poorly) in the comfort of their homes. We will then look at what happens when behavioral economics affects organ donation choices, which are made by every citizen, and fertility decisions, which are agonizingly made by few.

But first, let's talk about home decor.

RHAPSODY IN BLUE

If you had sneaked into my office one afternoon last May, you might have caught me red-handed, or rather blue-handed, with multiple tabs open in my browser to different paint company catalogs. I wanted to paint a drab niche in my living room so it would imbue the house with warmth and character. But there were over 3,500 shades to choose from. I narrowed down the assortment by ruling out everything except my favorite color, blue. Gorgeous squares of color now covered the screen, bearing names like St. Lucia Skies and Deep Ocean. But that was as far as I got.

Choosing paint was different from other consumer choices, such as buying cheese or picking a power-yoga video, and bore some similarities to the medical choices people have to make. For cheese and power yoga, I had already developed my own default choices, which minimized cognitive effort: Gouda for sandwiches, Saint-Maure as a treat (the riper the better), and the first power-yoga video that was the right length from among the top search results. The cost of cheese is low, power-yoga videos are free, and the choice of either can be quickly changed without long-term consequences.

Paint was a different shade of choice. I had never painted a niche before; I had no habit to fall back on. The catalogs offered no default to revert to, no "most popular" category that would allow me to enjoy the seductive selection without agonizing over finding "the one."

Herbert Simon, originator of bounded rationality, delineated two main choice styles people could use: maximizing and satisficing. Maximizers search for the very best option (be it cheese, a job offer, or medication), even when there are many options to choose from and the comparison between them is exhausting and wastes mental resources. Satisficers, on the other hand, are satisfied with what is sufficient—the first option that crosses their threshold of acceptance.[4] Maximizers end up with the better option, but satisficers have more fun.

I would happily have satisficed, I just needed a reason for choosing. People like to be able to justify their choices, but justification requires some knowledge. Since I was no paint expert, the parameters for choosing eluded me. I could not gauge sheen, saturation, dramatic effect, or luster—and satisfice on them.

Varsity Blues was described as "recalling the spirited sports competitions of bygone school days." It was unrivalled—or maybe it was a bit rivalled by the

Caribbean Azure with its "sense of romance and magic . . . as full of promise as a moonlit stroll along a tropical beach." I wavered between the championship football jacket and the moonlit stroll. Each offered different advantages. I scrolled further, as if this would help me choose.

There were no clear rights or wrongs and no rules to guide me through this task or tell me when to stop looking. This endless freedom also worked against me. Barry Schwartz had claimed that too much freedom from constraint is a bad thing. Without constraints or rules within which to operate, we feel helpless.[5]

Fear of error and the emotional concerns of self-blame and regret gnawed at me. And the consequences . . . a world war could break out if I chose Washington over Prussian Blue! Okay, unlikely . . . Still, if I had to reverse my decision and paint over the new shade, this would involve time, money, and mess.

I might have been happier choosing from a four-year-old's restricted palette of primary colors. In fact, extrapolating from experiments in other domains of choice, I probably would. I sighed, closed the multiple tabs of color catalogs, and with a palpable sense of relief went back to studying medical decision-making. That didn't mean I hadn't decided. By avoiding making an active choice, I had decided to stick with my drab-colored niche.

CHOOSING PAINT WITH NO EXPERIENCE IS AS CLOSE AS HEALTHY PEOPLE can get to making a medical decision. It's a one-time choice for which they are ill-equipped and where the choice makes a lasting difference. It is a decision where their own preferences play a key role, so guidance can only help up to a point. No design expert could have handed me a tin of paint and guaranteed I would like it. Choice overload, a need for guidance, fear of making a mistake, fear of dealing with the consequences of said mistake, and hope of living to regret it—these are the feelings patients often face nowadays as they have an increasingly active role in medical decisions and choice.[6] And health choices aren't a wall that can be painted over.

When we feel unfit to make a given choice, three things happen.

First, we experience cognitive difficulty. The more options we need to choose from, the harder it becomes to compare them and the more mental resources we must use up. Options may differ on several dimensions, such as price, quality, risk, and familiarity. We now need to decide which dimensions matter to us and, of these, which matter more and which less. In behavioral economics this process is known as the construction of preferences because we don't always have set preferences or know how we feel about options and dimensions.

We also need to evaluate each option on each of the dimensions. This process is beginning to sound like a lot of work, even if I'm just debating among three shades of blue. Cognitive overload may ensue, where the amount of information to be processed exceeds what we can handle. In such cases, because we are cognitive misers who like to spend as little mental energy as possible, we simplify and choose based on just a few dimensions.

Second, we face an emotional toll for making a choice. Self-blame, for example, often accompanies choice, and being responsible for choices increases self-blame if results are poor, because presumably we feel there were enough options that we could have chosen a decent one. Self-blame can happen even if, at the time we made a choice, we could not have known it would turn out to be a mistake.

Chronologically speaking, we should first make a choice and then, if we experience a poor outcome, feel self-blame or regret and learn a lesson so we don't face a similar situation in the future. Behavioral economists, however, have found that regret is also an anticipatory emotion: sophisticated creatures that we are, we know that we might come to regret a choice and have to face its consequences. Therefore, we factor possible mistakes into our considerations ahead of time when choosing, as if they are some cautionary tale.[7]

By imagining possible futures and consequences of our choices, we feel preemptive regret associated with various choices and their undesirable outcomes. Previewing teaches us to avoid potentially regretful options, often by choosing the more established, less risky option. This is why, for example, we are more likely to buy a branded, more expensive appliance than a lesser known, cheaper one.[8]

And third, we may not end up with the best option.

A FISTFUL OF CHOICES

Clint is an overweight smoker in his fifties with a chronically bad temper. A leading economics reporter, he spends his days poring over tables displaying data that make little sense to most of us. The numbers, he says, speak to him. Clint was certain he was well equipped to make smart choices. Then Clint came in for a routine checkup with his cardiologist. Even though Clint was feeling fine, the cardiologist noted some issues and recommended that Clint have a coronary bypass. It's an invasive procedure in which the chest is cut open through the breastbone, and it needs two to three months for full recovery. Clint obediently signed up for the bypass his doctor suggested and returned home.

Clint's acquiescence is worrying in and of itself; he was so overwhelmed that he did not ask the basic questions he would recommend to others. It didn't occur to him to employ Ask Me About What Matters to find the risks involved in the surgery, the benefits, and the alternatives.

When he told his wife and daughters what happened, they called him an idiot. At their insistence, Clint got a second opinion. The second cardiologist also called Clint an idiot. He elaborated, "Why would you agree to a risky procedure when there are no clear clinical indications that you need it? All in all, you're doing well. If your condition worsens, you should consider a bypass. But not now. You should not volunteer to have your chest cut open."

Clint now had two options to choose from. Getting a bypass involved having major surgery, significant pain, and an extended recovery period, whereas waiting involved none of those. Clint also felt confident he would regret a bypass more than he would regret waiting. The bypass lost by a knockout.

But as often happens when choosing, having chosen to cancel the bypass surgery, Clint lost his peace of mind. He lacked the reassurance of knowing that he had chosen well. Clint wanted a no-brainer, an option that clearly outperformed the others. He understood that different doctors could have different opinions. He just did not like having to pit those opinions against each other.

When he ran into the director of the largest medical center in town, Clint blurted, "Your jackass doctors can't make up their minds over anything." (I did say he had a chronically bad temper.) Then, of course, Clint was referred to a third cardiologist, allegedly one of the best.

Clint was serene, expecting the doctor to tell him what to do and thus relieve him of the burden of choice. But instead of this blissful scenario, the cardiologist said, "You have three options." Clint's sickly heart sank as the doctor asked him, "How about we use a stent?"

A stent is a tube that is inserted into a blood vessel, or any other natural passage in the body, to keep it open. If inserted as a preventive measure, the patient should be able to recover quickly and return to work within a few days. Without a stent, the blood vessel might narrow down to the degree that no blood could pass. The result would be a massive heart attack. A stent would solve the same problem as bypass surgery, but a stent is much less invasive.

Hoping he might still be able to avoid choosing (now between three options instead of the original two), Clint asked the doctor, "What would *you* do, if you were in such a situation?" "I would go for the stent," the doctor replied. Then, after a tiny pause, he added, "But it's up to you."

THE DOCTOR'S RELUCTANCE TO DECIDE FOR CLINT IS TYPICAL OF MODERN-day medicine. For decades now, medicine has been moving away from a paternalistic model, in which the doctor determines what will happen, to one in which the patient increasingly partakes in the decision.

Choosing on one's own can be hard, especially given the vulnerabilities associated with being a patient. So hard, in fact, that Oxford philosopher Benjamin Davies and Manchester physician Joshua Parker have recently proposed that "patients should have the option to formally hand over decision-making authority to their doctor, who thus acts as an 'appointed fiduciary.'"[9] This may seem to be the same as paternalism—it isn't. Under Davies and Parker's proposal, the choice of whether or not to delegate decision-making is the patient's, who can revoke the doctor's decision-making authority at any point. These thinkers were acknowledging the burden of responsibility that was weighing on Clint, one that his doctor couldn't, or at least wouldn't, resolve.

Choosing with a loved one is no picnic either, as Baba Shiv, marketing professor at the Stanford Graduate School of Business, found out. In a TED talk about his wife's breast cancer, he says, "The most horrifying and agonizing part of the whole experience was we were making decisions after decisions after decisions . . . and these were being thrust upon us by the doctors."[10] Shiv and his wife chose to actively defer choice. They chose to "take the passenger's seat" and let the doctors—who played along—decide for them.

CLINT DIDN'T HAVE AN APPOINTED FIDUCIARY. HE COULD NOT DEFER choice. He had to choose for himself, and there was no clear winner among his options. Waiting meant that Clint wouldn't undergo a procedure, but getting a stent meant he'd be taking care of the problem with only a minimal amount of risk. Ultimately what mattered was the ability to make an active choice with a sense of purpose, and that was what the stent offered. Taking a wait-and-see position felt like too passive an option.

A few days later, Clint was lying in the catheter room in preparation for the stent. He was fully conscious, under local anesthesia, emboldened by having chosen well. A tube was going from his groin to his heart, spraying radioactive material and tracing the flow of blood through his arteries. In what would have once been science fiction but is nowadays common practice, Clint was gazing at a screen that displayed the inside of his heart. His surgeon, an interventionist cardiologist, was gazing at it too, pensively. "You know," he told Clint, "the artery we were going to put the stent in, it's half clogged, but it's also half open." A profound observation suitable for a philosophy class.

"What does that mean?" Clint inquired.

"I propose we put a stent in another artery, one that is almost completely clogged. Here, see?" The surgeon pointed. Squinting at the screen, Clint agreed, getting that decision out of the way.

"OK," the doctor said, "but which stent should I use?"

How should Clint know? Was he really supposed to keep making these specialized choices—choices his doctor went to medical school to be able to understand? Indeed, he was. "There are two kinds," the doctor went on. "One that's just a stent, and one that is coated with slow-release medication. Which one do you prefer?"

Movement is restricted when you have a tube coming up your groin all the way to your heart. Still, Clint managed a full head turn and stared at his surgeon in disbelief. Panic was sinking in.

Deliberating over what to choose, along with the actual act of choosing, is depleting. Depleted people are either passive or impulsive. They don't engage in careful deliberation. They use mental shortcuts.[11] Clint was feeling depleted, with a capital D.

Clint's doctor could have anticipated this predicament. The doctor probably knew ahead of time that such decisions might need to be made. The doctor could—and should—have presented the choices to Clint in advance, giving him the opportunity—and genuine ability—to contemplate them under less compromising circumstances.

WHEN I DESCRIBED THIS SCENE TO MY FRIEND VARDIT RAVITSKY, A CANA-dian bioethicist, she said it was abandonment. I couldn't find this concept anywhere in a medical context, so I asked France Légaré, a physician and an authority on patient involvement, what she thought. "You seem to be tapping into something very interesting and novel," Légaré said. "Perhaps it has some relationship with the extreme of the continuum where the patient or client becomes, or is forced, into a pure consumer role and thus feels abandoned. . . . Overwhelmingly patients or clients want to be supported and not left alone totally by themselves."

This sense of abandonment, I thought, could occur when a doctor explained the diagnosis and the proposed treatment, with its risks and benefits, and then left the patient to decide. In such cases, abandonment was masquerading as empowerment.

Clint found himself abandoned in this situation. "How did you end up choosing?" I asked him.

"The medication-coated stent would reduce the risk of the artery clogging again by 40 percent. This was the pro," Clint explained patiently, "but it's not that big of a pro when you consider the chances of the artery reclogging anyway, since I would just be gaining a 5 percent increase in the probability that the stent would keep on working."

"So, what's the con?" I asked, impressed at his knowledge and his ability to apply System 2 thinking while lying on the operating table. "The con is that I would need to take a blood-thinning pill daily for at least a year, maybe forever."

Not the end of the world, I suppose. But perhaps not worth the mere 5 percent increase in the success rate.

"There's more," Clint continued. "As long as I'm on the blood-thinning pill, I can't be operated on. What if I do need to have bypass surgery done?" Clint had listed three different dimensions that his options involved: reducing the risk of a clogged artery, taking a daily pill, and being unable to have surgery.

"Which stent did you choose?"

"The simple one," Clint replied, almost disinterested. I could have analyzed Clint's choice for him, but there was nothing to gain from that. Clint had made his choice, leaving the agony of choosing behind. Discussing it now could only lead to self-blame and regret, which I was glad he wasn't experiencing, living happily postsurgery with his new stent. So I kept my mouth shut.

YOUR DRUG OF CHOICE—ISH

Our health choices are often less dramatic than Clint's, but they are no less significant. For example, many of us choose what medication to take. For each condition, our pharmacist or physician can offer several potential drugs. Drugs vary from one another on quite a few dimensions: their mechanisms of action, the frequency of taking them (once a day, twice a day, once a week, and so on), the pharmaceutical companies that manufacture them, and their price tag. Drugs matter to our health, so we had better choose well.

Atrial fibrillation (AFib) is a quivering or irregular heartbeat. It can lead to complications such as heart failure and stroke. There are several AFib medications on the market, and I've consulted a few of the pharmaceutical companies on prescriber behavior. But since the decision is ultimately the patients', I set out to discover how patients choose.

Along with two cardiologists, I reached out to 360 AFib patients.[12] The patients gave us, on average, fewer than two reasons for choosing their AFib medication. The main reason (according to 61 percent of the respondents) was that their treating physician had experience with the medication. The second reason (38 percent) was safety of use, which I'm guessing they'd also learned about from their physician. Then came two reasons patients could gauge for themselves: the frequency of taking the medication (26 percent), where patients preferred lower frequency, and side effects (21 percent). Only 13 percent of the patients chose based on the drug's mechanism of action. Much to the pharmaceutical companies' chagrin, few patients (6 percent) chose based on brand. Fewer still (5 percent) based their choices on price.[13]

The patients satisficed. To a large degree, they relied on their doctors' preferences, and to a smaller degree, on their own preferences and experience. The physicians weren't officially assigned the authority to choose, but in effect, their input was crucial for choosing. The patients seemed to appreciate the guidance.

YOUR DRUG PLAN OF CHOICE—ISH

What if the options you were offered were widely different from one another, and choosing suboptimally carried a hefty price, both financially and physically? What if you were no longer choosing just one medication but the insurance plan that would pay for all your medications? What if you—and millions of Americans—needed to engage in this choice each year? You will now see what happens when the government designs choice mechanisms with the best of intentions. I'm talking about Medicare Part D.

Medicare is a US government program that was established in 1965, long before universal healthcare was a glint in President Barack Obama's eye. It provides health insurance coverage, including hospital and doctor costs, for individuals over the age of sixty-five and for those who have permanent disabilities.

Originally, Medicare did not cover prescription drugs, but in the 1990s, a host of prescription drug treatments for common illnesses among the elderly entered the market, turning the gap in Medicare coverage into a gaping hole. In 2003 alone, Medicare recipients each spent around $2,500 on prescription drugs, which was more than double what the average American had spent on all healthcare expenses in total in 1965.[14] Angry recipients started calling Medicare, urging officials to address this gap. In 2003, Congress and the George W. Bush administration passed legislation called the Medicare Prescription Drug, Improvement, and Modernization Act, which added the Part D prescription and medication coverage to the Medicare program.

THIS IS WHERE THE STORY GETS INTERESTING. THE MOST STRIKING AND controversial feature of the Part D legislation is that benefits are delivered by multiple private insurance providers rather than by the federal government. That is, the Part D program allowed dozens of federally approved private insurers to offer a wide range of products. The marriage of government funding and free-market ideology gave birth to a significant freedom—and burden—of choice.

"Choice architecture" is the behavioral economics term for the way choice is served to the chooser. How choice is given is not random, accidental, or automatic. As Richard Thaler, Cass Sunstein, and John Balz note, "A choice architect has the responsibility for organizing the context in which people make decisions."[15] By varying choice structures and explanations, choice architects can influence people to choose one thing over another, to satisfice or to compare options thoroughly, to switch when they've found something better, to not look for an alternative, or to stay put even if they've found one. The first recommendation made by Eric Johnson and his colleagues, who looked at the tools available in choice architecture, was to "reduce the number of alternatives."[16]

Medicare Part D went in the opposite direction of what behavioral economics recommended. It promoted an abundance, even an excess, of choice. By November 2006, more than three thousand plans were offered to potential Part D enrollees. Every county in the nation had at least twenty-seven plans available; the typical county had forty-eight different plans, and some counties featured more than seventy, offered by companies both familiar and new.

People cannot effectively choose among seventy, forty-eight, or even twenty-seven options that may look alike to the untrained eye but aren't. Part D coverage was not standardized. Plans got to choose which drugs (or even which classes of drugs) to cover, at what level to cover them, and at what price. Comparing Medicare Part D plans is difficult and crucial: patients could end up paying hundreds of dollars more if they choose coverage that doesn't suit their needs.

Since people have significantly different medication needs from one another, it's hard to rely on a centralized ranking system. Add to this the fact that one's medication needs could change as time went by and that plan features change each year, and it becomes clear that Part D asks people to make impossible choices.

Medicare did intend to help its enrollees choose. When Part D launched, the Centers for Medicare and Medicaid (CMS) worked with more than ten thousand local partners, including senior centers, youth groups, and churches, to help people understand the plans and choose from them. However, many individuals found written communications and marketing material "confusing, written in jargon, or just too voluminous."[17]

RESEARCHERS TRIED TO BETTER UNDERSTAND HOW PEOPLE WERE DEAL-ing with the situation. They ran experiments in which they showed participants several sets of plans and examined how the number of options influenced the ability to choose. No such study ever used real-life Medicare Part D plans because of legal concerns and because, ironically, the real-life materials were too complicated. Instead, participants received one table that summarized the main features of all the plans, such as total estimated annual cost, annual deductible, and whether drugs could be ordered through the mail. (In fact, this kind of summary is precisely what Princeton University presented when they hired me. The university offered four different health plans and provided four leafy brochures, but it was the two-page summary table produced by HR that guided my decision.)

But back to the studies on Medicare Part D plans. One study examined people's ability to choose between three, ten, or twenty simplified medical coverage plans.[18] For example, participants were asked to choose the program that minimized annual costs so long as drugs could be obtained by mail order, or the plan that provided access to the most pharmacies. There was always only one right answer. Unsurprisingly, the more plans people had to sort through, the less likely they were to identify the *best* plan based on each criterion.

Participants over the age of sixty-five, who qualified for Medicare, did worse than younger participants. The older individuals were more confident in their choice, which suggests they would stick with it instead of switching to a plan that was better for them.

Using the study materials, Dr. Alex Federman of Mount Sinai Hospital, Yaniv Hanoch, and I ran a study of our own. Our participants—medical students and internal-medicine residents at a prestigious New York hospital—also struggled to identify the optimal plans when they were given more choices. Even for the brightest, once the number of choices increased past a certain point, the choice architecture started to work against them.[19]

IN REAL LIFE, FEWER THAN 10 PERCENT OF ENROLLEES CHOSE PLANS THAT were optimal for them in terms of total cost.[20] The rest overspent, on average, around $370 on their plan per beneficiary per year. One out of five beneficiaries overspent by at least $500 a year.

It might be that people didn't aim to optimize by price and that, therefore, they didn't care if they ended up paying more. For example, they could choose a plan that granted them more certainty so they would not be saddled with a surprise payment, or a plan that offered access to the nearest pharmacy. But such choices didn't explain away all cases where people chose a more expensive plan. Some were paying higher premiums for plan features they didn't need, such as generic drug coverage.

People who overspent initially were more likely to change their plan later, suggesting that money was a major consideration and that they didn't stand behind their initial, more expensive choice.[21] Part D enrollees are allowed to switch once a year. Most of those who switched (80 percent) reduced their overspending by $300 on average.

Jack Hoadley of Georgetown University tracked Medicare Part D enrollees for four years and found that only around 13 percent of them switched to a new drug plan within that time period.[22] People preferred to stick with the plans they had.

This conservatism may be due to decision costs—the mental effort associated with comparing all the relevant options. Or enrollees might be displaying what behavioral economics call the status quo bias: the preference to maintain an existing situation rather than make changes. The fear of losing what they have looms more heavily than the prospect of gaining something that they don't have. To maintain the status quo, people avoid switching from their previous choices. Kahneman and Tversky showed that failure to make a change also happened when people inherited investment portfolios. Regardless of whether the portfolio was risky or conservative, those who inherited it left it as it was.[23] They chose (yes, that is a choice) not to switch.

Like so many issues we saw in healthcare, too much choice is a problem that institutions create and individuals are forced to negotiate. Choice-architecture problems needed to be solved using choice-architecture measures—tackling the number of plans and their complexity—in a way that would encourage people to choose better initially and to switch to a better option when necessary.[24] I knew just the person to discuss this with.

THE WILD LIFE OF MEDICARE PART D

Here is a little secret. Please don't share it with college administrators who reimburse faculty members for travel expense. When at a conference, some academics will sleep late, go shopping, or skip a few sessions to explore the local zoo.

But not this geek here. During a health conference in DC, I saw a two-hour break between sessions in my schedule for the next day, so I reached out to

Jack Hoadley. I wanted to meet my hero in person, and I was hoping to discuss the intricacies of choice in Medicare Part D. I'd read so much of his work that I began to think of him as Medicare's zookeeper.

Hoadley, now retired, was a research professor at the McCourt School of Public Policy at Georgetown University, and he served as a member of the Medicare Payment Advisory Commission (MedPAC) that advises Congress on the topic. This put him in a unique position for an academic: he not only studied but also influenced the policies that shaped the nation. I could not believe my good fortune when he agreed to meet me the following day.

I waltzed into Hoadley's office thinking I had all the answers, or at least some answers for how to streamline and improve choice on Medicare Part D. After all, I was a decision scientist, and I knew how choice architecture could be improved. Choice sets had to be smaller and more unified so people could compare alternatives on fewer dimensions. Nudges could be put in place to promote switching and proper comparisons. Maybe if choice were removed altogether and replaced by defaults, people would fare better. Having all the answers put a spring in my step. As a bonus, Hoadley had decorated his office with wildlife photographs; between the lion, the giraffe, and the zebra, it was almost as good as playing hooky to go to the zoo.

But as Hoadley would soon show me, there were barriers upon barriers to simplifying choice. The government did mandate that insurers send out annual messages regarding changes in their plans. But these five-to-seven-page documents were not personalized, so it was hard to understand exactly how the changes affected any particular recipient. A hundred-page document was sent out describing the plan design with all the contingencies and the fine print. Hoadley once heard someone say, "I talked to my mom, and it was still there in the envelope."

In fact, *Medicare & You 2021: The Official U.S. Government Medicare Handbook* is 124 pages long.[25] My guess is that even when it is out of the envelope, it is impossible for Mom or Dad to read cover to cover.

I asked Hoadley why different plans could not be made simpler by focusing only on their key dimensions, such as low premiums. This would make it very easy to compare plans.

Hoadley nodded. He had already considered this and realized it was a bad idea, because one dimension could not capture all that a plan offered or lacked. For example, a plan could advertise by saying, "We've got a low premium." But there was a hitch, he told me: "This may not be done with the best motives and can also be a bait-and-switch kind of approach." He added that in such cases, medication coverage has significant gaps. "There might be a low premium because [medication] coverage is minimal."

MEDICARE PART D WAS MEANT TO DO GOOD BY PEOPLE, AND PEOPLE OFten chose suboptimally. So why not go all the way and relieve enrollees of both the burden of choice and its blunders?

Of course, Hoadley had considered this too. He said that ever since plans started implementing tiered pharmacy networks—that is, certain plans only worked with certain pharmacies—it was now even harder for him, or the government, to recommend an option. "I can find which plan would offer the lowest premium, and also the lowest cost for medication. Now I need to figure out which pharmacy this plan works with and how far it is from the beneficiary's home. If it takes three buses to get there, does it still make sense that I recommend it?"

So much for making choice significantly simpler for seniors or choosing for them. Even if taking into account how well a plan performed on one, two, or even three dimensions, there were always more to consider.

Choice is seldom simple. But the American health system makes choosing particularly complicated, often with severe financial implications. It's an unwelcome side effect of the ethos of choice, which is deeply rooted in the American dream, along with a distaste for governmental control over commercial companies, even when it comes to the business of health. While I do most of my work in the United States, I have spent most of my life in Israel, where medicine is socialized, everyone is insured, and patients pay nothing when hospitalized. Still, in Israel, a country that only has four health maintenance organizations (HMOs), each offering a different geographical spread, digitization level, and services, only 2.2 percent of the population switches their HMO each year.[26] People—regardless of location—walk away from choice.

Medicare Part D, imperfect though it may be, did help seniors pay for their medications. Even Hoadley did not expect Medicare Part D to be perfect—just better. As he walked me to the entrance of the secured building, he concluded, "In trying to get these choices better, we need to get smarter. Researchers and policy makers trying to use this research need to lower barriers and encourage smarter decision-making."

I searched for cases where smarter decision-making and better, simpler choices occurred and found that they were possible. I also found that getting there could be well above the patients' pay grade, and sometimes above their doctors' pay grade as well. It required clear definitions of what choosing well meant. Just as Hoadley advocated, researchers and policy makers would have to work jointly toward better choice architecture.

CHOOSING WISELY, STOPPING WISELY

When I teach about attitudes, I ask my students to raise their hands if they have a positive attitude toward organ donation. Then I ask them to put their hands down if they are *not* registered as donors. The low number of hands that stay up proves that attitudes are not enough to get people to act.[27]

When I gave a keynote address for Donate Life America, I proudly mentioned that all my eligible family members were registered as donors. My youngest, too young to register at the time, had donated her hair for cancer patients. As a family, we held strong views in favor of organ donation, strong enough to drive us to take action.

Donate Life America reported that while 95 percent of Americans were in favor of organ donations, only 58 percent were registered as donors.[28] In February 2021, there were over 109,000 men, women, and children on the national transplant waiting list. Twenty of them died each day while waiting for a transplant. One donor could save eight lives, but only three in one thousand people died in a way that would have allowed for organ donation.[29] If we were all registered as donors, it would not solve the problem completely, but it would markedly improve the situation.

Richard Thaler remarked that "signing up to be an organ donor should be at least as easy as downloading a song to your phone."[30] In some countries, it is even easier: people are automatically registered as donors. Such a system is libertarian paternalism in action: libertarian, because a person has the choice to opt out of being a donor; paternalistic, because it guides people's actions like a caring father. It also takes care of society's best interests, increasing the number of potential donors and one's chances of receiving a donation if needed.

Eric Johnson and Dan Goldstein asked, "Do defaults save lives?" The answer was a resounding yes—globally.[31] For example, in Germany, where the default is to not be registered to donate (aka an "opt-in" country), 12 percent of the population were registered as donors, compared with 99.98 percent in neighboring Austria and other "opt-out" countries where the default is donation, such as Poland, Portugal, and Hungary. These huge differences went beyond people's personal decision styles and beyond the influence of doctors. They demonstrated that when choice architecture points the way, people follow (unless they're opposed—in which case they can opt out), and community health benefits.

STOPPING POINTS ARE ANOTHER CLEVER PSYCHOLOGICAL MEANS OF SIMplifying choice, with the goal of reducing decision effort and improving outcomes. Stopping points help us resist becoming entrenched in our choices: of whom we're dating, whom we vote for, even what we eat. When my older daughter had been vegan (mostly subsisting on pastries) for a year, my friend Dr. Leah Gniwesch, a life coach, asked her, "How's it going for you?" It didn't take a second for my daughter to reply, "I'm tired and weak all the time." The initial considerations in choosing the vegan diet had been admirable. It just wasn't working out. Sayonara vegan diet. Stopping to form an evaluation gave her permission to revise her choices and to be released from them.

Since cheerful life coaches don't usually just appear on our doorsteps, we need to be the ones to reevaluate our choices. A birthday or a holiday—anything that happens routinely—can define a point when we stop to reconsider how we deal with our health.

ONE DECISION IN WHICH PEOPLE NEED TO CHOOSE VERY WISELY, AND which weighs heavily upon them, involves fertility treatments. The consequences can be having another child, having *a* child, or, if the treatments do not succeed, having no (biological) child at all. This is a very personal choice, but it occurs in an institutional context.

Fertility specialist Dr. Avi Tsafrir and I received a grant entitled "Choosing Wisely" from Israel's National Institute for Health Policy Research. We targeted women aged forty-three to forty-five undergoing in vitro fertilization (IVF).

Israel is a "pronatal" country where all families are expected to have children, plural. I was an only child; if my mother and I got into a cab, walked into a hair salon, or ordered at a falafel stand, someone would invariably reproach her, asking why she only had one. (Yes, it's also a country where a strong sense of community can veer into intrusion.) Accordingly, Israel offers generous public funding for fertility treatments to women who are trying to conceive a first or second child, until they reach the age of forty-five.

Women may interpret this generosity as a sign that having as many treatments as possible is medically advised—it isn't. Optimistically, women's chances of becoming pregnant through IVF using their own eggs (oocytes) at these ages are approximately 5 percent per cycle and 15 percent across all IVF cycles.[32] We wondered what drove women to persist, cycle after cycle, with treatments using their own eggs, when their chances of conceiving would have been substantially higher had they used egg donation. And they knew it.

In most other countries, public and private insurance funds up to four IVF cycles. Israel's bottomless funding made it a natural lab for studying women's fertility decisions almost free of constraints.

Our participants, on average, had already had almost five IVF treatment cycles.[33] One woman had had as many as seventeen previous treatments. Most women's doctors shared with them fairly accurate information about the potential success rates of their treatments.

But when we asked the women what they thought their chances were of conceiving in their current treatment, their estimates were almost ten times higher than the objective assessments! Their estimates for their overall IVF conception chances were four times higher than the objective ones. Receiving information from the doctor—or not—did not make a dent in their overoptimism.

One of the anonymous women—I like to call her Aliza—wrote on her questionnaire, "Luckily, I don't believe in statistics." *Aliza* is Hebrew for "cheerful." In keeping with her made-up name, she drew a smiley face next to her puzzling statement. This was heartbreaking: how cheerful was Aliza going to be when she found herself on the wrong side of forty-five with many IVF treatment cycles under her belt but no cute baby in her arms?

Furthermore, if Aliza didn't "believe in statistics," what guided her choice of how many treatment cycles to have and when to switch from IVF to pursue egg donation or adoption, or to give up trying to have a baby altogether? The truth was, once Aliza and her peers started the IVF treatments, they did not actively set further criteria for choosing. Most women (71 percent) said they would have attempted treatments regardless of estimated chance. So much for choosing wisely.

Though the treatments were publicly funded, women paid out of pocket for private consultations, complementary medicine, and sperm donations (half of the women did not have a partner). Women spent 3.5 times the average monthly wage during the year of the study—just shy of $10,000.[34] When we asked the women if they had a financial cutoff point for out-of-pocket spending beyond which they would give up treatments, most (62 percent) said, "I don't know." And 24 percent said there was no such cutoff.

Treatments also came with a mental price tag that increased from one cycle to the next. According to Alice Domar, the executive director of the Domar Center for Mind/Body Health in Boston, fertility treatments imposed a significant psychological cost on women, often leading them to discontinue treatment.[35]

Fertility doctors were caught between a rock and a hard place. Doctors did convey to women how low their chances of conceiving were. But they also didn't want to discourage the women and be labeled as mean and soul-crushing on every fertility forum and Facebook group. Cancer patients, and others in dead-end scenarios, sometimes posed similar dilemmas to their doctors, as I will discuss in the next chapter.

Tears were shed. And no baby appeared. Money—public and private—was spent on futile treatments. Such lose-lose situations prevailed in Dr. Avi Tsafrir's professional life and his patients' personal lives. This situation was taxing to both parties and not the best use of public coffers—though anyone mentioning this risked being called callous, or worse.

Choice gives people a sense of control, but it is meant to help people achieve their goals in the best, most personalized manner. The choice architecture here offered no predetermined points for stopping or reconsideration. Women may have interpreted this open-endedness as a sign that they not only could, but possibly also *should*, have additional IVF cycles and that there was no need to examine whether they were achieving their goals, possibly recalibrating their course.

Avi and I suggested a tentative stopping point after four treatment cycles, when the chances of conceiving from further treatments plateaued. Women and doctors, having given IVF a chance, would then discuss the statistics behind the treatments and perhaps recalibrate instead of persisting with the status quo. This plan would follow the tradition of libertarian paternalism: libertarian, in that women have the liberty to overrule the discussion and continue treatment; paternalistic, in that the discussion would be mandatory because it was deemed in the woman's best interest.

One possibility we cannot overrule, opt out of, or choose differently is dying: we'll all die one day. What we *can* choose is how much to disclose, how much we'll know about our death in advance, how to act, and how much control we'll have over how it will happen. The decisions become more complex and our nerves become more exposed the closer we get to the death bed, as we'll see in Chapter 7 on the end of life.

TAKEAWAYS

The takeaways for this chapter come from the auto industry, specifically, from Henry Ford, who, in the early 1900s, manufactured the Model T car. The secret to his success was an efficient assembly line. When he discovered that black was the fastest-drying color, helping to reduce costs and speed delivery, he removed all other color options from the menu. His most famous quote is, "Any customer can have a car painted any color that he wants so long as it is black." In 1914, for example, Ford manufactured more cars (all black Model Ts) than all other auto manufacturers combined.[36]

This somewhat extreme, albeit benign, example of lack of choice demonstrates the trade-offs that choice entails. It shows how both the person choosing (the consumer or the patient) and the person offering the choice can gain from reducing the number of available options.

FOR PATIENTS:

1. Choice is confusing, even difficult. Acknowledge it.
2. Many options you'll need to choose from will have multiple dimensions. Define ahead of time which dimensions matter to you. If you're not sure, ask your doctor for guidance.
3. Sometimes you can benefit from switching away from what you initially

chose. You rarely feel like changing, but gather up the energy to compare alternatives and switch. It could be worth it.

4. Better yet, identify ahead of time (before you're attached to the choice you've made) a stopping point when you will reevaluate your choice based on the new evidence you've gathered and maybe switch. No judgment passed.

5. Remember that maximizers may end up with the better option, but they spend a lot of energy in the process and may feel regret when they compare what they eventually choose to all the options they've seen. Satisficers do well enough at a lower cost, both cognitively and emotionally.

FOR HEALTHCARE PROFESSIONALS:

1. Help your patients construct their preferences. Don't abandon them under the guise of applying a scientific approach.

2. If your patients ask, disclose to them the dimensions you find pivotal to the choices they have to make.

3. Let your patients choose how to make choices: from deciding on their own, all the way to making you their appointed fiduciary, which means you can choose on their behalf.

4. If there's a choice that you believe a patient may benefit from revising, initiate the conversation. Better yet, identify ahead of time—before you, the patient, or both become attached to the choice that was made—a stopping point where the choice will be discussed and perhaps changed, as well as the evidence you will want the patient to consider before making a decision.

5. Everything you say, from the number of options you present to how you present them, influences your patient's choice. Nothing is 100 percent objective.

6. Don't pretend that your patients' choices aren't constrained by the choice architecture. They certainly are.

FOR HEALTHCARE SYSTEMS:

1. Everything you say, from the number of options you present to how you present them, influences your doctors' and patients' choices. Nothing is 100 percent objective.

2. Choice architecture influences choice. And you are in charge of it. Just as you hire a professional architect to design your building, use a professional to help you design the choices you present to your doctors and patients.

3. Ease patients into choice. Create materials that explain common choices and help patients compare their dimensions.

4. If there's a choice that you believe patients might benefit from revising, create an institutionally mandated (or at least recommended) stopping point to allow for reconsideration and discussion—anything to stop the inertia and status quo bias leading to nonswitching.

5. Create good defaults for doctors. Facilitate their decision-making processes in an evidence-based way while allowing them to overwrite these defaults based on their professional judgment.

6. Eric Johnson of Columbia University led a great team of scientists in designing behavioral economics choice hacks. Read their work carefully and emulate it as much as you can.[37]

7. Always choose to be aware of choice architecture and to improve it when possible.

CHAPTER 7

DANCE ME TO THE END OF LIFE

We come with an expiration date; we know that. What we don't know is what the date is exactly and what path we'll take to get there. Some will die in very old age, like Chitetsu Watanbe, the world's oldest man, age 112, at the time of his death. Others, like Pete Frates, an athlete rendered ALS patient who helped promote the "Ice Bucket Challenge," left this world at the young age of 34. Some won't even get this far. Of every 100,000 people aged 25–34, 38 will die of an overdose.[1] Some unfortunate 20-year-old students will fall from a cliff while hiking. And, every year, 300,000 teenagers will be treated in emergency departments following car accidents that kill 2,300 of their peers.[2]

What doesn't kill you can put you on life support. Which is all to say that at a certain point, most of us will be required to make end-of-life decisions, for ourselves or for someone else. We need to be prepared—but we're not. We need to prepare our loved ones—but we don't.

In this chapter, I take a hard look at the choices we can make about death and dying, arguably the hardest medical choices of all. The challenges surrounding end-of-life decisions epitomize the ones I have covered so far: navigating the sensitive interaction with physicians (who might view death as their failure), fighting for health literacy, understanding probabilities (for those lucky enough to be informed of probabilistic estimates of treatment effectiveness, risks, and mortality), and making consequential, emotion-laden choices.

A lot of the problems surrounding end-of-life decisions come down to the same basic issue: nobody wants to talk about death. But speaking candidly and openly about end-of-life matters is essential to receiving adequate care. You can only fully exercise your right to choose (actively, or by relinquishing decisions to medical staff) if you know and understand your situation, are familiar with your options, have had the opportunity to give your options some thought, have figured out your preferences, and can make those preferences known.

Drawing on centuries-old tradition, I propose a solution that can help overcome the silence around end-of-life care, providing clarity and reducing loneliness. I call it Talk About Death (TAD), a program through which end-of-life discussions are held at regular intervals, family members and loved ones are included in the decisions, and some of the tensions around decisions are deflated. Discussions even gain a celebratory tint instead of a tragic one.

But first, let's look at what comedians, poets, and filmmakers tell us about dealing with the great beyond.

EVERYBODY WANTS TO GO TO HEAVEN BUT NOBODY WANTS TO DIE

Groucho Marx (whom my father adored) famously said, "Die, my dear? That's the last thing I'll do." Acerbically accurate and adamantly against discussing the end of life. Avoidance is typical of so many of us, not only of this mustachioed fellow.

Dylan Thomas's "And Death Shall Have No Dominion" is a villanelle, a poem whose beginning and end are one. It further suggests continuity with such defiant lines as "though lovers be lost love shall not." This bewitching poetry is a glorious example of denial.

The Invention of Lying is a movie about a world in which people can only speak the truth. In the movie, we met Mark Bellison, played by Ricky Gervais, at his dying mother's bedside, facing the monitor. The doctor had just informed them that the mother was likely to have a fatal heart attack very soon and that it was fajita night at the cafeteria. The mother turned to her son and told him she was scared: "People don't talk about it, but death is a horrible thing . . . an eternity of nothingness." Thereupon, an alarm sounded as the frightened mother's vitals dropped.

Her son was the only person in their entire world who was capable of diverging from the truth. He told his mother that she was wrong, that when she died, she would go to her favorite place, she'd meet everyone she'd ever loved, and she would be young again. No pain. Just love and happiness. And a mansion. For eternity.

The mother hung onto every word her son said. Her countenance changed. With a serene smile on her face, she died. No medical choices were required regarding the mother, just a psychosocial one: what to tell her and how. The doctor took the direct, blunt road. The son beautified her impending death with a promise of everlasting, improved existence, a promise we could call heaven, or one we could call merciful denial.

While exploring artistic portrayals of death, I found strong undercurrents of shielding and sheltering through avoidance and denial. The loved ones shielded the dying, while the dying sheltered their dearest. Art both reflects life and guides it.

Avoidance of speaking about death, as well as denying it, is so common that Pulitzer Prize winner Ellen Goodman created the Conversation Project, designed "to help people with a serious illness think through and talk about what matters most to them."[3] They also have tools for people who are not ill but want to discuss their end-of-life preferences.

Etiquette is clunky; we fear stepping on others' toes and having them yell at us for raising the topic. We need not fear. The Conversation Project found that an overwhelming 95 percent of Americans were willing (or wanted to) talk about end of life, but only 32 percent have ever had such a conversation. Almost a quarter, 21 percent, said they did not initiate such conversations so as to avoid upsetting their loved ones.[4]

We need a better way to discuss end-of-life preferences, or at least to make it possible for the discussion to occur. I believe that for this to happen, these conversations need to stop being a harbinger of death and become a customary part of life. I propose having them at regular intervals, near milestone birthdays. This isn't an obvious idea, I realize. But we simply cannot rely on these conversations occurring "when the need arises" because, as you will see below, all too often they don't.

"DO NOT PERCEIVE THEY HAVE HAD A DISCUSSION"

Heart failure captures the complexity and delicacy of end-of-life discussions. It's a progressive, incurable, and unpredictable condition that can be, but doesn't have to be, immediately fatal. More than half of heart failure patients who die within three days of being diagnosed were originally predicted to survive another six months.[5] One out of every four patients dies within a year of their initial diagnosis.[6] Though heart failure patients may rush to their attorneys and start being nice to their loved ones, two out of every ten patients survive for more than ten years after being diagnosed.

Dr. Stephen Barclay of the University of Cambridge writes about these topics, teaches them, and also engages in the general practice of medicine and in palliative care. He examined heart failure patients' and healthcare professionals' practices and preferences concerning discussions of care at the end of life.[7] He reports that the vast majority of patients "do not perceive they have had a discussion" with their healthcare professionals. The spectacularly understated wording allows for two possibilities, either that the discussion never took place or that it went over the patient's head and emotional capacity.

Heart failure patients reacted to end-of-life discussions in three main ways:

1. Cognitively, either they did not want to think about death, or they accepted a low level of knowledge and didn't think they would understand the information provided by their doctor. They didn't want the full prognosis information, or they didn't think end-of-life issues were relevant to them. (My late father told me that he had set up a small pension for my mother in case he died, but he also said that he would not die.)
2. Emotionally, patients wanted to fend off the worry—their own and their families'—involved with such conversations. But some patients appreciated the opportunity to discuss their fears; it was a welcome change from the coerced spastic effort to put a smiley face on reality. Some heart failure patients even found the prospect of sudden death desirable.
3. Pragmatically, knowing about their heart failure prognosis prompted some patients to put their affairs in order and make plans for their families.

Barclay found that heart failure patients who wanted to talk wanted sensitivity and honesty. Some feared that they wouldn't feel good enough to have this discussion. They wanted an opportunity to have it a second time so that everything wouldn't hang on one conversation alone. To me, this underscores the importance of engaging in TAD habitually, so you consider what your preferences are, and they become known to your dear ones.

Patients feared that their doctor would be reluctant to talk or would provide them with incomplete information. They worried about putting their doctor in an uncomfortable position. This was a painful indication of how well these heart failure patients knew their doctor. Barclay found that doctors focused on the immediate aspects of disease management rather than on the fact that heart disease is a terminal illness that patients needed to prepare for.

EMOTIONALLY, DOCTORS MIRRORED PATIENTS' FEELINGS: THEY FEARED causing unnecessary alarm, anxiety, and depression, driving patients to give up the fight for life and shattering their hopes. They juggled being frighteningly informative in their explanations of the disease and being falsely reassuring, since they saw their patients as being unwilling to face the reality of their condition. Just like the patients, some doctors were confounded by etiquette, thinking it was inappropriate for the doctor to initiate the conversation. They waited for cues from their patients. This ordeal sounded as unsure and awkward as a middle-school dance.

A colleague of mine commented that death makes doctors and patients mutually disappointed. It's funny, in a sad sort of way.

Other researchers commented that the nature of heart failure gave doctors a sense of failure since they could not offer a cure or an unambiguous prediction. These researchers contrasted this with end-of-life conversations with cancer patients, whose disease trajectory was clearer and whose bleak prognosis was more certain.[8] Therefore, I looked at research on life-threatening illnesses: advanced cancer, chronic obstructive pulmonary disease (COPD), or chronic kidney disease. Contrary to the predictions, between 60 and 90 percent of patients who had these conditions reported never having discussed end-of-life issues with their clinician.[9]

Etiquette and cultural sensitivity prevail around end-of-life discussions—for example, between elderly Chinese patients and their doctors.[10] Han-Lin Chi of UCSF found that, with patients of all ages, genders, and ethnicities, "there is little guidance on how to initiate and facilitate such discussions."

Much like the TAD (which should occur at predetermined points in time), Han-Lin Chi suggested embedding end-of-life discussions in the protocol of check-ins or intake in a medical setting, as long as the elderly were asked if they agreed to discuss end of life. In the study, they all agreed.

With progressive diseases, the timing of these conversations is also of the essence. "Later" may end up being "never" if a patient dies or loses consciousness. I read (and reread to make sure I hadn't missed anything) a review of forty papers stating that doctors expected to make care choices collaboratively with people living with dementia and their families as their patients entered the *end stage*.[11]

Delaying the conversation until the person with dementia completely deteriorated and his or her involvement became moot was absurd. Such a delay was unfair to the patient and placed an unfair burden on their family. The authors acknowledged the absurdity. They recommended starting advance care planning well before the dementia worsened to the point that it prevented the patient from taking part in the decision (which brings us back to the advantages of using TAD at early stages in life).[12]

Critical care settings faced practical barriers. The competing demands on healthcare professionals' time in the intensive care unit (ICU) hindered advance care conversations and planning at the end of life. Discussions could only happen if they were "workable within complex and time pressured clinical workflows."[13]

Dagoberto Cortez, a sociologist from the University of Wisconsin, found that fitting these conversations in was unlikely. He listened to one hundred recorded conversations between terminal cancer patients, their caregivers, and their oncologists. These discussions were evasive. Addressing doctors' constraints, Cortez says, "Talking about what scans mean may add minutes to that part of the clinic visit but can create efficiencies that conserve overall time."[14] Bargaining over minutes—this is how pressured for time doctors were.

Time constraints are very real, but they can be overcome. Health professionals' emotional hardship, on the other hand, is here to stay. Delivering bad news takes a toll of its own, and, like patients and family members, doctors often take shelter in avoidance and denial.

In *Being Mortal: Medicine and What Matters in the End*, surgeon Atul Gawande recounted a conversation he had with a patient who came in for a minor gynecological procedure that led to the discovery of metastatic colon cancer.[15] What ensued was maneuvering in which the patient strove toward the truth while Gawande moved forward and back, approaching but never reaching full disclosure of the patient's condition and its implications.

Delivering bad news was an ordeal—more than one heart could break in the process. Thus Gawande backtracked, sweetening the bitter news with hope and minimizing what he had said. He promised the patient that he would bring in an oncologist. He did not lie and promise her that chemotherapy *would* be very effective. But he did say that it *could*, even though he had little faith in that happening. The patient asked if she was going to die. For that unique piece of information regarding her body, her prospects, and her end, she couldn't Google, Yahoo!, or Bing the answer. Her doctor alone could help her. According to his own account, Gawande flinched. "No, no," he said to this patient whom he barely knew. "Of course not."

The end of a patient's life also signifies the end of her doctor's ability to help her. It is the ultimate expression of his helplessness. How can we judge a physician for fumbling with the fact that there was a good chance that his patient was dying? Gawande later wrote that most doctors did not dare tell the truth: that they were sorry, but treatments were futile. Instead, they skirted around it in avoidance or denial.

Renowned neurosurgeon Henry Marsh, author of *Do No Harm* and *Admissions*, sometimes treats patients with slowly evolving brain tumors. Over time, he develops a familiarity and a friendship with them. He reported having "guarded conversations about their future—trying to provide hope, but not too much hope." Marsh revealed the extent to which a doctor would go to avoid crushing his patients' hopes of recovery. "On several occasions, I operated yet again when I should not have done," he admitted, explaining that he did so "because it was so unbearably painful to spell out the truth to them."[16]

Gawande and Marsh aren't the only physicians who perceive end-of-life conversations as failing one's patients. Doctors' reluctance to talk about the end of life is widespread, born of compassion, an intense workload, lack of communication skills, fear of conflict, and many other phenomena, all of which reflect the doctors' humanity. Nevertheless, it leaves patients to their own devices, too often incapable of devising an exit plan because nobody told them they were nearing the end of their life. It reduces patients' agency, their ability to act on behalf of themselves, to be prepared for, and somewhat shape, their end.

Friends and family also become casualties. A loved one's dying confronts you with the inconceivable notion that you are about to part with them, and with your own helplessness. When Dr. B. J. Miller was managing a hospice, he checked in on a twenty-seven-year-old patient who was wasting away with a rare and terminal cancer. The patient was surrounded by friends, whose suffering "was palpable, and some of their suffering was these spastic efforts to put a smiley face on things."[17]

THE NEW *ARS MORIENDI*

Having discussions near death, at home or in the hospital, is hard. Emotions are so raw. My solution emphasizes discussing end-of-life preferences regularly with friends and family and uses key insights from behavioral economics to help make those discussions happen. Subtle nudges can make it easier and more natural to have the dreaded discussions while also protecting the right to say no—both to having the conversation and to signing any sort of advance directives.

Nudges encourage people to take certain actions that will benefit them, such as saving for retirement or eating more vegetables.[18] Nudges make these behaviors as easy and emotionally painless as possible. I propose a gentle nudge that would regulate the timing and content of end-of-life conversations.

To better understand where mores surrounding end-of-life discussion come from, I sought some historical perspective from Monsignor Renzo Pegoraro, chancellor of the Vatican's Pontifical Academy for Life. He offers guidance on all issues pertaining to our bodies, whose mechanics predate all religions— issues from abortions to vaccines to death sentences. After a warm preface, I shared my frustration with end-of-life conversations. I told him about my idea to promote having them at predetermined times and asked for his thoughts. These issues had also been on his mind. The Academy for Life knows only too well how life ends:

> Doctors are unprepared and have great difficulty talking to a seriously ill person and encouraging the person to express opinions and preferences about the end of life. Even in the family there is little or no mention of these subjects, and

it is a pity that people do not prepare themselves at the time and there is no sharing with loved ones.

Certainly, there is work to do at the cultural level to talk, to discuss the reality of death, our mortal condition, the role and limits of medicine, and how to prepare for the end of life (a new *Ars moriendi*). And there is work to do with the doctors to deal with and manage communication, dialogue, listening to the patient and his family, and planning certain decisions in time.

I looked up *Ars moriendi*: two Latin texts dating to 1415 and 1450, written in the Christian tradition, that taught people how to die well.[19] In the mid-1300s, the Black Death killed between 75 and 200 million people in Eurasia. Death was a houseguest, and clergymen became scarce as they caught the disease from dying parishioners. People were left unguided and unconsoled. The *Ars moriendi* filled the void. *Ars moriendi* literally means the art or skill of dying. It is a DIY guide for one's final hour.

The long *Ars moriendi* instructed the friends and family of a dying person on how to behave around the deathbed. The main concern was the state of the soul as it approached death. Therefore, the questions posed to dying persons revolved around their faith and their salvation. Delegating some spiritual duties—such as saying the last rites and asking certain questions of the soon-to-be-deceased—to people other than clergy was a novel idea. Maybe the idea was born out of necessity, or maybe it was a consolation to the soon-to-be-mourners helplessly standing by the soon-to-be-deceased.

By the turn of the sixteenth century, the *Ars moriendi* had almost a hundred editions. Their vast popularity and translation into most western European languages attest to the immense hunger people felt for their teachings and solace.

NOWADAYS—IN FACT, FOR QUITE A WHILE NOW—PEOPLE DIE DIFFERently. In the middle of the twentieth century, Geoffrey Gorer, a Cambridge-educated anthropologist, wrote "The Pornography of Death." He noted that sex, which was once taboo, unmentionable, and out of sight, has traded places with death, the new unmentionable. He wrote, "It can have been a rare individual who, in the 19th century with its high mortality, had not witnessed at least one person dying, as well as paying their respects to 'beautiful corpses' [corpses displayed in open caskets and made to look as though they were sleeping]."[20] Children were encouraged to think about death: their own deaths and the deaths of others, both of which were tangible in those times.

Death is no longer so tangible. People hardly ever die at home where others can bear witness to the process. Children are no longer part of wakes, nor do they see open caskets in their living rooms. We no longer take weekly strolls to the cemetery in the center of the village to visit the dead. We are sheltered from death—it is out of sight and far from our daily discourse.

Gorer foreshadowed the antiaging movement, too, stating, "The natural processes of corruption and decay have become disgusting."[21] If we Botox, we don't wrinkle. And if we have already wrinkled, we nip and tuck. Either way, we don't show our age. If we don't age, we will never die, and there is therefore no need to talk about it.

Similarly, the Pulitzer Prize–winning book *The Denial of Death*, by the late anthropologist Ernest Becker, posits that the elemental motivation for human behavior is the need to control our anxiety by denying the fear of death. One way to presumably transcend death is through our possessions and achievements.[22] This idea fits with an increase in our home sizes and consumption.[23] Popular culture encourages us to awaken our inner giants, adopting habits that will turn us into extraordinary people—in short, to be omnipotent, as close as we can get to being superhuman immortals.

But people still age, die, mourn, and crave solace. We need a new *Ars moriendi*, one that will legitimize talking about death, creating a contemporary ritual surrounding it. A new *Ars moriendi* could help us rebuild a long-lost practice of inviting the presence of death into our life, in a way that we can live with. It will help us gather knowledge about our preferences, but, more importantly, it will help us walk through the unfathomable experience, with its pain and its silences, some clumsy, some tenderly intimate.

I am spelling out an etiquette to guide you through speaking about end-of-life preferences and what they ultimately lead to. Since few of us speak Latin, I propose we call it TAD, Talk About Death.

WHEN TO TAD

Given the gap between people's wishes to discuss death and the fact that such talks rarely happen, setting times to talk about our preferences for the end of life is key. "Right before I die" won't do because we don't know when that will happen or if we will still have our mental acuity when it does. "Whenever is convenient" won't do either because it's *never* convenient. We need designated times, a series of temporal anchors.

Behavioral economics underscores the value of anchors—numbers that can be random and irrelevant but are still influential. Think of the full price at a luxury hotel, which is unthinkably high, and we would never pay it. It becomes a point of reference, an anchor. We think we can ignore it, but we cannot. We adjust from it. Sale prices in the same hotel seem low compared to the anchor price, and thus we are more likely to think of them as reasonable. Temporal anchors provide a time for doing things, such as having five-o'clock tea or cocktails.

A widely shared temporal anchor for discussing preferences could be a powerful means of encouraging people to do it. As persuasion researcher Robert Cialdini showed, the fact that everybody does something provides social proof that it's what you should do too.[24] Yet the temporal anchor for such a delicate process cannot be completely arbitrary. The time for discussing end-of-life preferences must be artfully chosen. It must balance between catching people when they're prepared to talk about it and not weighing them down with heaviness. It must also be clearly defined and widely shared.

I propose birthdays as the temporal anchor for TAD conversations. Birthdays punctuate our lives, imbuing them with meaning. I specifically propose milestone birthdays, the big, round-number ones that warrant an extravagant party, skydiving, or a sports car—and that are pregnant with contemplation.

BIRTHDAYS HAVE A STRANGE CONNECTION WITH DEATH. BY LOOKING AT data sets comprising almost three million people, sociologist David Phillips from the University of California, San Diego, found that women were least likely to die in the week before their birthday and most likely to die in the week following it compared to any other weeks of the year.[25] Men, on the other hand, were most likely to die in the week before their birthdays. Their birthdays weren't a lifeline; they were a deadline.

Milestone birthdays amplify this effect. For example, in Japan, suicide rates rise on the twentieth, thirtieth, fortieth, and sixtieth birthdays, especially for men.[26] In the United States, Phillips also found that suicides occurred more often around milestone birthdays.[27] He called these birthdays "symbolic events"—times when life didn't change per se, as it did when a person retired or had a baby. Phillips speculated that at round-number birthdays, people felt compelled to engage in "stocktaking": appraising their accomplishments and their goals.

Rajesh Bhargave, Glen Doniger, and I wondered whether milestone birthdays changed how people thought about their life and how they formed judgments about it.[28] We examined women who were in milestone-birthday years and ran a statistical regression analysis to determine what these women's life satisfaction depended on.

We found that body mass index (BMI) and how women felt about their health mattered more to life satisfaction for milestone women than for non-milestone women. In the spirit of stocktaking their achievements in life, health provided a reality check: it reflected their past life choices and constrained their future abilities. For milestone women, health suddenly became an issue. Or perhaps not so suddenly.

People mentally build up toward milestone ages. Adam Alter and Hal Hershfield of the business schools in New York University and UCLA, respectively, examined tens of thousands of people from one hundred countries.[29] They found that those approaching their milestone birthday, "9-enders," are most likely to be "life auditing"—thinking about life's meaning and purpose. More than people of any other age suffix, 9-enders engaged in maladaptive behaviors, such as suicide and extramarital affairs, and in adaptive behaviors, such as signing up to run a marathon for the first time. They even ran faster than people whose age does not end with a nine.

Whether we walk or run toward our milestone birthday, we reach it after an entire year of stocktaking, meaning contemplating, and life auditing. This is why I propose to discuss end-of-life preferences at every milestone birthday: twenty, thirty, forty, and so on (or rather, on the day before the birthday, so as not to put a damper on the celebrations). The dark implications of the daunting conversation are somewhat brightened, if not completely neutralized, by the joyful temporal anchor. Through repetition, we learn how to step into the process. The idea might be strange, I'll grant you that. It's also vitally important.

HOW TO TAD

The issues I lay out here are similar to those that appear in the formal instruments I mentioned, such as advance care directives, though these vary over time and between states and countries. Dr. Joan McIver Gibson founded the Health Sciences Center Ethics Program at the University of New Mexico. She told me that what was most important in end-of-life conversations was "teaching family members that they are experts in your goals, and that this part of the syllogism is front and center of the decision-making process." That is, I should worry less about the content wording, and more about the meaning and the intention. TAD is the first step toward discussing and then, if desired, documenting and formalizing end-of-life preferences.

The core issues you must consider are these:

1. Think of where you stand on each of the medical choices you may at some time have to make (listed in item 3).

2. Choose a surrogate or proxy—someone whom you trust and who knows you well enough to gauge what you would have wanted for the blurred cases that the forms and conversations do not cover.

3. Share with your proxy your preferences on the following issues:

   Would you want to be resuscitated, should the need arise, and under what conditions?

   Would you agree to being placed on a ventilating machine or to undergoing a tracheostomy? (A tracheostomy is a more invasive procedure in which a breathing tube is inserted into the throat through a cut in the neck. Once the tube is inserted, legal restrictions limit removing it.)

   Would you agree to a feeding tube?

   Is there anything else you want your proxy to know? Are there any guiding principles you would like them to follow?

4. A number of forms are available if you want to formalize the process: Living wills can be filled out that allow you to make important decisions ahead of time about the type of care you wish to receive—such as instructing your physician not to use artificial methods to prolong the process of dying if you become terminally ill. Similarly, each state provides its own forms for advance care directives. There are also forms for becoming an organ donor.

5. Consider TAD as good planning. If you live to have your next milestone birthday end-of-life conversation, don't consider the previous one a

waste of time. TAD encourages you to think about things that can truly matter in dire times, and practice makes perfect.

I AM NOT ALONE IN OFFERING TO START TALKING ABOUT DEATH TO RELA-tively young people. Physicians B. J. Miller and Shoshana Berger propose that eighteen-year-olds should nominate someone to decide for them in case they need it and should also consider filling out an advance directive.[30] But they don't specify when these choices should be revisited.

One reason for engaging in TAD every decade, on your own and with those closest to you, is to make it part of your practice, getting over the uncomfortable silence and the urge to ignore the need for TAD. Gibson spoke of TAD as a rehearsal; it is an act of capability building, which cannot happen for the first time in the ICU or the ER.

Another reason to TAD habitually is that we change, and so do our preferences. As we age, loved ones die and we come to understand more viscerally that death is an unpreventable reality. The same questions remain, but our state of mind may change from invincible to pensive, from combative to accepting, or vice versa.

HOW TO TAD AT CRITICAL TIMES

Conversations can fall outside the routine and happen when accident or illness strikes—for example, if a twenty-two-year-old is hit by a car or a sixty-three-year-old develops lung cancer. People who TAD routinely become accustomed to discussing matters of life and death. This skill can carry over to times when the conversations are immediately necessary and no longer hypothetical. In those cases, if the patient is coherent, we need to go back to our most recent TAD discussion, verifying that everything they said and requested still applies. Retrieving preferences is a lot easier than having to come up with those preferences from scratch while in fear and suffering pain.

In addition, we should discuss matters that pertain to the immediate, severe circumstances:

1. What, and how much, does the patient want to know? "Protecting" a patient from the truth might be hurting them and only making the situation easier for ourselves. On the other hand, as far as the patient is concerned, ignorance may be bliss.

2. What is the patient being offered in terms of treatment? As always, apply Ask Me About What Matters: What are the risks? What are the benefits and the chances of them occurring? What are the alternatives? Is palliative care being offered alongside, or instead of, curative treatment?

At no time are these questions more crucial than now, giving an opportunity for both fact-based and hope-based decision-making.

IN ADDITION TO THE FORMS I HAVE ALREADY MENTIONED, THERE ARE also Portable Medical Orders, or POLST for short. This is what they are called at the national level, but different states have different names for them—legally recognized documents, similar to the widely used do not resuscitate orders (DNRs).[31] Both are signed by doctors, which means that they qualify as doctors' orders and must be followed by the medical system. The POLST form is used for patients with a serious illness or whose life expectancy is a year or less. It outlines a plan of care reflecting patients' wishes concerning medical treatment and interventions at life's end. The POLST form complements an advance directive by turning a patient's treatment preferences into actionable medical orders.

TAD provides people with a protocol to follow and words for things unspoken. I hope it will be found more comforting than the shelters of avoidance and denial, more beneficial than the spastic effort to put a smiley face on something that is not at all funny.

Protocols and acronyms aside, what is important is the intention. When one autoimmune teenage patient was dying at the hospital, her mother asked if, in the event that she were unable to breathe on her own, she would want a trach (tracheostomy). The girl looked at her and said, "Mom, fuck the trach." Rougher language than her usual speech, but what an unambiguous directive.

I proposed a way to discuss end-of-life preferences, TAD. Now I will show that people have options—even toward the end of their life. Then I will demonstrate that end-of-life care discussions won't hurt patients or their loved ones who suffer alongside them.

CLOAK ME TO THE END OF LIFE

End-of-life discussions can lead to the choice to utilize palliative care. "Palliative" comes from medieval Latin. It means "to cloak": to wrap a warm garment around someone for protection from the cold. Palliative care increases quality of life, helps families cope during illness and bereavement, offers patients psychological support, and opens up the necessary communication lines.

Dr. Diane Meier, a Mount Sinai Hospital geriatrician, received the MacArthur Foundation genius award for recognizing that "modern medicine's focus on curing disease and prolonging life failed to treat the physical and psychological distress of patients in both early and advanced stages of serious illness."[32]

Meier shapes and nationally promotes palliative care that provides dying patients with relief from pain and other distressing symptoms, such as depression, anxiety, and lack of appetite. It can be used instead of or alongside curative care. This is revolutionary because doctors are trained to treat illness. We've seen that they follow their training even when chances that the treatment will work are slim.

Unabashedly, and against the backdrop of rampant denial, palliative care "affirms life and regards dying as a normal process."[33] This is the biggest revolution of all. The palliative approach "also improves the quality of life of patients and their families facing challenges associated with life-threatening illness."[34] The acknowledgment that families and close friends suffer alongside the patients during their illness and after their passing is also revolutionary (though the ancient *Ars moriendi* touched upon it).

We should not leave people—the patient, the friends, the family members, and the healthcare professionals—to make choices during the tender moments where feelings cloud decision-making. Avoiding TAD conversations could come at an emotional and physical cost.

TALK ABOUT TALK ABOUT TALK ABOUT MOVIN'

To evaluate the effect that end-of-life conversations have on patients, comparisons have to be made between people who had such conversations and people who didn't. Furthermore, the comparison has to be made experimentally so that having or not having the conversation was randomly determined, and it wasn't the sicker, smarter, more anxious, or any other specific group of patients who held these discussions.

Elizabeth Weathers from University College Cork, in Ireland, conducted a systematic review of studies that randomly assigned over 3,500 patients, aged between seventy-two and eighty-eight, to either having or not having end-of-life conversations.[35] Seven of the studies were of people still living in the community, and two were of seniors in nursing homes. The interventions implemented in these studies began with offering end-of-life discussions to people who had the option to decline; patient choice began with the ability to say no.

Interventions came in all shapes and sizes. Some patients received video and written materials through the mail on advance care directives (ACDs). Others had a session with a nurse or health worker who helped them reflect on their goals, values, and beliefs. The nurse also helped patients consider their future medical treatment preferences, appoint a surrogate or a proxy who would decide for them in case they could not decide for themselves, and document their wishes.

Interventions could involve a lighter touch—for example, an intervention could be a brief information session that emphasized the importance of end-of-life communication between patients and their proxies or surrogates. These trusted friends or family members were sometimes invited to be present in the ACD discussion with the patient or to review the ACD that the patient completed.

The studies measured multiple outcomes, in three domains:

1. *Cognitively*, patients gained knowledge of ACDs and life-sustaining treatments. Surrogates had more knowledge of patient preferences or were more likely to discuss them.
2. *Pragmatically*, five studies found an increase in documenting end-of-life care preferences or in completing durable powers of attorney or standardized ACDs. This led to eventual implementation of end-of-life care preferences. Two studies tracked patients for six months after the intervention and found an increased concordance between patients' end-of-life wishes and the treatment they received. Clearly, there is no ultimate goal for end-of-life care: it can be palliative or it can seek every chance to beat death.
3. *Emotionally*, patients were more satisfied with their care following the interventions, and so were their family members.

   Oh, the family members were not to be envied. Family members of people with dementia incurred a double whammy: first their beloved patients could no longer be partners in the end-of-life conversations, and then they died. The family caregivers are on their own unless the clinical team and the researcher show up to assess the dementia patient's palliative care needs, document them into a management plan, and then share these plans with the caregivers.[36] When this happens, family caregivers have higher life satisfaction and less distress, and they experience less decisional conflict.

Two studies examined the feelings of bereaved family members whose loved ones had passed away after the interventions. They felt better, thanks for asking. They experienced less stress, anxiety, and depression than relatives who had not had an intervention promoting end-of-life discussions. Though lovers be lost, those who stay behind don't have to be devastated. And what a relief that is.

TEA, COOKIES, AND DISCUSSIONS

Long before "nudge" became a buzzword, researchers at McMaster University in Ontario conducted a study where they created a nudge: a time, a place, and materials for having the conversation.[37] In my mind, they also provided ease—tea and cookies.

Three nursing homes received what we would now term a "nudge intervention." In these homes, registered nurses first met with nursing home residents to assess their mental competence. Then came the nudge: competent residents and proxies of mentally incompetent residents learned about CPR, intubation, and nutrition.

Residents and proxies then received the opportunity to complete advance directives. Residents had plenty of choice in the matter: 17 percent of competent residents in the "nudge" homes refused to participate. And some of those who initially participated did not end up stating their preferences. These nursing homes were carefully matched with a control group of three other Ontario nursing homes, where life went on as before with no special training or education relating to advance directives for staff, residents, or proxies.

What were the outcomes? On the emotional side, the residents' overall satisfaction with healthcare over an eighteen-month period was similar in all nursing homes. This helped relieve concerns that nudging people to talk about the end of life would hurt their well-being.

By the end of the eighteen-month study, more residents in the "nudge" group had completed advance directives than in the control group. A staggering 91 percent of the competent residents in the "nudge" homes requested not to be resuscitated if they reached an intolerable or irreversible situation (when they couldn't recognize their family members or communicate). Two-thirds did not want resuscitation even if their situation was potentially reversible.

Almost all the "nudge" group residents (89 percent) opted for a Let Me Decide (LMD), a comprehensive document that covered life-threatening illnesses, cardiac arrest, and feeding options and what to do in cases of disability.[38] Variations of such documents are available in the United States. Nobody in the control group filled out an LMD. Not one. Instead, 71 percent of the control participants went for the simpler and narrower DNR form. DNRs vary by state but the gist is similar: they either ask that a person not be resuscitated under all conditions, or only if by the time resuscitation was needed he or she was already incapacitated.

Both groups were offered both forms. Why did the control group settle for signing DNRs instead of the more comprehensive, personalized LMDs? Because one needs guidance to comprehend and fill out an LMD, and the "nudge" intervention provided this help. The staff in "nudge" nursing homes received appropriate education on the complicated LMDs and were allocated precious work hours to explain them and answer questions. Having struggled through similar forms with my mother and my in-laws, I can attest to how necessary such help is. Without it, the invitation to determine one's destiny toward the end is a mock invitation.

Real-life consequences followed. Over time, people in the "nudge" group had fewer hospitalizations regardless of whether they had filled out forms. I attribute this to the staff training; they now knew that the hospital did not offer harm-free miracles and may have preferred to care for the deteriorating patients in their familiar environment. This lowered healthcare costs. Whenever money is involved, suspicions arise, along with hints that people might be pushed to their deaths. But they weren't. "Nudge" and control homes had similar mortality rates. Cost savings resulted from following patient preferences.

I OPENED WITH AVOIDANCE AND DENIAL, BECAUSE THEY ARE SO RAMPANT, so potent in silencing us and restricting our emotional range. Dylan Thomas wrote, "Do not go gentle into that good night. / Rage, rage against the dying of the light." Expecting the dying to rage might empower some, but it doesn't leave room for discussing their fears or accepting what is about to follow.

When essayist Barbara Ehrenreich was diagnosed with breast cancer, she raged, not against the disease, but against the tyranny of forced cheerfulness that surrounded her illness.[39] In her book *Bright-Sided: How the Relentless Promotion of Positive Thinking Has Undermined America* (published in the UK as *Smile or Die: How Positive Thinking Fooled America and the World*), she asserted that positive thinking wasn't a cure for cancer. Presumably, it shielded patients from the narratives of fear, pain, and anxiety, but to Ehrenreich, the compulsory gaiety stifled truthful, open discussions with doctors and loved ones, where women could admit to experiencing fear, anger, and pain and didn't have to always be brave warriors.

TAD, talking about death and end-of-life preferences both routinely and at critical times, will, I hope, help keep conversations real. Because in real life, patients, their doctors, and their loved ones, rage, ache, smile, and die. I end this chapter with an event that was beyond sad but could maybe have been a smidge less sad if TAD had been implemented.

WHEN CHOICE BECOMES DEATH

David holds a managerial position in the college where I am a faculty member. There is something reserved about him. He is also an amateur guitar player and singer and a very decent guy. I negotiated some of my contract terms with him when I was hired over a decade ago, but there's more to our relationship than that. We have a running joke about eating chocolate chip cookies together, which we never get to do. Like me, he has a son and two daughters. Since both our sons are our eldest, we talk about them the most, always very proudly.

You can imagine my shock when I woke up one morning to an email from our college administration announcing their sorrow at the death of David's son. I read and reread the note, called one of my more in-the-know colleagues, and verified: devastatingly, it was true.

I went to pay my respects. We all did. The *shiva*, the seven-day period of strict mourning Jews observe, was packed with visitors. As is often the case, we talked of anything but the circumstances. I did learn through my friend that the son—a young man of twenty-five, a computer science student—had been the picture of good health. He fell down unconscious during martial arts practice and was rushed to a hospital where the doctors diagnosed a lethal virus that was attacking his heart. After almost a fortnight at the hospital, never once regaining consciousness, David's son passed away.

In my mind, the event involved many medical choices, and one big looming choice to top them all. I wanted to ask David about it, but it took me more than a year to venture there. I asked for a private meeting. Coward that I was, I didn't have it in me to tell him what I wanted to discuss. For all he knew, it could be my salary or a sabbatical.

For the first time since we started the chocolate-chip-cookie joke, I placed a box of them on the table and told David about the book I was writing. Starting with the general theme, I gathered up the courage to mention the chapter on choice. The real courage here was David's, who didn't flinch at me asking him to go back to that time in the ICU.

The head of the ICU explained to David and his wife Jasmine that their son's brain had been deprived of oxygen for a substantial amount of time and had stopped functioning. The heart wasn't functioning either, so their son was ventilated (though not intubated).

"The head of the ICU was so patient, he spoke so clearly," David recalled, "that we both got it right from the start." David seemed incredulous as he told me how he and his wife went from knowing that they had a healthy, thriving son to accepting that they were about to lose their firstborn. That they had in fact already lost him. If any brain activity was registered, there might be some recovery. However, even if such recovery did occur, it would extend only to the most minimal brain functions. At the very best, their son would be in a lifelong vegetative state.

After two days, their son's heart resumed functioning as though nothing had happened. But the brain was already gone, and soon the body's various systems started shutting down. First their son's kidneys stopped working, so the doctors offered dialysis as a solution. "Without it," David repeated the doctor's explanation, "your son's body will be infected, and the infection will kill him."

"That's very in your face," I said.

"Maybe he did not quite phrase it like that, but that was the gist of it," David replied. "Then followed a few hours where we were preoccupied with whether or not they'd give him dialysis. Jasmine, my wife, was even more determined than me against the dialysis because then what would we do if his body recovers when we know the brain is gone. And we didn't want to be in a position where we have to make decisions." But they did decide, and no dialysis was performed.

"Those twelve days at the ICU feel like a single day to me," David said. "It's like a casino. The lights are always on, and we never left his bedside." He and his wife decided to get a second opinion from a senior neurologist at another medical center in town. "He confirmed what the first doctor said, and that was a relief." How could this be a relief, I wondered, but I didn't interrupt as tears rolled down David's face. He clarified, "What would we do if he had told us something that contradicted the first doctor?"

Still, they wanted to consult another doctor, a man who was regarded as one of the topmost experts in the field. He was incredibly busy, but they managed to reach him through a friend of a friend. This expert made the time and sat with David and Jasmine three or four days prior to their son's death.

"He explained what the other doctors had already told us: that the brain did not get oxygen. That he [their son] was not coming back. There would not be consciousness. There would not be comprehension. Best case scenario was a vegetative state. He said what the others had said, but maybe something about the way he said it, about his rhythm of speech, made us understand and accept and decide that we were not making any more inquiries."

The doctor and his team were doing their best and were open to hearing other opinions.

"We don't believe in miracles. This is just not who we are. And we knew that if we started believing in them, it would only be harder. We knew we had to believe what the doctors said because it's evidence-based and again, the alternative would only be harder. We had hordes of visitors, and people said all sorts of things and told us all sorts of miracle stories. And then it's important to say—'it's really incredible how your uncle recovered from being a vegetable, but this is a different case altogether.'"

"Did you know what your son would have chosen or what he would have preferred?" I asked.

"I went to therapy," David volunteered. "Very short therapy." Which was his gentle way of saying he found it useless. "She asked what my son would do. Or what my father would do. Well, my father passed away a year before my son did. Just one more thing that unhinges you. But, with all due respect, my father never lost a child. And my son—I know how he thought about everyday matters. He would have wanted his sisters to be happy and the family to keep going. But this? I've no way of knowing." I noticed David did not say his son would want his parents to be happy, which may not be a viable option for David, though he kept on living, working, traveling with his family, and playing the guitar.

"We didn't really have any choice," David half apologized for not providing me with material for my book.

I did not interrupt him, but what I would like to suggest here is that there was a choice, and that there almost always is. You decide what to do, how to react, how much information to gather and from whom. You choose whether it is a time to question the information or to believe it. You choose whether it is a time to fiercely press for options or to accept that only one exists. Whether it is a time to concede to the dreadful reality or a time to fight for what you think is the best for your boy. A time to be born and a time to die.

David's son's heart stopped beating. There was no point in discussing organ donation, because all the systems in his body had collapsed.

Jasmine and David are one of those solid, handsome couples who have been together since their late teens. They stood by one another. "Even when you have a disaster happen, you need luck. And we had luck," he tells me.

We had those twelve days to say goodbye, to prepare. And things happened. That was luck too, not having to decide. If we would have had to decide, we would have. You find strength. You withstand things you never thought you could. But this would be difficult.

When two people sit in front of the same doctor, they each have their different interpretation; they each perceive different nuances in what the doctor says, how he speaks, whether or not he looks you in the eye. You hang on to everything, to every nuance in these situations. You become so dependent.

Jasmine and I would leave the room remembering things differently. And this was when all doctors were saying the same thing. What would we do, had they contradicted one another? That could have torn us apart.

The cookies lay orphaned on the table. I reached past them and held David's hand. We sat in silence for a while, in the place where words became platitudes.

Leaving the administration building, I couldn't find the energy to walk to my office. Instead, I made my way to the landing outside the music department where some visionary who oversaw the construction, possibly David himself, had placed rocking chairs and white sofas. Opening my laptop, I tried to write down a faithful account of what he had told me but ended up gazing at the screen, seeing in my mind the relentlessly lit ICU. I gave up, took off my shoes, curled up on the sofa, closed my eyes, and let my mind try to process David and Jasmine's ordeal in my sleep.

Being a patient is hard, and so is being a caregiver and a healthcare provider. Some ordeals cannot be avoided, but perhaps they can be mitigated. Perhaps we can be less alone when going through them. Other difficulties can also be smoothed by solutions, institutional and otherwise. This is what the next part of the book focuses on.

TAKEAWAYS

The takeaways for this chapter are inspired by Leonard Cohen's indescribably beautiful song "Dance Me to the End of Love." The indescribably sad story behind it exemplifies that even in the darkest hour, there can be grace.

FOR PATIENTS:

1. When you think about death as an inevitable part of existence, you can accept end-of-life decisions as being on the continuum of choices you make throughout your life. You can still rely on your values, beliefs, and preferences when making them.

2. TAD—talk about death—routinely. Do it the day before milestone birthdays, when you're already taking stock of your life, evaluating what

you've accomplished and where you're headed. Make it part of your practice so that on your birthday you can celebrate with a clean mind.

3. TAD—talk about death—at critical times.

4. You have the right to choose not to talk about your own death and not to make any choices regarding it. This too is a choice. Consider that it leaves the people caring for you—loved ones and professionals—at a loss for what you would have wanted and whether they did right by you.

5. For further instruction, look up the National Academies of Science, Engineering, and Medicine's two-part webinar "Advance Care Planning: Challenges and Opportunities."[40]

6. Know that death isn't the end of love, just as speaking about death isn't the opposite of love.

How to TAD:

1. Think of where you stand on each of the medical choices you may at some time have to make (listed in item 3).

2. Choose a surrogate or proxy—someone whom you trust and who knows you well enough to gauge what you would have wanted for the blurred cases that the forms and conversations do not cover.

3. Share with your proxy your preferences on the following issues:

   Would you want to be resuscitated, should the need arise, and under what conditions?

   Would you agree to being placed on a ventilating machine or to undergoing a tracheostomy? (A tracheostomy is a more invasive procedure in which a breathing tube is inserted into the throat through a cut in the neck. Once the tube is inserted legal restrictions limit removing it.)

   Would you agree to a feeding tube?

   Is there anything else you want your proxy to know? Are there any guiding principles you would like them to follow?

4. If you want to formalize the process, living wills, DNRs, LMDs, advance care directives, POLST, and organ donation forms can be filled out that allow you to make important decisions ahead of time about the type of care you wish to receive and what you would want to happen to your body, before and after you die.

5. Consider earlier TAD as good planning if you live to have your next milestone birthday end-of-life conversation. TAD encourages you to think about things that can truly matter in dire times, and practice makes perfect.

How to TAD at Critical Times:

1. What, and how much, does the patient want to know?
2. What is the patient being offered in terms of treatment? As always, apply Ask Me About What Matters: What are the risks? What are the benefits and the chances of them occurring? What are the alternatives? Is palliative care being offered alongside, or instead of, curative treatment?

FOR HEALTHCARE PROFESSIONALS:

1. People die. Do your best to help them live (hopefully also live well), but acknowledge that, eventually, their life will end. This is a fact of life, not evidence of your failure.
2. If your health system supports this, TAD—talk about death, or rather, end-of-life preferences—at predetermined points, such as when checking into a hospital or during annual checkups. This can be part of routine paperwork. But verify that your patient agrees to discuss this. Revise this at milestone ages.
3. TAD—talk about death—at critical times. Do what Leonard Cohen asked for when he sang, "Dance me through the panic till I'm gathered safely in." Keeping quiet, offering useless treatments, or slapping on a smiley face won't do the trick.
4. Let TAD—the new *Ars moriendi*—guide you in asking what and how much your patient wants to know. Tell them their options, the risks, and the benefits.
5. Mention the forms that patients can sign to formalize their choices.
6. If relevant, suggest palliative care, alongside (or instead of) curative treatment.
7. Avoiding this particularly painful TAD isn't protecting patients; it's depriving them of the right to make some of the most significant choices of their life.

FOR HEALTHCARE SYSTEMS:

1. Create procedures and allocate resources (time, training) to TAD when checking into a hospital, as well as during annual checkups. This can be part of routine paperwork and around milestone birthdays. Make it part of routine care. But verify that your patient agrees to discuss this.

2. Create procedures and allocate resources (time, training, intervention) to TAD at critical times and around looming diagnoses.

3. Create procedures and allocate resources (time, training, interventions) to support your physicians and staff around the death of patients. Dance them to the end of love.

PART III

DESTINATION: BETTER MEDICAL DECISION-MAKING

CHAPTER 8

IT TAKES AT LEAST TWO
TO TANGO

(BUT WHO IS KEEPING THE BEAT?)

We've learned what the major barriers to making medical decisions are, along with some tools for overcoming them. We've also learned that while there's a lot that patients can do, we still need help—health choices are not a DIY endeavor. Choice happens in a clinical setting, with a healthcare professional. It takes place within a social and political context and within an organization that, for the most part, does not consider having a good decision process a priority in and of itself. All this poses unsurmountable difficulties for patients, and to claim otherwise would be misleading.

The burden of bringing about change and improvement cannot rest solely on individuals, regardless of how tech savvy they are and how well versed they are in behavioral economics. Some solutions will have to come from doctors and health institutions. Some already do, with tremendous variation.

Over the last few decades, a new solution has emerged in response to the problem of making medical decisions: shared decision-making (SDM). SDM is a school of thought intended to inform and empower patients by reconfiguring doctors' and patients' roles. SDM goes beyond establishing a relationship. It's about patient-centered care in the sense that patients' process of choice is supported through doctor-patient collaboration, whose creation is the shared responsibility of both doctor and patient. Doctors give patients evidence-based, comprehensible information and help patients construct and elucidate their preferences, which then guide their choices.

In theory, SDM has always seemed to me like an obviously good idea. SDM is a generous way of lending a hand to patients rather than abandoning them to make decisions alone. The people who founded the concept of the doctor-patient partnership did so in the 1970s, in an era when the notion was anything but obvious. The concept bloomed out of a deep conviction in the values it represented. I revere the people who carry the SDM torch, some of whom are close friends of mine. So it agonizes me to say that in practice, SDM isn't universally applied or even accepted.

In this chapter, I show the legitimacy and following that SDM has gained over the decades. I then hunt for evidence on how SDM is being implemented and the effect it has had on patients.

But first, let's talk about dragons and dogs.

TO SALZBURG AND BEYOND

Early morning, Frankfurt, Germany. France Légaré, physician and advocate for SDM, and I were practicing yoga on a stretch of lawn overlooking the Main river. I was filled with gratitude for having the time and ability to do yoga and for being a part of this mission. Soon we would return to the hotel where Gerd Gigerenzer had summoned a few dozen scholars to contribute to a book envisioning better healthcare decisions.[1] My group was discussing health literacy, and I was turning our conclusions into a chapter for the book. This is my milieu. These are people I look up to and whose dedication to supporting physicians and patients I admire.

Some patients resent the idea that they require any support. Sun is such a person. We met at a party Facebook threw in Palo Alto. When I told Sun what I did and how it related to SDM, she replied that she liked to decide on her own. She is a senior partner at an accounting firm and runs a tight ship at home with her wife and three boys. Her hair is always tied in a bun, with no stray ends peeking out. Sun's friends seek her advice. After all, she was born in the year of the dragon, which means she has innate leadership.

She told me about her father, Jianhua, a retired tailor who was born in the year of the dog. He is honest and prudent, but not a leader. He appreciates a medical authority he can rely on when making decisions.

My colleagues and I—doctors and psychologists—have long aimed to ensure that the medical system worked just as well for people like Sun as it would for people like Jianhua. Most of us thought the best way to cater to Sun's and Jianhua's needs was through shared decision-making.

To fully understand SDM and determine its merits, it's important to examine it against the backdrop of other models. SDM mainly stands in contrast with the paternalistic model, in which the doctor decides based on medical knowledge and with the intention of improving the patient's health but without consideration for the patient's preferences. This makes sense in emergencies but is less reasonable in routine care.

In 1992, doctors Ezekiel Emanuel and Linda Emanuel listed several models of medical care: the paternalistic one and other models that followed the call for SDM to varying degrees.[2] The differences between the models they listed may explain why implementation of SDM varies widely. Nevertheless, the term "shared decision-making" caught on and has now become the name of an entire movement.

The title of a 1997 paper says it all: "Shared Decision-Making in the Medical Encounter: What Does It Mean? (Or It Takes at Least Two to Tango)."[3] The patient is invited to the discussion as an equal—receiving comprehensible information from the doctor, as well as giving information: the patient's input, likes, and dislikes are taken into account. After all, choice concerns the patient's mind and body. The doctor and patient then reach a consensus about the preferred course of treatment.

In 1998, physicians, scholars, and policy makers involved with SDM convened in Salzburg, Austria. They were invited by the Salzburg Global Seminar, a nonprofit organization dedicated to challenging current and future leaders to shape a better world.[4] A sentence stuck from the meeting and became a slogan: "Nothing about me without me."[5] "Me" is the patient, who now was invited to assume an active position. Coincidentally, this slogan is also used in disability activism.[6]

"Nothing about me without me" is a slogan simple enough for children to remember (they'll use it when you least want them to) or for adults to utter in pain, asserting their rights when longer statements are impossible. Sun reminded her father of this sentence when he hesitated over the prostate cancer surgery his doctor suggested.

As SDM GAINED SUPPORT, IN 2001, THE INTERNATIONAL SHARED Decision-Making Society was founded—a transdisciplinary group of researchers, clinicians, psychologists, and educators. Managers and policy makers were invited too: making SDM a standard practice would require resources, retraining of medical professionals, and plenty of goodwill and conviction from the health systems. SDM has grown substantially since the society was formed.

In December 2010, thought leaders from eighteen countries met at the Schloss Leopoldskron hotel for another Salzburg Global Seminar. This seminar produced a full statement on how to achieve the doctor-patient dialogue. The statement called on clinicians to "recognize that they have an ethical imperative to share important decisions with patients," "stimulate a two-way flow of information," "provide accurate information about options," and "tailor information to individual patient needs."[7]

The statement encouraged patients to express their concerns, to seek information, and to "recognize that they have a right to be equal participants in their care." It also called on clinicians, researchers, editors, and journalists to provide clear, evidence-based updated information. Lastly, it also called on policy makers to promote SDM and to embed it in informed-consent laws.

I thought the Salzburg statement was well poised to pave the way to solidifying a worldwide consensus around SDM. The meeting ended close to Christmas Eve. It tied up SDM with a ribbon and presented it to the world as a gift.

In 2019, I called John Lotherington, the program director of the Salzburg Global Seminar, who said, "The need for the statement was because progress towards SDM over the previous 30 years had been so patchy."

SDM now had more than half a million Google Scholar mentions and counting, which can no longer be considered "patchy" progress. Surely all patients were now welcomed and guided into a collaborative dialogue with their physicians, so they had sufficient understanding of their conditions and options and could choose according to their values and preferences.

However, this was not necessarily the case.

Glyn Elwyn is a physician at the forefront of implementing SDM in clinical settings and directs the Dartmouth College Patient Engagement program. We first met in Dartmouth in 2007: he was on the faculty of a summer institute on SDM where Dan Ariely, Yaniv Hanoch, myself, and others were participants.[8]

Elwyn was one of the lead voices in the drafting of the Salzburg statement. Therefore, I was surprised when he told me, "The idea was that organizations would adopt the statement as policy. Some did—but I do not think it has had that much uptake." Could I cite him on that, I asked? I feared his colleagues might view his response as belittling the Salzburg achievement. Glyn answered, "Of course . . . we are on a Sisyphean journey."

Dave deBronkart, cofounder of the Society for Participatory Medicine, expressed puzzlement as to why I even bothered to ask about the statement: "What makes such statements interesting, when they (seem to) make no difference in the long run?"[9]

Much as I appreciated the rationale behind the statement and the SDM movement, I cared more about their enduring effects. My next step was to examine its implementation.

HUNTING AND GATHERING

Eager to see what changes SDM has made in the world, I hunted for the latest evidence on its practice. I looked at systematic reviews—compilations of results from tens, hundreds, sometimes thousands of academic papers. I looked at so many studies that my head was spinning.

First, I examined the extent to which SDM was being rolled out. A review of close to three hundred papers spanning ten years found that patients and providers in the United States have generally positive attitudes toward SDM, but "actual engagement in SDM behavior is lagging."[10]

Ouch.

The review's authors suggested a top-down remedy: policies that encouraged SDM could lead to revised guidelines and influence the allocation of resources, such as doctors' time, or the use of decision aids.

This is probably easier said than done. The notorious fifteen minutes per doctor's visit do not leave us enough time with our doctors to become informed participants in our care or for them to elicit our values and preferences.[11] In the emergency department, doctors spend 44 percent of their time entering data and only 28 percent of it with their patients. In ambulatory care practices—family medicine, internal medicine, cardiology, and orthopedics—doctors spend 37 percent of their time on desk and electronic health-record work.[12]

Doctors examine patients, diagnose them, retrieve information from the electronic health record, and enter data. It amounts to *four thousand* clicks per physician on a ten-hour shift at the community hospital emergency department.[13] In the midst of this, how can our physicians employ the candid dialogue that the Salzburg statement called for?

It gets more discouraging. Remember Victor Montori's study: he found that when doctors elicited their patients' concerns, they interrupted them after only eleven seconds.[14] The recorded doctor-patient conversations Montori analyzed came from studies that were designed to examine the effect of shared decision-making. The doctors were as likely to listen or not listen to the patient's agenda and to interrupt them regardless of whether or not they were using decision aids—tools to support discussions!

Decision aids could facilitate SDM, especially given physicians' time constraints. Aids are tools that inform patients about their options and help them construct their preferences: defining what pros and cons matter the most to them and trying to imagine the physical, social, and/or psychological effects of living with each option. Glyn Elwyn, Michael Barry, and their colleagues cautioned against subpar decision aids, which could sway patients in dubious directions. They called for setting up a national patient decision aid certification process. A persistent hindrance to certification is "the lack of a sustainable financial model to support the work."[15] Money, not ethical imperatives, makes the world go round.

RACE AND CULTURE CAN ALSO BE BARRIERS TO SDM. HISPANIC AND AFrican American patients sometimes felt they lacked the knowledge to participate in decision-making. Occasionally they feared that health providers would not react favorably if they were to take a more active role during the encounter.[16] These obstacles must be dealt with on an institutional level. For the most part, we are still waiting for that to happen.

While we are waiting, I also examined how SDM was improving outcomes. The more SDM accomplished, the more likely it was that health systems—who are, so to speak, in charge of the dance floor: of doctors' training, time, and priorities—would endorse it by allocating the resources required for its success.

I followed systematic reviews by disease area. I started with hypertension—high blood pressure—because it's so common. According to the World Health Organization, in 2015 one in four men and one in five women around the world had hypertension.[17] So many patients, and yet so little relevant research. Up until September 2017, only six controlled studies evaluated the effects of SDM interventions on adults with hypertension in a way that merited being included in the review.[18] The interventions ranged from training for healthcare professionals, decision aids, and patient coaching to a patient information leaflet. I was conflicted about this last device of mass education—did it count as SDM? A booklet was better than nothing and it might be a wonderful leaflet, but it wasn't interactive and it didn't involve the physicians.

The outcomes were abysmal. Only one study reported that patients participated more in SDM following the intervention. And the health impact? No difference was found in blood pressure between intervention and control groups.

I wondered what SDM would do for people who suffered from conditions like carpal tunnel syndrome or a herniated or ruptured disk. These are the most common workplace injuries and are responsible for almost 30 percent of all worker's compensation costs.[19] A review looked at almost two hundred studies on SDM and clinical health-related outcomes in patients with a variety of musculoskeletal conditions.[20] Disappointingly, no study compared SDM to a control group or measured patients' quality of life, costs, health-related pain, or disability. Maybe it was too much to expect that SDM would influence costs and disability. Likewise, we wouldn't expect it to improve global health and bring world peace.

Randomized controlled trials that looked at 1,065 men who were making decisions about prostate cancer screening found that those whose treatment involved SDM knew more and, for a short period of time, had a higher quality of life than men who received the usual care.[21] But, at a three-month follow-up, the effect on quality of life had all but disappeared.

Michael Saheb Kashaf, Elizabeth McGill, and Zackary Berger of Johns Hopkins University School of Medicine reported an association between

SDM and improved decision quality, patient knowledge, and patient risk perception in type 2 diabetes.[22] However, they couldn't associate SDM with glycemic control (the holy grail of diabetes treatment) or with medication adherence, patient satisfaction, or quality of life.

BUT WHAT DOES IT MEAN WHEN AN ARTICLE OR TREATMENT PLAN SAYS, "SDM was implemented"? Does it mean that the prerequisites for SDM were fulfilled, that an up-to-date decision aid was used, or that the patients got an information leaflet? If SDM were a cup of coffee, would it be made from freshly ground premium beans or from semi-stale coffee crystals?

In response to this question, Glyn Elwyn and Adrian Edwards tried to standardize SDM. They created Option Grids, a summary table allowing quick comparison of options, guided by patients' frequently asked questions. It's branded as "shared decision making made easier" and is publicly available, so you can bring it to your next doctor's appointment.[23] This dovetails with my recommendation of Ask Me About What Matters, which encourages patients to inquire about risks, benefits, and alternatives.

Option Grids are short, their language is relatively simple, and the onus is on the health professional to use them. Doctors reported that the grids made it easier to explain options to patients. Option Grids have been widely adopted in the UK. Patients who used Option Grids often shifted their treatment or procedure preferences—usually to more risk-averse options.[24] The grids are being tested with various populations and levels of patient health literacy.[25] I suspect the outcomes will look good. I also suspect, given the substantial obstacles, that widespread dissemination is a Sisyphean journey.

PATIENT PREFERENCES AND ALL THAT JAZZ

A few years ago, SDM champion Dr. Martin Härter edited an issue of the *German Journal for Evidence and Quality in Health Care (ZEFQ)* on implementing SDM around the world. Along with colleagues, I contributed a piece about SDM in Israel.[26] We published a longer version that Dr. Harvey Fineberg, then head of the Institute of Medicine, wrote a commentary on.[27] His words were an illuminating, well-deserved slap on the wrist. Fineberg noted that patient choice also means patients could choose to let their doctor decide for them or that patients could decide on their own without a doctor's involvement.

To have patients truly participate in their care, they had to be offered several models of participation, not just the one we thought best: a smorgasbord agenda, if you will.

I tended to believe in the ethical superiority of SDM, so Fineberg's analysis was hard to swallow. But he was absolutely right. Sun may want SDM, but perhaps not all the time. Jianhua may prefer a more passive role, but this too could change. Who were we to tell them what they wanted or needed? No one had the right to tell Sun, her father, and all the people born in the years of dragons, dogs, and everything in between how to go about making their health choices.

Fineberg was not the only one who thought this way. At an early dinner by the ocean in Boston, Dr. Matthew Katz, former director of radiation oncology at Lowell General Hospital, made the same point: that while he is obliged to offer various modalities of involvement, patients don't always want to partake in decisions and should be allowed to take a back seat. In his community settings at Lowell and in Manchester, New Hampshire, Katz encountered many patients who, he said, nodding gravely, "want answers. They need the confidence that I know what I'm doing."

Katz clarified that at Massachusetts General Hospital and Memorial Sloan Kettering Cancer Center where he had previously worked, he saw patients with active, shared, and passive styles. He added, "More people don't seek information on the internet in my communities; they want it from the doctor." He was describing the appointed fiduciary model in action. It made me think of the doctor as being the son of God and therefore, regardless of religion, offering some solace. Who could deny patients that comfort, and by what moral upper hand?

IF EVERYBODY WANTS YOU, WHY ISN'T EVERYBODY CALLING?

When I was invited to speak at an annual conference of child psychiatrists, I thought I would put SDM aside for a moment and focus on kids' adherence to medication. Then I read about interviews with children ages seven to seventeen who had attention deficit hyperactivity disorder (ADHD).[28] A third of the kids wished that their doctor had spoken more to them about their ADHD. But these kids had never asked their doctor to do so. In fact, they said it was hard to speak with their doctors about ADHD because they felt uncomfortable with the doctor, with being in an exam room, or with discussing their condition.

A quarter of the kids wanted their doctors to ask them more questions about ADHD, and 16 percent wanted their doctors to tell them more about symptoms and medication side effects. Some of these young people needed to be actively invited to dance and to be given the option to decline. If we were to wait for these patients to initiate the active-patient role, we would wait a very long time. Doctors need to lay out a smorgasbord of communication models and invite patients to choose among them.

Just when I thought I was done with SDM, it pulled me back in. And children were a fascinating population to examine in this context. Or maybe SDM was now being examined, to see if it fit in all circumstances.

Pediatric care offers extra complications since children are the patients but their parents are their legal guardians, and are therefore allowed to decide for them. France Légaré, Dawn Stacey, and others examined studies, from all over the world and spanning over twenty years, that looked at SDM in pediatric medicine.[29] They found that healthcare providers and parents were more willing to involve children in decisions when the potential outcomes were less risky. Children too preferred to be involved only in lower-stake decisions, if at all.

Erica Carlisle and her colleagues explored SDM in pediatric surgery, mainly in outpatient clinics such as ear-nose-throat, plastic, cardiac, urological, and neurosurgery.[30] Most of the studies they looked at (73 percent) showed that either the parents or the patients favored SDM. Only eight out of the relevant thirty-six studies Carlisle found looked at surgeon preferences; in only half of those eight did the surgeons favor SDM.

Carlisle's work was limited to low-stakes situations: almost all the studies (94 percent) examined elective or nonurgent procedures where there was a choice between surgical and nonsurgical approaches. Regardless, the thought of your child having surgery is stressful. Period. And in such settings, she concluded, patients or parents may prefer more guidance from their surgeons. She proposed "developing a more nuanced understanding of how patients would prefer to be counseled during discussions regarding complex, urgent and emergent surgical procedures."[31]

Patients seemed to have a perfectly nuanced understanding of their own preferences. They reported that their willingness to engage in SDM was determined by specific details of the encounter with their doctor, including their emotional state at the beginning of a consultation and "desperation of pain."[32] Emotional state also came up in Légaré and Stacey's work as an obstacle to SDM. But more importantly, it highlighted just how uncomfortable being in the patient's shoes could be. It's no wonder patients don't always want to dance, or at least don't want to do the SDM tango.

A CAUTIONARY LESSON FROM INFORMED CONSENT

The cursory, merely pragmatic way informed consent is handled does not bode well for SDM or for the smorgasbord agenda, which are both more diffuse and prolonged than informed consent and harder to reduce to mere lip service. Informed consent is mandated by law: doctors must hand out the form and get it signed, which means that the signature will happen, cursory though it may be; otherwise, doctors risk liability.

To follow the informed consent example, for SDM or the smorgasbord agenda to happen, organizations would need to be legally bound to standardized practices. Currently, there is no established liability for failing to exercise SDM or failing to present multiple doctor-patient interaction models, even at a perfunctory level. Liability could lead to lawsuits, and these translate to money, which organizations care about more than they care about philosophical principles and ethical imperatives.

Overall, the resources that could make SDM happen are outside the control of any doctor or patient. SDM ostensibly has merit, as does any agenda that would present all participation options to patients. But the push to empower patients has come without the necessary practical supports, such as teaching patients how to understand probabilities or teaching doctors how to translate complicated medical jargon into easy-to-digest language. Not all patients feel that they want to participate in decisions or that they are up to it anyway. And can we pretend that all patients, regardless of who they are and what their other concerns are (housing and income, for example), can muster the courage to speak up? Can we pretend that they all would be heard?

Rome and Salzburg weren't built in a day, and neither was shared decision-making. In the grand scene of medical history, it is still a new idea. When we achieve SDM—or whatever agenda offers more options—we will have empowered patients to gain a deeper understanding of their treatment options and will have given them greater say over their healthcare.

In the next, and final, chapter, we will explore solutions that soar higher than us and our physicians, solutions that digital health, insurance payors, and academia offer in favor of improving our health choices.

TAKEAWAYS

The takeaways for this chapter are inspired by the restaurant industry, where people have set roles—the patron, the waiter, the chef, the owner. But the interpretations of these roles vary: they are different at a salad bar than in a fine-dining establishment. The interpretations can also change from one person to another and from one day to another. Even someone who was born in the fierce year of the dragon can feel like a meek dog sometimes, and vice versa. And everyone deserves to eat.

Keep in mind that the restaurant analogy is incomplete: people choose whether to go to a restaurant, whereas dealing with medical treatment is often forced upon us.

FOR PATIENTS:

1. "Nothing about me without me" asserts your place at the table.
2. You have the right to determine how involved you want to be in making decisions about your health. At a restaurant, you can choose what to eat and how to modify your dish. You can also choose to ask the waiter or waitress what they recommend. Whichever way you want to handle choosing your dinner is fine, because it's your dinner, just as your medical treatment is about your body and nobody else's.
3. You have the right to receive information in a way that lets you understand it, just as you understand a Shake Shack burger menu. If there's anything that's unclear to you, ask that it be explained. Otherwise, how can you choose?
4. If you're a patron, stay out of the kitchen. SDM, and any type of patient involvement, has its limitations. Medicine is not a takeout menu from which you can choose to have your salad without the shallots. You as

patient are an expert in your own body, your experience, and your preferences, but not in how medicine is handled. Some things doctors and nurses know best.

FOR HEALTHCARE PROFESSIONALS:

1. Not everyone is cut out for coming to the cash register to order. Some people prefer to have the waiter come up to them and ask, What would you like? Some patients will not tell you what they prefer unless you actively and genuinely invite them to the discussion.
2. Not every doctor is cut out for having patients place their order, ask questions, or voice their preferences, but this is where we are heading, if we're not there already. A doctor-patient conversation is not a monologue.
3. Be prepared to offer your patients a range of participation options alongside treatment options, regardless of what you consider the preferred options. Some chefs wince when a customer pours ketchup on a dish, but they are not the ones eating it.

FOR HEALTHCARE SYSTEMS:

1. While SDM isn't mandated by law, it's supported by the imperative of informed consent and other ways of engaging your patients in their care. It is also an important part of the smorgasbord agenda: laying out a rich buffet of participation options for patients to choose from.
2. Find the degree to which you want to implement SDM. Be transparent about your plan and pursue it, whether it be a leaflet, an Options Grid, or any other means of pulling the patients into the discussion.
3. Realize that if you want your patients to be involved, you need to take steps toward it. Ensuring that the patients understand the communications they receive—that they can grasp the probabilities and not be baffled by choices—is essential, no matter where you stand on the SDM continuum. Waving a menu written in a foreign language under your clients' noses doesn't count as asking them what they would like to eat.

CHAPTER 9

BRAVE-ISH NEW WORLD

In this chapter, I focus on what digital health and innovation can do for us. Fortunately, in recent years researchers, companies, and entrepreneurs have devised some incredibly creative solutions. A thousand flowers are blooming, or more. There is so much creativity out there. So much initiative, fueled by technology. From social media, celebrity doctors, nongovernmental organizations, specialized health organizations, and researchers, as well as national efforts at the government and industry level. So much compassion. So much inspiration for large-scale solutions. So much optimism.

With technological advances, public awareness, and computational power, perhaps patients' challenges can be more easily overcome, not just by us and our physicians, but on a system level. This can be done through digital health and the promise it carries, as well as through policy changes and reforms to support our health choices for our overall health. These factors must work in tandem to create much-needed synergy. The debate between the two approaches—technology and public policy—deeply rooted in ideological differences, is simplistic, and fraught with blind spots regarding the role each one can fill and the role it cannot. Different entities can help us in different ways.

We need smart, innovative tools to facilitate health and related choices. We've been using them for quite a while, and the COVID-19 pandemic has boosted the use of remote medicine and placing some of the responsibilities doctors and nurses used to have in our own hands. Digital health has shown us how to accommodate patients' decision-making processes and emotional needs to improve overall health and well-being. These are glimpses into what healthcare looks like when digitized and elevated through psychological insights.

We must also recognize that psychology and new technologies can only go so far. They cannot completely replace good practices and policies. They do not obviate the need for higher-order social, political, and economic reforms that improve the way health is delivered and everyone's access to healthcare. We need all the help we can get. From every possible stakeholder.

We need smart, innovative policies to encourage the use of digital tools and to go beyond what these tools can do. COVID-19 has shown us that we need regulations and reforms to ensure that we are protected, in our health choices and in our health in general.

For example, the CDC stated that masks help prevent a person from getting or spreading the virus.[1] And then states could choose to help curb the spread of COVID-19 by requiring people to wear face masks in public (hello, New York and thirty-six other states, as of December 2020), or not (hello, Nevada, and twelve other states).[2] Without such a requirement, streets and public transportation may be unsafe for us. These issues can only be resolved on state and federal levels. We cannot rely just on ourselves or count on private enterprise alone to do the work for us.

This brave new world has its limitations. Solutions—both technological and political—require money and intention. They require that our interests align with those administering the solutions. This isn't always the case—bounded optimism, then.

But first, let's talk about selfies.

DEATH BY TEA

A few years ago, after a TV interview, smartly dressed and with my makeup deftly applied by the studio artist, I asked the interviewer if we could take a selfie together. Right before the camera clicked, we simultaneously took off our glasses. That had to be a sign. Off with the spectacles, for good. I decided to get LASIK surgery.

I was a deluxe patient. I became a patient out of vanity, not out of pain or danger. I chose the timing of my surgery. I chose the surgeon, who had operated successfully on my son and chatted with me in French. I got a second opinion for extra reassurance. I had the time and wherewithal to read related scientific articles and go on the US Food and Drug Administration website, making sure I was not subjecting myself to too much risk. I took a few days off from work. My husband drove me to the clinic and back and made me lemonade.

Cutting into one's eyes reduces the ability to focus, mentally as well as visually. The eye clinic acknowledged this and developed a secret weapon to ensure that we patients would take our medication as prescribed. Before the procedure, the nurse pulled out a thick black marker and marked my eye drops with 1, 2, 3, to match the instruction sheet she gave me. To be on the safe side, she went over it with me and told me to call if I had any questions.

The thick, clear numbers the nurse drew on the box, together with the instruction sheet, told me all I needed to know: what medication to take and when ("1 drop x 8 times a day, every two hours"), and a short explanation ("artificial tears"). There were also answers to frequently asked questions, such as what to do if I missed a dosage. They printed out two copies for me in case I lost one or spilled a cup of tea all over it. My imagination ran wild, visualizing tea spilling on hospital discharge notes after, say, open heart surgery—and then what? The frantic calls to the ward, trying to figure out what to do and when, the hospital readmissions when you failed to follow orders, maybe even the deaths—death by tea.

The measures taken by the eye clinic reduced the number of confused phone calls from patients who missed a dose or weren't sure which drops to apply when, and they might have also reduced postoperative complications. They could increase success rates, boost customer recommendations, and help the bottom line too.

I was a deluxe patient, and yet I was still a patient, complete with the desire to flee right before the excimer laser cut into my eyes, the sting when it happened (the nurse held my hand), and the discomfort at home when my lids felt glued together. I would have messed up the drops and the times if it hadn't been for the thick black markings and the instruction sheet (both copies). With them, I aced it.

Now I am always ready for a selfie. But it took some help getting there.

THE NEXT PHASE OF THE JOURNEY

Humanity is exploring the possibilities of living on Mars, and yet here I am marveling at thick black markers. It's the thought that counts, not the machinery delivering it. The key to better healthcare is to anticipate and cater to the psychological needs of making good medical decisions.[3]

The marker-printer combo is readily available for other practices to use, in many other contexts, without substantial investment in technology or infrastructure. Indeed, the black marker and the printer that produced the copies of the medication regimen elegantly address these basic criteria, which are also applicable to more sophisticated solutions:

1. A need that patients have (e.g., to take their meds as prescribed after surgery)
2. The difficulties patients might have in fulfilling that need (e.g., forgetting their eye drop schedule, or getting the bottles mixed up)
3. The facts that these difficulties abound and that help must be offered to everyone in a way that is free of barriers to access and allows for optimal comprehension
4. The resources required to administer the solution (e.g., a team member whose job it was to explain, and an entire process that her job was built into, such as the prescription for obtaining the eye drops ahead of time so they could be properly marked)

A thousand flowers are blooming. A thousand solutions. However, most of those solutions are ones that we cannot apply on our own. Let's look at some of them and how they help overcome the main barriers to good medical decision-making that I described in this book.

NICE TRY!

Like children, in order for us to remain in the game, we need the coach to say "Nice try!" when we've let a slow pitch slip from our hands. Of course, health isn't an extracurricular activity—we should be self-driven. Nevertheless, we need an affective reward to keep us on top of our medication, physical activity, smoking cessation, and the like. We need positive feedback, because it is more effective than negative feedback in creating behavior change.[4] We need that feedback not only when we're doing well, but also when we don't exercise or don't take our medication. Companies that design behavior change solutions for us must keep this in mind.

More than a decade ago, I was hired to consult for Healarium, a digital health company. I was at my Princeton office, on the phone with four or five company executives. They were awaiting my opinion on their platform that gave people feedback on their health. My eyes skipped from one dial to the other, each reflecting a different health measure, as I was trying to gauge the health of the person whose measures were on display. Their cockpit-like interface was complicated. "You can tell this was designed by engineers," I remarked.

The CEO wasn't thrilled to hear this, though he knew they had ignored the psychological aspects of the platform, which is why they had come to me in the first place. We then worked together to bring clarity to the system and increase the motivation of those using it, making sure the feedback they receive was not discouraging.

A similar process occurred with an international mobile health company that created an adherence-to-medication platform. Their product was functional, but functionality was not enough. They needed people to want to use the platform for extended periods of time, and emotion would be a strong driver of that.

To drive sustainable behavior change, health and fitness apps should predispose us toward the health behavior, providing us with the knowledge, the attitudes and values, and the confidence and motivation to act upon them. Then they should enable us: teach us the skills we need or allow us to track progress. Finally, they should reinforce our behavior by rewarding it.[5] Providing such tools is up to our app designers, up to advertising agencies, HMOs, and anyone who commissions such solutions—it's not up to us.

SO FAR AND YET SO NEAR, AND SOMETIMES, TOO NEAR

The first barrier to patient decision-making is forming a connection with one's doctor; Chapter 3 showed how important and challenging that is. And for some, it proves to be more challenging than for others. Take transgender people: they often feel uncomfortable when receiving medical care. Sometimes they are even physically assaulted.

Plume is a digital health company cofounded by two doctors. One of the cofounders, Jerrica Kirkley, is transgender. Her cofounder and CEO,

Matthew Wetschler, said that 20 percent of transgender people report being discriminated against or harassed during in-person medical visits.[6] In another interview, he noted that in order to avoid going to doctors' offices, 30 percent of transgender people in urban areas buy hormones on the black market.[7] Through digital health, Plume offers a trans-friendly environment, allowing trans patients to connect with doctors who are respectful and sympathetic, thereby removing reliance on one's physical vicinity and eliminating adversity from the medical encounter.

Physical proximity was also a barrier for tuberculosis patients in Kenya. These patients needed to receive their medication at the clinics on a daily basis, but social stigma associating TB with HIV made it undesirable to be seen at the clinic. That stigma is yet another hindrance to forming a strong connection between patient and doctor and led to unsuccessful treatment outcomes: the patient died during the treatment, the treatment failed (the patient tested positive for tuberculosis within five months or later), or the patient ceased treatment for two months or more. The solution relied on a change of policy: giving the more adherent patients large batches of medication they could take at home. However, the change of policy was not enough. Patients also needed to feel that someone cared about their health. This personal touch was delivered using "dumb" phones, though the intervention involved was anything but dumb.

A team led by MIT researchers and Keheala, a mobile health company that operates in resource-constrained environments, sent daily text messages to these patients, asking them to verify adherence to treatment. If there was no response, more automatic messages were sent, followed by messages and then phone calls from study-team members who knew firsthand how to complete the treatment for tuberculosis. Still no response? They notified the clinic, who would contact the patients, motivate, and assist them. This gave patients resources and support for overcoming barriers to nonadherence without exposing them to stigma.

The team tested the intervention in seventeen clinics in Nairobi. They performed a randomized controlled trial between patients (so that a patient could be included regardless of which clinic he or she was in). It worked. In the control group, out of five hundred patients, seventy had unsuccessful outcomes, compared with only twenty-four in the intervention group—a remarkable result.[8] But resources were needed for this solution to be sustained and implemented at the necessary scale.

Sometimes you want the relationship to be as unobtrusive as possible. Amwell, an American telemedicine company, reported that 42 percent of women aged eighteen to forty-three would prefer to get birth control prescriptions online, as opposed to walking into a hospital or clinic.[9] It could be that the women do not wish to have their contraception discussed in person, or that they view getting the prescription as a functional need that doesn't involve a personal connection.

THE HEALTH DOMAIN ENCOMPASSES MORE STAKEHOLDERS THAN US, OUR doctors, and our health systems, and some relationship etiquette applies there too.

An American health insurer developed an innovative, credit-card-like way of paying for doctors' visits and tests and hired me to review his model before going to full-on dissemination. I found that the insurer expected the patients to trust him with their financial details but gave them no reasons for doing so. This oversight would cause major aggravations at the doctor's office, once the patients realized that the card did not work (because they had never entered their financial information!). To talk about caring in this context would be stretching it, but we should talk about trust as the cornerstone of any relationship. Therefore, trust has to be established, even in a relationship between a person and an institution.

Having a relationship happen on your own terms is tricky when the other party is much bigger and stronger than you, such as when the relationship you're in is with the company you work for.

Employers now offer wellness, mental health, and lifestyle interventions. They do it to increase productivity, lower health insurance premiums, and reduce the number of sick leave days, and, hey, because they care. All these reasons translate to a huge employee benefit market: in 2019 it was estimated at $57.2 billion globally.[10] The plan works: randomized controlled trials show that mental health interventions increase psychological well-being and work effectiveness.[11] It also works for physical activity and/or diet. The results on metabolic risk factors are, however, mixed. And here's a hint into why this might be.[12]

An employer offered employees with type 2 diabetes an expensive support package, but six months later, only eight out of every hundred employees were still using it. The health advertising agency that had brokered the deal asked me to solve the mystery. I found that nobody had asked the employees if they wanted or needed the new glucometers the employer had paid for. I also found that the onboarding process, where employees learned of the generous offer, was missing some crucial pieces, such as telling the employees that they would be receiving phone calls from health coaches when their blood sugar levels spiked. What the employer intended to be a VIP service was instead perceived by the employees as an intrusive breach of the terms of their relationship with their employer.

PATIENTS AND THEIR PHYSICIANS RELY ON HEALTH SYSTEMS TO BE ATTUNED to patients' needs, not just medically but also in terms of what kinds of support and care they wish to receive and what they wish to avoid. The same goes for people using health insurance, employee wellness programs, or any related product or service. The solutions offered by Plume, Keheala, and Amwell provided a means to accommodate the right kind of, and the right amount of, contact with medical caregivers, with as little friction as possible. And others, like the health insurer I consulted, or whoever devised the type 2 diabetes support plan, didn't realize there was human contact between them and their clients, and that they had to nurture it, or at least not overlook it.

These are all solutions in which patients need health systems' help in order to implement positive change. Plume illustrates how far from regional providers digital health can take a patient. Keheala, using less sophisticated measures, helps keep patients connected to local support while removing stigma and saving lives.

Innovative insurance models, wellness interventions, and anyone aiming to benefit their clients can do even better if they treat them as dinner party guests, or simply as individuals who have emotional, not just health, needs. There is great promise here, but we are yet to see if it is fulfilled broadly.

FUN, FACTS, AND FUNCTIONALITY

Health literacy is yet another challenge patients encounter. Patients need to understand medical information. That's hard when the information is slathered in jargon, and harder still when the information is viewed with sus-picion. Who, then, can give people access to clear information that they can trust to be unbiased and factual? Due to physicians' time constraints, they cannot be the only ones performing this role. For example, given the consid-erable distrust of the medical establishment on the issue of vaccination (to such a degree that the World Health Organization included the reluctance or refusal to vaccinate among the top ten threats to global health in 2019), some-one needs to convey vaccination-related health information in a credible, dis-arming manner.[13]

Enter Dr. Mikhail (Mike) Varshavski, a dashing American doctor in his early thirties, who specializes in conveying valid medical information with special attention to the fun-to-fact ratio. His short, masterly videos are always useful and always presented in an honest and impartial manner.

It's no wonder that Dr. Mike's YouTube channel has more than 6.9 million subscribers and that his videos have exponentially more views than those pro-duced by official medical agencies. Watching this likable physician is a treat. He's always on the move, in the car, outdoors, crinkling his forehead above those blue beamers of his, inserting quirky visuals to the clips, and never using SAT words.

I'll do my best to convey the magic.

One of his child-vaccination videos has been viewed more than a million times.[14] Early in the video, he said, "You hear people screaming all of these things, you don't know what to believe, and I empathize with the person who doesn't have a great medical education to understand what's true and what's not," thus disarming people who hang on to one vaccination position or another because they feel incapable of evaluating them. Then he stopped a woman on the street and asked her what she thought about vaccinations. "I don't believe in them," she said. He asked her why, and whether her doctor tried to push her or convince her to do it (he didn't use the verb "to vaccinate," I noticed). "They get paid for this s—t!" the woman giggled. Dr. Mike smiled, said, "Thank you so much, appreciated," and raised his hand in a farewell or an unrequited high-five.

When we spoke, I asked him about that. He complimented me on noticing the high-five. I complimented him for not losing his cool with the woman, even though the clip immediately included a short explanation of why vaccinations aren't a source of profit for doctors. Mike said he had learned a lot about communication and persuasion from Dale Carnegie and Robert Cialdini. He was treating people with respect, not dismissing their beliefs. Viewed from the lens of health literacy, he was lowering people's resistance, thereby raising their motivation to listen.

For me the pleasure in watching his clips was doubled when I considered his genius in making health information approachable and giving people the motivation to access it. People can view the clips regardless of where they are and regardless of how good the doctors in their vicinity are at conveying medical information. It's the magic of Dr. Mike, delivered on the magical platform of digital media.

But there is only one Dr. Mike, and tens of millions of people with low health literacy. Only one Dr. Mike, and an entire universe full of people who need to be motivated to learn about their health, and hopefully to also do something about it.

IN SEPTEMBER 2020, BEFORE THE COVID-19 VACCINATION WAS ANnounced, 17 percent of Americans surveyed said that they "somewhat disagree" to COVID-19 vaccinating, and 16 percent said they "strongly disagree."[15] In Italy the responses were 17 percent to both, and in the UK they were 9 percent and 7 percent, respectively, which is good news, because a 75 percent vaccination rate is required to reach a level that will extinguish an epidemic if the vaccination is at an 80 percent level of efficiency.[16] Once you figured out the medical aspect of COVID, the psychological barriers to making better health choices emerged, big time. For our society to live free of fear of diseases for which effective vaccinations exist, a great many people need to learn what the vaccine does and why they should take it.

But when people were offered vaccinations, some said, "No thanks I don't want to be a guinea pig!," "No to this poison," and "Ridiculous. No one needs a toxic vaccine to 'protect' themselves against a glorified cold virus."[17]

I suggested applying several psychological tactics to increase vaccination rates, including using temporal anchors such as "Vaccinate by Valentine's Day—Show the Love," or "Vaccinate by Easter—Show You Really Care." These slogans also apply the affect heuristic, fighting fear with a more positive emotion.[18]

Vaccine reluctance is just one of many threats to global health, all of which require massive educational campaigns to get public buy-in. Noncommunicable diseases—including diabetes, hypertension, and cancer—are another such threat. Of the main risk factors for noncommunicable diseases, only one—air pollution—lies outside the individual's control. The other risk factors are in people's hands: tobacco use, physical inactivity, the harmful use of alcohol, and unhealthy diets. Behavior change is hard, as anyone who ever tried to quit smoking will tell you. But acquiring the knowledge on what your unhealthy behaviors are and gaining the motivation to change them are important steps toward making better choices.

SCOTT RATZAN, FORMER VICE PRESIDENT OF HEALTH POLICY AT JOHNSON & Johnson, is well aware of health literacy issues. Ratzan asked me to create a comprehensible tool that would illustrate to people their health status and the behaviors leading up to it. I created a short scorecard based on medical evidence, using wording people could easily understand and criteria they could measure themselves against, discuss with their doctors, and then apply in order to increase their score, improving their health in the process.

If your behavior-related indicators were perfect, you scored 7. But if, for example, you smoked, you went down to a 6. Didn't exercise five times a week, 30 minutes each time? A 5. Had more than two units of alcohol a day for a man and one for a woman? Your score was a 4. You also lost a point for having a BMI outside the healthy range (or won one if you were in the healthy range), likewise for blood pressure, cholesterol, and blood sugar level.[19]

Curbing noncommunicable diseases is a global health issue. We prepared the scorecard in time for the UN's high-level meeting about noncommunicable diseases.[20] The scorecard, or a variation thereof, could reach people of high and low health literacy levels and help reduce their communicable disease risk, but no health system ever picked it up for extensive use.

A HOME VISIT FROM THE APP MAN

I speak a lot about health literacy (see Chapter 4), but when medicine goes digital, technological literacy becomes just as important, adding another layer of complexity.

During COVID-19, telemedicine allowed us to meet our doctors free of contagion risk. According to *Forbes*, in 2020, 46 percent of US consumers used telehealth, compared with 11 percent the previous year.[21] Telemedicine is now a force to be reckoned with. It provides tremendous relief for the health system, and for patients. But not for all of them. More than 80 percent of adults aged fifty-five and above who had access to telehealth have not had a virtual or telemedicine visit (the numbers were similar for adults younger than sixty-five). Telemedicine, and especially telephone-based consultations, was particularly challenging for seniors with mild (or severe) hearing loss.[22] The bright telemedicine picture may not be so bright for everyone.

Years before COVID-19, at a *Financial Times* event in New York, I sat on a panel with the impressive Jonathan Linkous, the then twenty-year president of the mighty American Telemedicine Association, an organization that has thousands of companies as members. Linkous proudly told me that telemedicine visits are becoming increasingly prevalent. "Do you have medical guidelines for them?" I asked. "Of course," he answered. "And psychological ones?" Well, no. By "psychological" I meant a range of issues, relating to how the doctor and patient connected and how information was communicated, but also to the design and usability aspects of the experience. I thought—and still think—they are pivotal.

Some people share my belief. Dr. Joseph Kvedar is the president-elect of the American Telemedicine Association. He is vice president of connected health at Partners HealthCare, and professor of dermatology at Harvard Medical School. He is also a practicing dermatologist with a placid attitude. Sitting in the Google offices in downtown New York one drizzly morning, he told me that he never cuts off a patient. He lets them speak for as long as they want, and only once in every hundred or so patients does it become too long.

When COVID-19 broke, I reached out to him. I acknowledged that with the pandemic, telemedicine was popularized by necessity. I added that it made us more aware of the fact that technology alone couldn't solve everything. We needed a good understanding of the human factor. Did he agree?

Kvedar's response recognized technology's advantages as well as its limitations: "Now that telehealth is a household word and the majority of both patients and doctors have experienced it, we move into a hybrid, multi-channel healthcare delivery world. The next phase of the journey will be thoughtfully deciding which healthcare interactions must be in person, which can be done either way, and which are ideal for telehealth."[23]

My colleagues and I, including nephrologist Stefan Becker, offered our own blend of a hybrid model.[24] You could say we put the "house" in "household word." We made digital health accessible for all individuals, and practically held their hands during their first use of the technology, which occurred in their homes.

We identified a need: patients in cardiac rehabilitation had to take five or six types of medication at different times during the day, plus measure their blood pressure. We identified a difficulty: keeping track of the complicated regimen, and we realized this difficulty was common. We offered help: we created an app that told the patients what to take when and made it fun to check "Done" when they reported they had swallowed their pill. And, what we were most proud of: we created and implemented a technique that allowed people who were not particularly digitally savvy to use the app. These folks—patients around the age of seventy-four who had never owned (or even held) a smartphone or a tablet—liked our medication reminder tablet app better than the familiar pen and paper journal.

The seniors did not make the leap from "never held a smartphone or a tablet" to loving an app on their own. Instead of dumping the new technology in the seniors' laps, we introduced them to the technology and helped them ease into it. We did home visits—the app man came knocking! We brought each senior a tablet, put a sticker where the on button would be in a less novel design, muted everything on the screen so only the medication app was showing, and punched into the app the medication names and doses for the particular person. Then they got it, used it, loved it, and adhered to their medication, and almost all of them wanted to keep on using the app after we wrapped up the study.

Some of the seniors may have been able to handle the app on their own. Others needed us to remove the barriers. The study's success proved that interventions can and should include patients of all ages and all levels of technological familiarity and literacy.

SOLVING THE PROBLEM WITH PROBABILITIES

As we've already noted in Chapter 5, a person who receives a diagnosis wants to know, What do I do now, and what can I expect? PREDICT is an online tool that helps women who have had surgery for early invasive cancer decide which other treatments to have.[25] It is offered free of charge by the British National Health Service (NHS), and it is endorsed by the American Joint Committee on Cancer (AJCC).

PREDICT was established and validated by professors Gordon Wishart of the University of East Anglia and Paul Pharoah of the University of Cambridge. It models the way probabilities regarding medical events can be accessible and useful to people with no medical training (aka patients). It encompasses decades of research, with dedicated researchers, and with an expert team specializing in risk communication. Finally, PREDICT illustrates the immense professional effort that goes into rendering probabilities accessible and useful—definitely not a DIY.

Following extensive testing and visualizations by the Winton Centre for Risk and Evidence Communication at Cambridge, where I'm a visiting researcher, PREDICT received an update so that it now uses frequentist wording such as "69 out of 100 women treated with surgery live at least 10 years from surgery." PREDICT was already widely used, but the Winton Centre saw a traffic boost from about twenty thousand users a month to thirty thousand users after relaunch. Women can choose how they view the information: in a table; on a curves graph, a chart, or a graph; or with icons (frequentist presentation). To the degree that "user-friendly" can apply to breast cancer knowledge, PREDICT is highly user-friendly.

The greatness of PREDICT is not just in presenting the information clearly and accessibly, although that is paramount. The true greatness of PREDICT is in the scientific research that it captures and the analytical effort it represents. Women and oncologists can now enter a woman's age, genetics, and other relevant features and, with just a few clicks, learn what she might gain from each additional treatment.

Over a million doctors and women have used this free tool so far.[26] It became so ubiquitous in the UK—virtually every oncologist was showing it to patients—that the Winton Centre had trouble forming control groups to conduct further testing because they couldn't find enough people who hadn't already used it. But we can anecdotally look at its effect.

A WOMAN WHO WAS TAKING HORMONAL THERAPY FOR BREAST CANCER postsurgery was enduring such devastating effects on her mood and behavior that her daughter said, "Mom, I feel I don't know you anymore!" The patient hated it, but she felt as though she would be giving herself a death sentence if she were to go off the medication.

Then she punched her numbers into PREDICT—her age, relevant genetics and tumor features, and whether she was postmenopausal, characteristics that determined her estimated benefit from continuing the hormone therapy. The results established that given her information, her medication offered less than a 4 percent increase in survival rates. Out of one hundred women in her situation who receive the treatment, only four will see a benefit. She read the text in disbelief. She clicked to see the "curves" display and had to strain her eyes to see the small curve associated with benefit due to her treatment:

This graph shows the percentage of women who survive over time after surgery.

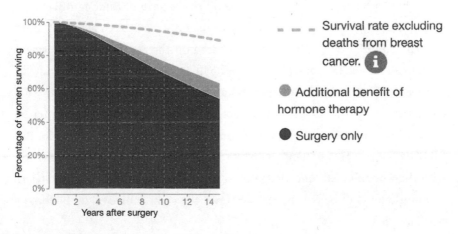

Curves graph showing survival over time after breast cancer surgery

Could this be true? She switched to the "icons" display, which told her the same story.

This display shows the number of women who survive at least 10 years after surgery.

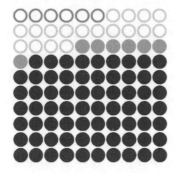

○ 6 deaths due to other causes

○ 18 deaths related to breast cancer

● 7 extra survivors due to hormone therapy

● 69 survivors with surgery alone

Icon (frequentist) presentation showing survival over time after breast cancer surgery

Shocked at the results, she went back to her oncologist and asked whether she was using PREDICT correctly. She brought up her numbers, and her doctor confirmed that, yes, she was doing it correctly. The doctor agreed that since she was still experiencing harsh side effects despite having been on the medication for a while, she could stop taking it, without significantly increasing her risk of recurring cancer. She went off the medication and got her life back.

Without PREDICT, this patient would never have become familiar with these numbers, which her doctor may or may not have been aware of. Both of them would have blindly continued based on the assumption "Treatment saves lives," which they translated to "Stopping treatment leads to death."

PREDICT doesn't encourage patients to make rash decisions, or any decisions, on their own or with their doctors. Just as I noted in the chapter on probabilities, no test or computerized system can tell you what to do. But PREDICT does arm patients with the information needed for a discussion with their oncologist. Knowledge of probabilities and chances translates to action and leads to better choices, whatever the right choice might be for any particular patient.

SPOILED FOR CHOICE

We are used to having choices. We like it and view it as a prerogative. But Chapter 6 showed that choice requires mental resources from us, as well as from our physicians. In some cases, the cost imposed on our health because our physicians choose incorrectly, or even suboptimally, is exorbitant. In such cases, we benefit when the choice process is reconfigured to be less demanding. But, as with probabilities, it's the health system, not a single doctor, that needs to create better choice architecture. Luckily for us, computerized systems, when properly handled, can do the trick.

In England, when the NHS noticed people who were referred to specialists sometimes had to wait over a year for an appointment, it brought in the Behavioral Insight Unit (nicknamed the Nudge Unit). The Nudge Unit talked to doctors and discovered that each time a doctor searched for a specialist for a patient, on average, ninety-nine specialists were offered. Given everything we've learned about choice, we know that doctors could not compare options efficiently from such a large choice set. Therefore, many used a heuristic and referred their patients to the local hospital as a default, even if that meant excruciatingly long wait times.

The solution was to change the choice architecture. Referring doctors were still presented with a large array of specialists, but choosing was made easier. At the top of the list, referring doctors now saw a green box with three local clinics that offered the same service with reasonable wait times. Three were easy to choose among (easier than from ninety-nine!). If a doctor wanted to refer to a specialist's office that had a red box next to it, noting a prohibitive wait time, a pop-up appeared, urging the doctor to discuss this with the patient.

Referral rates for the congested hospitals went down by 40 percent.[27] This trial, which first took place in East London, was later rolled out nationally.[28] It had the potential to shorten wait times for forty thousand people a month, instead of leaving them to hang in there, in pain, consoling themselves with a cuppa tea.

EVEN WHEN MEDICAL GUIDELINES EXIST AND SHOULD, IN THEORY, GUIDE physicians' choices, they are not fully implemented. In the United States, Geisinger Health System has a Pharmacy Innovations Team whose role, somewhat related to the Nudge Unit's, is to help address suboptimal or inappropriate prescribing. They aimed to use data from the Epic electronic health records to help doctors keep up with the latest medical guidelines and best practices. In one project, they nudged doctors to screen children aged nine to eleven for early detection of high cholesterol and familial hypercholesterol-emia, thus allowing for early treatment and prevention of poor cardiovascular outcomes in the future.

The company chose to work on such projects in order to improve patient outcomes while cutting costs or keeping them at the same level. Amir Goren is the program director for the Behavioral Insights Team at the Steele Institute for Health Innovation within Geisinger. Goren applied A/B testing (showing version A or B at random) to the messages sent to doctors, just as companies test consumer-facing campaigns. He found that by combining a best-practice reminder with an alert for the need to order screening, the number of screening orders went up more than three times compared to sending no alerts at all.[29] This led to 2.6 times as many screenings, because some parents ended up not taking their kids to the screening. The fun of medical decision-making never ends.

Some choices are not up to the patients but can cause them great harm. Prescribing for ventilated patients formed another context where choice architecture reduced doctors' burdens while simultaneously increasing health outcomes with minimal effort. Ventilated patients run the risk of developing pneumonia. And, being ventilated, there's nothing they can do about it. It is up to their doctors to prescribe chlorhexidine mouthwash, which significantly reduces the risk of developing pneumonia while ventilated. This mouthwash was available to order at the University Hospitals Bristol NHS Foundation Trust, and yet only 55 percent of patients received it. Choice architecture to the rescue! When the mouthwash was added as a default, an already checked box, to the electronic order form doctors filled out for patients, 90 percent of them got it.[30] These advancements in choice architecture left the physicians room for consideration but made choosing the "right thing" easy, thereby reducing doctors' cognitive effort and saving patients' lives.

Why did such things fall through the cracks? Were the doctors depleted? Was there choice overload, with too many things to decide on? I am sure that the doctors—who were referring patients to overbooked specialists (or not), who were sending children to high cholesterol screenings (or not), and who were ordering mouthwash for their ventilated patients (or not)—wanted what was best for their patients. Clever nudges and defaults helped them get there.

SHOW ME THE MONEY

In Part I of this book I discussed the inherent laziness of our minds. Being cognitive misers, calculatedly preserving our mental resources, is the chief reason we rely on heuristics, defaults, and nudges, why we let ourselves be convinced by emotional tokens of hope and fear. I spent most of Part II showing how this plays out and most of Part III talking about solutions that can help us make better decisions about our health.

Some of the solutions are deceptively simple. Pulling out a black marker and writing "3" on the artificial tears box does not sound like something that wins you a Nobel Prize. Making home visits to seniors and putting stickers on their tablets may not sound like psychology or behavioral economics. Nevertheless, behavioral economics is about understanding our motivations and removing barriers to desired behaviors. It helps us do what we intended to do but still haven't (even for intentions that are important—like saving for retirement or living in a society where organ donation is widely available).[31]

We are reliably human. Reliably, we mess up. Even when our health is at stake.

DR. KATHERINE (KATY) MILKMAN IS A WHARTON PROFESSOR, FORMER president of the Society for Judgment and Decision Making, and author of *How to Change: The Science of Getting from Where You Are to Where You Want to Be*. She is terrific at applying behavioral insights to real-life settings. Via email I asked her, "What prompts organizations to create nudges and better choice architecture? Because this isn't commonplace. The follow-up question is: can we rely on them to do this for us, and under what circumstances?"

She was not even boundedly optimistic: "My immediate answer is 'no.'" She referred me to a paper to that effect.[32] She then added, "Unless trained to use choice architecture wisely, it doesn't seem at all obvious that even well-intentioned organizations will create good architecture since people mis-intuit what 'works.'" She noted that choice architecture is taught only in very few elective classes around the country, not in the widespread curricula. Yet this rare specialization isn't the only reason we're not getting all the help we need. Milkman added, "And then of course there are conflicts of interest (for instance, Big Tobacco would love to use choice architecture to get you hooked on cigarettes, presumably)." Misaligned financial incentives, anyone?

Milkman is a great proponent for health and behavior improvement. She is not a pessimist but merely a realist. Black markers, an instructions sheet (two copies!), text messaging and calls to patients, a close analysis of the medical literature that translates to computerized systems evaluating risk, tablets, and nudge units all cost money. They also help increase satisfaction and improve health, which hopefully somebody cares enough to pay for.

In order to remove barriers, caring about patients is not enough. It is also not enough to recognize their needs, identify their difficulties, and suggest ways of meeting those needs. The resources required to administer the solutions and remove barriers are crucial. A thousand flowers are blooming. And they require water and fertilizer. For us to receive the best possible support in making health decisions and maintaining our health based on behavioral economics and other best practices, someone has to care.

The eye clinic I attended cared enough to dedicate resources—they needed my positive word of mouth. University of Utah Health cared—they wanted to improve their HCAHPS scores. Healarium cared—they wanted to attract customers and keep them on board. Plume cared—it was their business to deliver supportive treatment. Keheala, support agencies, and governments cared—fewer people died of tuberculosis. Dr. Mike cared—he became a recognizable, well-trusted brand name. My colleagues and I cared—we wanted to publish the app study. The researchers at Cambridge University and the Winton Centre cared about getting the science right and communicating it correctly. And, luckily for women with breast cancer, Cambridge University paid them to do it. The NHS cared—longer wait times hurt patient health and the NHS would have to pay more to take care of them. Geisinger Health cared—costs were lowered or maintained and satisfaction increased. Someone had to foot the bill for all those efforts. But are the financial incentives aligned with yours? Don't count on it.

Keheala CEO and founder Jon Rathauser doesn't count on it. He told me it was difficult to obtain continuous funding for the tuberculosis project, despite the fact that its success had been proven. Funding agencies were keen on new, innovative projects, even though their success wasn't guaranteed. No optimism here either.

Dr. Nicholas (Nick) Peters is a cardiologist, and, among other things, he is also the clinical adviser for Google Fit. He established the Connected Care Bureau at Imperial NHS Trust in London, which offers innovative solutions for diagnosis, triage, and self-care for "the sole aim of delivering better care more cost effectively."[33] Those are two aims, I thought. But perhaps they are so intertwined that they can only be materialized together. Better and more costly care won't happen unless someone explicitly pays for it. And shabbier, cost-saving care should not happen.

Given Peters's involvement in implementing novel solutions, I expected him to be an optimist. But when we spoke, he proved to be no optimist at all. "With the lack of understanding in the US that good health is a continuum through to ill-health, I don't believe that the behavioural levers to promote healthy decision-making have a chance in that context."

In other words: we decision scientists consider ourselves kings and queens where in fact we are nothing but pawns. That hurt. But his position did make sense. Even though I come at the question of healthcare as a psychologist, other, greater, forces are at play. Dollars are key here, but digging a bit deeper reveals that the issue is not just about spending money; the ideology of where to spend it, and on whom, becomes equally salient.

Maybe this is how the situation in the United States is viewed from across the ocean, I thought, still hanging on to a shred of optimism. But as it turned out, health decision-making isn't viewed any better from Connecticut, where Kerry Robinson, president of FoundationHealthMed, is based. Robinson sells solutions for patient and provider empowerment. His clients, the potential buyers, are health organizations. When I asked Kerry if improvements to the bottom line would encourage organizations to buy the solutions he sold, he reminded me that insurers were very traditional in their spending (I suppose this translates to them not liking to spend much), whereas pharma, which paid for almost all of American physicians' continuing medical education, aimed to sell more medication.

"If I'm a patient I need to be an advocate for myself—a truer statement was never made because these stakeholders don't care about you. Ultimately, the idea is that all institutions try to improve health, but there are a lot of things that get into that when you go from point A to point B," Robinson explained.[34]

He is right. If a health organization cared and paid for it, you would be offered behavioral solutions for better adherence, doctor-patient communication, and more. If a medical device company or other med-tech company created gadgets that helped you stay on top of your health, and if you could figure them out and pay for them if needed, your health choices, and consequently also your health, would be better. If a governmental agency set out to protect health consumers, no cancer treatment center would get away with offering medication that helps only three out of one hundred patients and marketing it as "hope."

In January 2020, when COVID-19 was only reported in Wuhan City, China, the World Health Organization director-general, Dr. Tedros Adhanom Ghebreyesus, said, "We need to realize that health is an investment in the future. Countries invest heavily in protecting their people from terrorist attacks, but not against the attack of a virus, which could be far more deadly, and far more damaging economically and socially. . . . This means advocating for national funding to address gaps in health systems and health infrastructure."[35] If governments heeded this notion, and more so if they implemented it with overcoming psychological barriers in mind, our health would be significantly improved, and our health choices, easier.

However, these are a lot of ifs.

So here you are, learning your barriers and important ways to overcome them. Great, because your life depends on it. After all, it is your life, nobody else's.

TAKEAWAYS

The takeaways for this chapter are inspired by Antoine de Saint-Exupéry's novella *The Little Prince*. It is the story of a pilot whose plane crashes in the Sahara. There he meets a little prince who asks him, "Draw me a sheep." After three failed attempts, the pilot draws a box with three holes, and explains that the sheep is in it. The prince is finally pleased.

Like the little prince, patients sometimes wish for things beyond what is immediately available to them. Like the pilot, doctors and health systems should listen to what patients ask for, even when this sounds unlikely or incomprehensible and even when it pushes them outside of their comfort zones. They should attempt to cater to patients' needs, be it inside or outside the box.

FOR PATIENTS:

1. You may have desires and needs around your healthcare and medical choices that seem unattainable. Still, it is worth expressing them to your providers.
2. You may have desires and needs around your healthcare and medical choices that seem unattainable. Still, it is worth looking around. Somebody out there might be developing just the thing you are wishing for.
3. If you did not find the solution you were seeking, keep looking. It took the little prince and the pilot four attempts to nail the drawing of the sheep.

FOR HEALTHCARE PROFESSIONALS:

1. We live in a time of incomparable innovation and technological capabilities. There is no excuse for only doing things the old way, especially since parts of it are broken.
2. Some professionals find technology exciting, others do not. Regardless of where you stand, don't let your comfort zone get in the way of giving your patients the care they deserve.
3. You can identify your patients' needs and find ways to ease them, at any level of technological ability. You may not be a programmer, but you can buy black markers. You may not be a skilled illustrator like Saint-Exupéry, but you can draw a box.

FOR HEALTHCARE SYSTEMS:

1. We live in a time of incomparable innovation and technological capabilities. There is no excuse for only doing things the old way, especially since parts of it are broken.
2. The fox tells the little prince that important things can only be seen with the heart. Close your eyes, ignore the way you currently see healthcare delivered, and open your heart to reimagine how you can better cater to your patients' and staff's needs.

3. Solutions that help patients also help you. Think of the competitive advantage the eye clinic achieved with mundane, inexpensive means. Think of the money the NHS saved by reducing patients' wait time for specialists, thereby reducing repeated complaints and complications.

4. The pilot tried to grant the prince his wish several times. He kept on trying, and finally succeeded with what some may call a cop-out but the prince called a coup. Aim for the intention behind the patients' expressed needs. Keep on trying.

ON TRAGEDIES AND BOUNDED OPTIMISM

I opened this book with my experiences as a thirteen-year-old patient and, more than twenty years later, as a professional who was too stunned by back pain to act like a professional and own her medication choices. But I did not write it to make peace with my past; I wrote for the sake of a better future. Mine, and everyone else's. I wrote it as a decision scientist, researcher, consultant, speaker—a person heavily involved in how healthcare and health information are served. A person who also happened to be a patient at a few points in time, who deserved to have it better, and who often did have it better and has received care from competent, even outstanding, caring physicians—just like all of us.

My experience having scoliosis was a minor tragedy that nobody would ever dramatize. What happened to me has happened to many people around me and around the world. It still does: not only were we afflicted with a medical condition, we weren't consulted and weren't involved in our care. We weren't taught the skills and knowledge we needed to be involved, and we lacked the ability to acquire these skills and knowledge on our own. I didn't realize they existed. I felt small and powerless. An ordinary tragedy.

My doctor, who prescribed me the loathsome back brace, did not know how to make our short scenes together less alienating for the both of us, which makes her a tragic figure too. In a way, the Child and Adolescent Orthopedic Center where I was treated, which gave me the chills despite making my back better, was yet another tragic figure.

Such ordinary tragedies befall people all the time; so much so, that people are convinced that they're not real tragedies, or that if they are, the sufferers themselves should shoulder the blame for it. They are wrong on both accounts. Aristotle defined the dramatic form of tragedy as an imitation of "an action that is serious, complete, and of a certain magnitude."[1] Being disempowered around one's medical condition is serious, complete, and certainly has magnitude. Our tragedies are very real.

Aristotle added that the tragic hero's misfortune "is brought about not by vice or depravity, but by some error or frailty."[2] And aren't we humans all frail by nature? We cannot avoid it. Understanding our blamelessness can provide relief and catharsis. Understanding our barriers and those our doctors face can help us act differently and relieve some of the tragic difficulty of handling medical adversity and making the necessary choices that come with it. Understanding the part that the health systems our doctors operate in have in forming these tragedies is no less crucial.

GREEK HEROES ALWAYS HAD A MISSION—MINE BEGAN WITH SHINING A light on patients' barriers and devising ways of overcoming them. In the course of doing so, I learned what every Greek hero knew: that we and our doctors are, at least to a degree, dominated by the epic forces of gods and fate. Replace those forces with health establishments and throw in the gods of politics and economics, gender, and race. Then we can acknowledge that some of the barriers we encounter in making health choices are insurmountable, regardless of our skills, knowledge, and might and our doctors' best efforts and empathy.

Change is in order.

Greek tragedy is radical, both in the sense that it's the root (*radix* in Latin) of modern theater and in the sense that it is politically dangerous: "capable of challenging and undermining accepted practice."[3] Barriers to having patients make the best medical decisions they can are radical, the root of our difficulties. Revealing and unraveling them is radical, demanding change to an accepted flawed practice.

FORTUNATELY, WE DO NOT LIVE ON THE PAPYRUS SCROLLS OF A GREEK play. We are not fated to fumble when making medical decisions. Armed with bounded optimism, we and our doctors, who want to be part of a meaningful, instructive dialogue, can help drive a change. And when we cannot drive it ourselves, we can demand that it happen. This dramatic shift requires commitment by modern gods and fate. Otherwise, people are hurt twice—physically, by being patients, and emotionally, by failing to perform, perfect, and own their health choices. Doctors, trying their best to curtail the tragedies, are hurt too. So are health systems, unawares, and the technological wizards who try to come to our aid.

Enough.

We can comb through health interactions and put the psychological knowledge on overcoming barriers to good use. We can make health systems, along with medical educators, even legislators, commit the resources to making it happen. No patient should be as tragically powerless as I was, no doctor should be as estranged as mine was, and no health system should get away with allowing such disempowering decision-making processes to take place. Together, we can be the heroes who make our health and medical choices much less tragic.

NOTES

INTRODUCTION

1. Jerome Groopman, *How Doctors Think* (Boston: Houghton Mifflin Harcourt, 2008).

2. Daniel Kahneman, *Thinking, Fast and Slow* (New York: Farrar, Straus and Giroux, 2011).

3. Talya Miron-Shatz, "Evaluating Multiepisode Events: Boundary Conditions for the Peak-End Rule," *Emotion* 9, no. 2 (2009): 206–213, doi:10.1037/a0015295; Talya Miron-Shatz, "'Am I Going to Be Happy and Financially Stable?' How American Women Feel When They Think About Financial Security," January 18, 2009, *SSRN Electronic Journal*, doi:10.2139/ssrn.1329806.

CHAPTER 1: OH, THE CHOICE YOU NOW HAVE

1. *Cambridge Dictionary*, s.v. "paternalism," 2020, https://dictionary.cambridge.org/dictionary/english/paternalism; Rolf E. Sartorius, *Paternalism* (Minneapolis: University of Minnesota Press, 1983); Mark Cartwright, "Greek Medicine," *Ancient History Encyclopedia Limited*, accessed January 17, 2020, www.ancient.eu/Greek_Medicine/.

2. ABPI Interactive Resources for Schools, "History of Medicine," accessed January 17, 2020, www.abpischools.org.uk/topic/history-of-medicine.

3. Barbara Ehrenreich and Deirdre English, *Witches, Midwives, and Nurses: A History of Women Healers* (New York: Feminist Press at CUNY, 2010).

4. American Medical Association, *Code of Ethics*, originally adopted at the Adjourned Meeting of the National Medical Convention in Philadelphia (Chicago, 1847).

5. Sachin Waikar, "When Are Consumers Most Likely to Feel Overwhelmed by Their Opinions?," KelloggInsight, October 3, 2017, https://insight.kellogg.northwestern.edu/article/what-predicts-consumer-choice-overload.

6. Jochen Vollmann and Rolf Winau, "Informed Consent in Human Experimentation Before the Nuremberg Code," *BMJ* 313, no. 7070 (1996): 1445–1447, doi:10.1136/bmj.313.7070.1445.

7. Iain Chalmers, "People Are 'Participants' in Research," *BMJ* 318, no. 7191 (1999): 1141, doi:10.1136/bmj.318.7191.1141a.

8. WMA World Medical Association, "WMA International Code of Medical Ethics," July 9, 2018, www.wma.net/policies-post/wma-international-code-of-medical-ethics/; WMA World Medical Association, "WMA Declaration of Helsinki—Ethical Principles for Medical Research Involving Human Subjects," July 9, 2018, www.wma.net/policies-post/wma-declaration-of-helsinki-ethical-principles-for-medical-research-involving-human-subjects/.

9. Ruth Faden and Tom L Beauchamp, *A History and Theory of Informed Consent* (New York: Oxford University Press, 1986).

10. Karen Appold, "High-Deductible Health Plans: A Brief History," *Managed Health-care Executive*, September 22, 2015, www.managedhealthcareexecutive.com/mhe-articles /high-deductible-health-plans-brief-history.

11. Beatrix Hoffman, "Restraining the Health Care Consumer: The History of Deduct-ibles and Co-Payments in U.S. Health Insurance," *Social Science History* 30, no. 4 (2006): 501–528, doi:10.1215/01455532-2006-007; Healthcare.Gov Glossary, s.v. "High De-ductible Health Plan (HDHP)," *HealthCare.Gov*, 2020, www.healthcare.gov/glossary /high-deductible-health-plan/.

12. Daniel Kahneman and Amos Tversky, "Prospect Theory: An Analysis of Decision Un-der Risk," in *Handbook of the Fundamentals of Financial Decision Making: Part I*, ed. Leonard C. MacLean and William T. Ziemba (Singapore: World Scientific, 2013), 99–127.

13. Theodore McDowell, "Mandatory Health Savings Accounts and the Need for Consumer-Driven Health Care," *Georgetown Journal of Law and Public Policy* 16, no. 1 (2018): 315.

14. Robin Cohen and Emily Zammitti, "High-Deductible Health Plan Enrollment Among Adults Aged 18–64 with Employment-Based Insurance Coverage," CDC, National Center for Health Statistics, NCHS data brief no. 317, August 2018, www.cdc.gov/nchs/products /databriefs/db317.htm.

15. Edward Berchick, Jessica Barnett, and Rachel Upton, "Health Insurance Coverage in the United States: 2018," report no. P60-267, United States Census Bureau, November 8, 2019, www.census.gov/library/publications/2019/demo/p60-267.html.

16. "Internet Users per 100 Inhabitants 1997 to 2007," ITU: International Telecommu-nications Union, ICT Data and Statistics (IDS), updated July 15, 2008, www.itu.int/ITU-D /ict/statistics/ict/; Monica Anderson, et al., "10% of Americans Don't Use the Internet: Who Are They?," FactTank, Pew Research Center, April 22, 2019, www.pewresearch.org /fact-tank/2019/04/22/some-americans-dont-use-the-internet-who-are-they/.

17. Emily A. Vogels, "About One-in-Five Americans Use a Smart Watch or Fitness Tracker," Pew Research Center, January 9, 2020, www.pewresearch.org/fact-tank/2020/01/09 /about-one-in-five-americans-use-a-smart-watch-or-fitness-tracker/; Irl Hirsch et al., "Role of Continuous Glucose Monitoring in Diabetes Treatment," American Diabetes Association, 2018, https://pubmed.ncbi.nlm.nih.gov/30958664/; Ara Jo, Bryan D. Coronel, Courtney E. Coakes, and Arch G. Mainous III, "Is There a Benefit to Patients Using Wearable Devices Such as Fitbit or Health Apps on Mobiles? A Systematic Review." *American Journal of Medicine* 132, no. 12 (2019): 1394–1400.

18. Matt Peterson, "A Vaccine Will Only Succeed if Americans Have Trust," *Barrons*, July 31, 2020, www.barrons.com/articles/how-americans-became-hesitant-about-covid-19 -vaccines-a-q-a-with-walter-orenstein-51596219473.

19. "Current Cigarette Smoking Among Adults in the United States," Centers for Disease Control and Prevention, page last reviewed December 10, 2020, www.cdc .gov/tobacco/data_statistics/fact_sheets/adult_data/cig_smoking/index.htm#: ~:text=In%25202018%252C%2520nearly%252014%2520of,with%2520a%2520 smoking%252Drelated%2520disease; "80% of Americans Don't Get Enough Exercise—And Here's How Much You Actually Need," Cleveland Clinic, "Health Essentials," November 20, 2018, health.clevelandclinic.org/80-of-americans-dont-get-enough-exercise-and-heres -how-much-you-actually-need/#:~:text=About%252080%2520percent%2520 of%2520U.S.,enough%2520exercise%2520for%2520optimal%2520health; "Health Risks of

an Inactive Lifestyle," NIH U.S. National Library of Medicine, MedlinePlus, last updated December 2, 2020, medlineplus.gov/healthrisksofaninactivelifestyle.html.

20. "High Cholesterol—Symptoms and Causes," Mayo Clinic, 2020, www.mayoclinic .org/diseases-conditions/high-blood-cholesterol/symptoms-causes/syc-20350800.

21. McVin Hua Heng Cheen et al., "Prevalence of and Factors Associated with Primary Medication Non-Adherence in Chronic Disease: A Systematic Review and Meta-Analysis," *International Journal of Clinical Practice* 73, no. 6 (2019): e13350, doi:10.1111/ijcp.13350.

22. Lisa Rosenbaum and William H. Shrank, "Taking Our Medicine—Improving Adherence in the Accountability Era," *New England Journal of Medicine* 369, no. 8 (2013): 694–695, doi:10.1056/nejmp1307084.

23. "High Cholesterol—Symptoms and Causes."

24. Ann Marie Navar et al., "Medication Discontinuation in the IMPROVE-IT Trial," *Circulation: Cardiovascular Quality and Outcomes* 12, no. 1 (2019), doi:10.1161 /circoutcomes.118.005041.

25. Pouya Saeedi et al., "Global and Regional Diabetes Prevalence Estimates for 2019 and Projections for 2030 and 2045: Results from the International Diabetes Federation Diabetes Atlas, 9th Edition," *Diabetes Research and Clinical Practice* 157 (2019): 107843, doi:10.1016/j .diabres.2019.107843; "Division of Diabetes Translation at a Glance," CDC, National Center for Chronic Disease Prevention and Health Promotion, last reviewed August 21, 2020, www .cdc.gov/chronicdisease/resources/publications/aag/diabetes.htm.

26. Cheen et al., "Prevalence of and Factors Associated with Primary Medication Non-Adherence in Chronic Disease."

27. "Type 2 Diabetes," CDC, Diabetes, page last reviewed May 30, 2019, www.cdc.gov /diabetes/basics/type2.html; "Complications," American Diabetes Association, 2020, www .diabetes.org/diabetes/complications.

28. Dario Giugliano et al., "Clinical Inertia, Reverse Clinical Inertia, and Medication Non-Adherence in Type 2 Diabetes," *Journal of Endocrinological Investigation* 42, no. 5 (2018): 495–503, doi:10.1007/s40618-018-0951-8; Kam Capoccia, Peggy S. Odegard, and Nancy Letassy, "Medication Adherence with Diabetes Medication," *Diabetes Educator* 42, no. 1 (2015): 34–71, doi:10.1177/0145721715619038.

29. Kimberly Holland and Valencia Higuera, "The Dangers of Abruptly Stopping Antidepressants," *Healthline*, updated May 11, 2020, www.healthline.com/health/depression /dangers-of-stopping-antidepressants#2; Randy Sansone and Lori Sansone, "Antidepressant Adherence: Are Patients Taking Their Medications?," *Innovations in Clinical Neuroscience* 9 (2012): 41–46.

30. Robby Nieuwlaat et al., "Interventions for Enhancing Medication Adherence," *Cochrane Database of Systematic Reviews*, November 20, 2014, doi:10.1002/14651858.cd000011 .pub4.

31. Meera Viswanathan et al., "Interventions to Improve Adherence to Self-Administered Medications for Chronic Diseases in the United States," *Annals of Internal Medicine* 157, no. 11 (2012): 785, doi:10.7326/0003-4819-157-11-201212040-00538.

32. Jan Horsky and Harley Ramelson, "Cognitive Errors in Reconciling Complex Medication Lists," *AMIA Annual Symposium Proceedings*, 2016, 638. The lowest annual sum they mention as spent per year on adverse drug events in the United States is $1.56 billion.

33. Brooke Hoots et al., "2018 Annual Surveillance Report of Drug-Related Risks and Outcomes—United States," CDC National Center for Injury Prevention and Control,

August 31, 2018, www.cdc.gov/drugoverdose/pdf/pubs/2018-cdc-drug-surveillance-report
.pdf; "Statistics on Addiction in America," Addiction Center, 2021, www.addictioncenter
.com/addiction/addiction-statistics/; Lawrence Scholl et al., "Drug and Opioid-Involved
Overdose Deaths—United States, 2013–2017," CDC, Morbidity and Mortality Weekly Reports, January 4, 2019, www.cdc.gov/mmwr/volumes/67/wr/mm675152e1.htm; "What Is
the U.S. Opioid Epidemic?," HHS.Gov/Opioids, last reviewed September 4, 2019, www.hhs
.gov/opioids/about-the-epidemic/index.html.

34. Tulip Mazumdar, "Are We Missing the Real Opioid Drug Crisis?," BBC News, February 1, 2018, www.bbc.com/news/health-42871641.

35. Heide Brandes and Nate Raymond, "J&J Liable for $572 Million in Oklahoma Opi-
oid Epidemic Trial; Shares Rise," Reuters, August 26, 2019, www.reuters.com/article
/us-usa-opioids-litigation-oklahoma/jj-liable-for-572-million-in-oklahoma-opioid-epidemic
-trial-shares-rise-idUSKCN1VG0V2.

36. Brigid C. Flynn, "You Never Know When You'll Need a Vicodin: An Era of Opioid
Abuse," *Journal of the American Pharmacists Association* 57, no. 3 (2017): 299, doi:10.1016/j
.japh.2017.02.024.

37. Jan Hoffman, Katie Thomas, and Danny Hakim, "3,271 Pill Bottles, a Town of 2,831:
Court Filings Say Corporations Fed Opioid Epidemic," *New York Times*, July 19, 2019, www
.nytimes.com/2019/07/19/health/opioids-trial-addiction-drugstores.html.

38. "The Process of Becoming a Doctor—How Many Years Does It Take?," The Apprentice
Doctor, April 17, 2017, www.theapprenticedoctor.com/the-process-of-becoming-a-doctor/;
"How to Become a Surgeon," The Apprentice Doctor, January 1, 2017, www.theapprentice
doctor.com/how-to-become-a-surgeon/.

39. "The Deceptive Salary of Doctors," Best Medical Degrees, accessed April 12, 2020,
www.bestmedicaldegrees.com/salary-of-doctors/.

40. "Fentanyl DrugFacts," NIH National Institute on Drug Abuse, February 28, 2019,
www.drugabuse.gov/publications/drugfacts/fentanyl.

41. Mariel Padilla, "After Dozens of Fentanyl Killings, Hospital C.E.O. and 23 Employees Are Forced Out," *New York Times*, July 12, 2019, www.nytimes.com/2019/07/12/us
/hospital-fentanyl-murder.html?searchResultPosition=5.

42. Erik Ortiz, "Nurses Defend Ohio Doctor Accused of Murdering 25 Patients in Lawsuit
Against Hospital," NBC News, December 19, 2019, www.nbcnews.com/news/crime-courts
/nurses-defend-ohio-doctor-accused-murdering-25-patients-lawsuit-against-n1102796.

43. Jim Woods, "Working with Dr. Husel at Mount Carmel Brought Trouble to Colleagues," *Columbus Dispatch*, May 17, 2020, www.dispatch.com/news/20200517
/working-with-dr-husel-at-mount-carmel-brought-trouble-to-colleagues.

44. Mark D. Smith, *Best Care at Lower Cost* (Washington, DC: National Academies Press,
2012).

45. Heather Lyu et al., "Overtreatment in the United States," *PLOS ONE* 12, no. 9 (2017),
e0181970, doi:10.1371/journal.pone.0181970.

46. NEJM Catalyst, "What Is Value-Based Healthcare?," *NEJM Catalyst* 3, no. 1 (January 1, 2017): 1, https://catalyst.nejm.org/doi/full/10.1056/CAT.17.0558; Thomas Feeley and
Namita Mota, "New Marketplace Survey: Transitioning Payment Models: Fee-for-Service to
Value-Based Care," *NEJM Catalyst: Innovations In Care Delivery*, November 8, 2018, https://
catalyst.nejm.org/doi/full/10.1056/CAT.18.0056.

CHAPTER 2: DELIVER ME FROM THINKING

1. Alison Kanski, "Healthline Beats WebMD in Monthly Visitors for First Time," Medical Marketing and Media, July 22, 2019, www.mmm-online.com/welcome/70648/single/~home~channel~media-news~healthline-beats-webmd-in-monthly-visitors-for-first-time/.

2. Herbert A. Simon, "Rational Choice and the Structure of the Environment," *Psychological Review* 63, no. 2 (1956): 129–138, doi:10.1037/h0042769.

3. Susan T. Fiske and Shelley E. Taylor, *Social Cognition*, 2nd ed. (New York: McGraw Hill, 1991).

4. Daniel Kahneman, *Thinking, Fast and Slow* (New York: Farrar, Straus and Giroux, 2011).

5. Stacy W. Gray et al., "Marketing of Personalized Cancer Care on the Web: An Analysis of Internet Websites," *JNCI: Journal of the National Cancer Institute* 107, no. 5 (2015), doi:10.1093/jnci/djv030.

6. Gray et al., "Marketing of Personalized Cancer Care on the Web."

7. Viorela Dan, "Audiences in the Dark: Deception in Pharmaceutical Advertising Through Verbal–Visual Mismatches," in *The Palgrave Handbook of Deceptive Communication*, ed. Tony Docan-Morgan (Cham, Switzerland: Palgrave Macmillan, 2019), 839–855.

8. Gray et al., "Marketing of Personalized Cancer Care on the Web."

9. "Side Effects of Cancer Treatment," National Cancer Institute, 2020, www.cancer.gov/about-cancer/treatment/side-effects; Laura B. Vater et al., "What Are Cancer Centers Advertising to the Public? A Content Analysis," *Annals of Internal Medicine* 160, no. 12 (2014): 813, doi:10.7326/m14-0500.

10. Kahneman, *Thinking, Fast and Slow*.

11. Amos Tversky and Daniel Kahneman, "Judgment Under Uncertainty: Heuristics and Biases," *Science* 185, no. 4157 (1974): 1124–1131; Daniel Kahneman, Paul Slovic, and Amos Tversky, eds., *Judgment Under Uncertainty: Heuristics and Biases* (Cambridge: Cambridge University Press, 1982).

12. Amos Tversky and Daniel Kahneman, "The Framing of Decisions and the Psychology of Choice," *Science* 211, no. 4481 (1981): 453–458, doi:10.1126/science.7455683.

13. Richard E. Petty and John T. Cacioppo, "The Elaboration Likelihood Model of Persuasion," in *Communication and Persuasion* (New York: Springer, 1986), 1–24, doi:10.1007/978-1-4612-4964-1_1.

14. "Commission on Cancer," American College of Surgeons, 2020, www.facs.org/quality-programs/cancer/coc.

15. Petty and Cacioppo, "The Elaboration Likelihood Model of Persuasion," 134.

16. Melissa L. Finucane et al., "The Affect Heuristic in Judgments of Risks and Benefits," *Journal of Behavioral Decision Making* 13, no. 1 (2000): 1–17, doi:10.1002/(sici)1099-0771(200001/03)13:1<1:aid-bdm333>3.0.co;2-s.

17. Paul Slovic, Melissa L. Finucane, Ellen Peters, and Donald G. MacGregor, "The Affect Heuristic," *European Journal of Operational Research* 177, no. 3 (2007): 1333–1352, 1336.

18. Vater et al., "What Are Cancer Centers Advertising to the Public?," 813–820.

19. Vater et al., "What Are Cancer Centers Advertising to the Public?," 818.

20. Vater et al., "What Are Cancer Centers Advertising to the Public?," Table 3.

21. James E. Maddux and Ronald W. Rogers, "Protection Motivation and Self-Efficacy: A Revised Theory of Fear Appeals and Attitude Change," *Journal of Experimental Social Psychology* 19, no. 5 (1983): 469–479, doi:10.1016/0022-1031(83)90023-9.

22. Daniel Kahneman and Amos Tversky, "On the Psychology of Prediction," *Psychological Review* 80, no. 4 (1973): 237–251, doi:10.1037/h0034747.

23. Vater et al., "What Are Cancer Centers Advertising to the Public?," 818.

24. Talya Miron-Shatz and Gershon Ben-Shakhar, "Disregarding Preliminary Information When Rating Job Applicants' Performance: Mission Impossible?," *Journal of Applied Social Psychology* 38, no. 5 (2008): 1271–1294, doi:10.1111/j.1559-1816.2008.00348.x.

CHAPTER 3: "WHAT KIND OF A DOCTOR IS THIS?"

1. Johnny Wood, "These Are the World's Most Respected Professions," World Economic Forum, January 15, 2019, www.weforum.org/agenda/2019/01/these-are-the-world-s-most-respected-professions/; Airtasker, "Who Do You Trust," *Airtasker Blog*, May 12, 2019, www.airtasker.com/blog/who-do-you-trust/.

2. Robert B. Cialdini, *Influence: The Psychology of Persuasion* (self-pub., Quill, 1993).

3. Daniel Kahneman and Shane Frederick, "Representativeness Revisited: Attribute Substitution in Intuitive Judgment," in *Heuristics and Biases*, ed. T. Gilovich, D. Griffin, and D. Kahneman (Cambridge: Cambridge University Press, 2002), 49–81, doi:10.1017/cbo9780511808098.004.

4. Mark D. Neuman et al., "Non-Operative Care for Hip Fracture in the Elderly: The Influence of Race, Income, and Comorbidities," *Medical Care* 48, no. 4 (2010): 314.

5. Talya Miron-Shatz et al., "'A Phenomenal Person and Doctor': Thank You Letters to Medical Care Providers," *Interactive Journal of Medical Research* 6, no. 2 (2017): e22, doi:10.2196/ijmr.7107.

6. Jing Liu et al., "What Do Patients Complain About Online: A Systematic Review and Taxonomy Framework Based on Patient Centeredness," *Journal of Medical Internet Research* 21, no. 8 (2019): e14634, doi:10.2196/14634.

7. Interestingly, these complaints map onto the principles of patient-centered care, as defined by the Picker Institute in Oxford, which strives to promote them internationally. "Principles of Person Centred Care," Picker, 2020, www.picker.org/about-us/picker-principles-of-person-centred-care/.

8. Beth Huntington and Nettie Kuhn, "Communication Gaffes: A Root Cause of Malpractice Claims," *Baylor University Medical Center Proceedings* 16, no. 2 (2003): 157–161, doi:10.1080/08998280.2003.11927898.

9. Huntington and Kuhn, "Communication Gaffes," 157.

10. Huntington and Kuhn, "Communication Gaffes," 158.

11. Glyn Elwyn, Benjamin Elwyn, and Talya Miron-Shatz, "Measuring 'Decision Quality': Irresolvable Difficulties and an Alternative Proposal," in *Shared Decision-Making in Health Care: Achieving Evidence-Based Patient Choice*, 2nd ed., ed. Adrian Edwards and Glyn Elwyn (Oxford: Oxford University Press, 2009).

12. Glyn Elwyn and Talya Miron-Shatz, "Deliberation Before Determination: The Definition and Evaluation of Good Decision Making," *Health Expectations* 13, no. 2 (2010): 139–147; Stephanie Sivell et al., "Increasing Readiness to Decide and Strengthening Behavioral Intentions: Evaluating the Impact of a Web-Based Patient Decision Aid for Breast Cancer Treatment Options (BresDex: www.bresdex.com)," *Patient Education and Counseling* 88, no. 2 (2012): 209–217, doi:10.1016/j.pec.2012.03.012.

13. Glyn Elwyn et al., "Developing CollaboRATE: A Fast and Frugal Patient-Reported Measure of Shared Decision Making in Clinical Encounters," *Patient Education and Counseling* 93, no. 1 (2013): 102–107, doi:10.1016/j.pec.2013.05.009.

14. Paul Kalanithi, *When Breath Becomes Air* (New York: Random House, 2016).

15. Naykky Singh Ospina et al., "Eliciting the Patient's Agenda—Secondary Analysis of Recorded Clinical Encounters," *Journal of General Internal Medicine* 34, no. 1 (2018): 36–40, doi:10.1007/s11606-018-4540-5.

16. Lawrence Dyche and Deborah Swiderski, "The Effect of Physician Solicitation Approaches on Ability to Identify Patient Concerns," *Journal of General Internal Medicine* 20, no. 3 (2005): 267–270, doi:10.1111/j.1525-1497.2005.40266.x.

17. Mary Catherine Beach, Jeanne Keruly, and Richard D. Moore, "Is the Quality of the Patient-Provider Relationship Associated with Better Adherence and Health Outcomes for Patients with HIV?," *Journal of General Internal Medicine* 21, no. 6 (2006): 661–665, doi:10.1111/j.1525-1497.2006.00399.x.

18. Deborah Lynne Jones et al., "Fertility Desires Among Women Living with HIV," *PLOS ONE* 11, no. 9 (2016): e0160190, doi:10.1371/journal.pone.0160190.

19. Deborah L. Jones, et al., "Reproductive Decision-Making Among Postpartum HIV-Infected Women in Rural South Africa," *International Journal of STD and AIDS* 29, no. 9 (2018): 908–916, https://doi.org/10.1177/0956462418766932.

20. Adriane M. Delicio et al., "Adverse Effects in Children Exposed to Maternal HIV and Antiretroviral Therapy During Pregnancy in Brazil: A Cohort Study," *Reproductive Health* 15, no. 1 (2018), doi:10.1186/s12978-018-0513-8; Vatsla Dadhwal et al., "Pregnancy Outcomes in HIV-Infected Women: Experience from a Tertiary Care Center in India," *International Journal of MCH and AIDS (IJMA)* 6, no. 1 (2017): 75, doi:10.21106/ijma.196; R. R. Cook et al., "A Bayesian Analysis of Prenatal Maternal Factors Predicting Nonadherence to Infant HIV Medication in South Africa," *AIDS and Behavior* 22, no. 9 (2018): 2947–2955.

21. Manya Magnus et al., "Linking and Retaining HIV Patients in Care: The Importance of Provider Attitudes and Behaviors," *AIDS Patient Care and STDs* 27, no. 5 (2013): 297–303, doi:10.1089/apc.2012.0423.

22. Neda Ratanawongsa et al., "Communication and Medication Refill Adherence," *JAMA Internal Medicine* 173, no. 3 (2013): 210, doi:10.1001/jamainternmed.2013.1216.

23. Thomas Lewis, Fari Amini, and Richard Lannon, *A General Theory of Love* (New York: Vintage, 2001). Thank you to Dr. Mayer Brezis for this reference.

24. Hal Shorey, "Dismissing Parents and the Rejected Adult Child," *Psychology Today*, May 7, 2019, www.psychologytoday.com/us/blog/the-freedom-change/201905/dismissing-parents-and-the-rejected-adult-child.

25. "Dr. Dudley Brown, MD," Healthgrades, www.healthgrades.com/physician/dr-dudley-brown-xjcf9; "Dr. Antonella Leary, MD," Healthgrades, www.healthgrades.com/physician/dr-antonella-leary-2t4qd.

26. Collin Searle, "Treating Patients as Human Beings," Intermountain Healthcare, Patient Stories and Blog, December 5, 2016, https://intermountainhealthcare.org/blogs/topics/transforming-healthcare/2016/12/treating-patients-as-human-beings/.

27. Agnieszka M. Kempny et al., "Patients with a Severe Prolonged Disorder of Consciousness Can Show Classical EEG Responses to Their Own Name Compared with Others' Names," *NeuroImage: Clinical* 19 (2018): 311–319.

28. "HCAHPS: Patients' Perspectives of Care Survey," CMS.Gov, last modified February 11, 2020, www.cms.gov/Medicare/Quality-Initiatives-Patient-Assessment-Instruments/HospitalQualityInits/HospitalHCAHPS.

29. Karlene Kerfoot, "Patient Satisfaction and the Bottom Line," GE Healthcare, *Healthcare in the Know Blog*, September 8, 2016, www.apihealthcare.com/blog/healthcare-trends/patient-satisfaction-and-the-bottom-line.

30. Vivian S. Lee et al., "Creating the Exceptional Patient Experience in One Academic Health System," *Academic Medicine* 91, no. 3 (2016): 338–344, doi:10.1097/acm.0000000000001007.

31. Alex B. Haynes et al., "A Surgical Safety Checklist to Reduce Morbidity and Mortality in a Global Population," *New England Journal of Medicine* 360, no. 5 (2009): 491–499, doi:10.1056/nejmsa0810119.

32. "Sins of Omission: How Government Failures to Track Covid-19 Data Have Led to More Than 1,700 Health Care Worker Deaths and Jeopardize Public Health," National Nurses United, September 2020, https://act.nationalnursesunited.org/page/-/files/graphics/0920_Covid19_SinsOfOmission_Data_Report.pdf; Audrey McNamara, "The CDC Says over 600 Health Care Workers Have Died from the Coronavirus. This Doctor Has Counted Hundreds More," CBSNews, August 14, 2020, www.cbsnews.com/news/dr-claire-rezba-tracks-healthcare-workers-coronavirus-deaths/. Dr. Claire Rezba, an anesthesiologist in Richmond, Virginia, identified one thousand deaths of healthcare and nursing workers from COVID-19 by August 14, 2020; "Global: Amnesty Analysis Reveals over 7,000 Health Workers Have Died from COVID-19," Amnesty International, September 3, 2020, www.amnesty.org/en/latest/news/2020/09/amnesty-analysis-7000-health-workers-have-died-from-covid19/.

33. McNamara, "The CDC Says over 600 Health Care Workers Have Died from the Coronavirus."

34. Jo Shapiro and Timothy B. McDonald, "Supporting Clinicians During Covid-19 and Beyond—Learning from Past Failures and Envisioning New Strategies," *New England Journal of Medicine* 38, no. 27 (2020): e142, doi:10.1056/NEJMp2024834.

35. Melinda Smith, Jeanne Segal, and Lawrence Robinson, "Burnout Prevention and Treatment," HelpGuide, last updated October 2020, www.helpguide.org/articles/stress/burnout-prevention-and-recovery.htm.

36. Maria Panagioti et al., "Association Between Physician Burnout and Patient Safety, Professionalism, and Patient Satisfaction," *JAMA Internal Medicine* 178, no. 10 (2018): 1317, doi:10.1001/jamainternmed.2018.3713.

37. Tait D. Shanafelt et al., "Burnout and Medical Errors Among American Surgeons," *Annals of Surgery* 251, no. 6 (2010): 995–1000, doi:10.1097/sla.0b013e3181bfdab3; Tait D. Shanafelt et al., "Burnout and Career Satisfaction Among US Oncologists," *Journal of Clinical Oncology* 32, no. 7 (2014): 678–686, doi:10.1200/jco.2013.51.8480.

38. David A. Rothenberger, "Physician Burnout and Well-Being," *Diseases of the Colon and Rectum* 60, no. 6 (2017): 567–576, doi:10.1097/dcr.0000000000000844.

39. Carol Peckham, "Medscape Lifestyle Report 2017: Race and Ethnicity, Bias and Burnout," Medscape, 2017, www.medscape.com/features/slideshow/lifestyle/2017/overview; Daniel S. Tawfik et al., "Physician Burnout, Well-Being, and Work Unit Safety Grades in Relationship to Reported Medical Errors," *Mayo Clinic Proceedings* 93, no. 11 (2018): 1571–1580, doi:10.1016/j.mayocp.2018.05.014.

40. Dave Lu et al., "Impact of Burnout on Self-Reported Patient Care Among Emergency Physicians," *Western Journal of Emergency Medicine* 16, no. 7 (2015): 996–1001, doi:10.5811/westjem.2015.9.27945.

41. John Elflein, "U.S.: Active Doctors Number by Specialty 2019," Statista, accessed January 20, 2020, www.statista.com/statistics/209424/us-number-of-active-physicians-by-specialty-area/.

42. Frédéric Michas, "Active Doctors of Medicine in Patient Care in the U.S. 1975–2015," Statista, November 6, 2019, www.statista.com/statistics/186226/active-doctors-of-medicine-in-patient-care-in-the-us-since-1975/.

43. Byron Beresford et al., "Preventing Work-Related Stress Among Staff Working in Children's Cancer Principal Treatment Centres in the UK: A Brief Survey of Staff Support Systems and Practices," *European Journal of Cancer Care* 27, no. 2 (2016): e12535, doi:10.1111/ecc.12535.

44. Beresford et al., "Preventing Work-Related Stress Among Staff Working in Children's Cancer Principal Treatment Centres in the UK."

45. Juliana Eng et al., "Patient Death Debriefing Sessions to Support Residents' Emotional Reactions to Patient Deaths," *Journal of Graduate Medical Education* 7, no. 3 (2015): 430–436.

46. Shapiro and McDonald, "Supporting Clinicians During Covid-19 and Beyond."

47. Sabir I. Giga et al., "Organisational Level Interventions for Reducing Occupational Stress in Healthcare Workers," *Cochrane Database of Systematic Reviews*, April 24, 2018, doi:10.1002/14651858.cd013014.

48. David Belk, "Hospital Financial Analysis," True Cost of Heathcare, accessed April 29, 2020, https://truecostofhealthcare.org/hospital_financial_analysis/#:~:text=The%2520average%2520profit%2520margin%2520for,are%2520to%2520non%2520Dprofit%2520hospitals.

49. Steven J. Atlas et al., "Patient–Physician Connectedness and Quality of Primary Care," *Annals of Internal Medicine* 150, no. 5 (2009): 325, doi:10.7326/0003-4819-150-5-200903030-00008.

50. Joy L. Lee et al., "A Qualitative Exploration of Favorite Patients in Primary Care," *Patient Education and Counseling* 99, no. 11 (2016): 1888–1893, doi:10.1016/j.pec.2016.06.023, quotation on 1893.

51. Jeffrey Ressner, "New Age: Four Questions to Inner Peace," *Time*, December 11, 2000, http://content.time.com/time/magazine/article/0,9171,998759,00.html; Byron Katie and Stephen Mitchell, *Loving What Is* (New York: Three Rivers, 2003).

CHAPTER 4: SAVING FACE OR SAVING YOUR SKIN

1. "Track 2: Health Literacy and Health Behaviour," WHO World Health Organization, 2020, www.who.int/healthpromotion/conferences/7gchp/track2/en/.

2. Don Nutbeam, "The Evolving Concept of Health Literacy," *Social Science and Medicine* 67, no. 12 (2008): 2072–2078, doi:10.1016/j.socscimed.2008.09.050.

3. Mengyun Zheng et al., "The Relationship Between Health Literacy and Quality of Life: A Systematic Review and Meta-Analysis," *Health and Quality of Life Outcomes* 16, no. 1 (2018), doi:10.1186/s12955-018-1031-7.

4. Albert Bandura, "Self-Efficacy: Toward a Unifying Theory of Behavioral Change," *Psychological Review* 84, no. 2 (1977): 191.

5. Sian K. Smith et al., "Supporting Patients with Low Health Literacy: What Role Do Radiation Therapists Play?," *Supportive Care in Cancer* 21, no. 11 (2013): 3051–3061, doi:10.1007/s00520-013-1875-7; Lisa Renee Miller-Matero et al., "Health Literacy Status Affects Outcomes for Patients Referred for Transplant," *Psychosomatics* 57, no. 5 (2016): 522–528, doi:10.1016/j.psym.2016.04.001.

6. Steve Leuck, "The Cost of Low Health Literacy," *Pharmacy Times*, April 10, 2017, www .pharmacytimes.com/contributor/steve-leuck-pharmd/2017/04/the-cost-of-low-health -literacy; Hongyan Liu et al., "Assessment Tools for Health Literacy Among the General Population: A Systematic Review," *International Journal of Environmental Research and Public Health* 15, no. 8 (2018): 1711, doi:10.3390/ijerph15081711.

7. Talya Miron-Shatz et al., "Barriers to Health Information and Building Solutions," in *Better Doctors, Better Patients, Better Decisions: Envisioning Health Care 2020*, Strüngmann Forum Report, ed. Gerd Gigerenzer and J. A. Muir Gray (Cambridge: MIT Press, 2011).

8. Roopa Mahadevan, "Health Literacy Fact Sheets," Center for Health Care Strategies, October 2013, www.chcs.org/resource/health-literacy-fact-sheets/. In 2020 there were nearly 330 million Americans. Therefore, based on Mahadevan's estimation that 36 percent of Americans have low health literacy, we might be looking at almost 120 million Americans in this situation. Wikipedia, s.v. "Demographics of the United States," accessed January 17, 2020, https://en.wikipedia.org/wiki/Demographics_of_the_United_States.

9. Ruth M. Parker et al., "The Test of Functional Health Literacy in Adults," *Journal of General Internal Medicine* 10, no. 10 (1995): 537–541.

10. Mark Kutner et al., "The Health Literacy of America's Adults: Results from the 2003 National Assessment of Adult Literacy. NCES 2006-483," *National Center for Education Statistics*, September 6, 2006, https://nces.ed.gov/pubsearch/pubsinfo.asp?pubid=2006483.

11. David W. Baker et al., "The Association Between Age and Health Literacy Among Elderly Persons," *Journals of Gerontology Series B: Psychological Sciences and Social Sciences* 55, no. 6 (2000): S368–S374, doi:10.1093/geronb/55.6.s368; David W. Baker et al., "Health Literacy and Mortality Among Elderly Persons," *Archives of Internal Medicine* 167, no. 14 (2007): 1503, doi:10.1001/archinte.167.14.1503.

12. Martina Fernández-Gutiérrez et al., "Health Literacy Interventions for Immigrant Populations: A Systematic Review," *International Nursing Review* 65, no. 1 (2017): 54–64, doi:10.1111/inr.12373.

13. Mariano E. Menendez et al., "Patients with Limited Health Literacy Ask Fewer Questions During Office Visits with Hand Surgeons," *Clinical Orthopaedics and Related Research* 475, no. 5 (2017): 1291–1297, at 1292.

14. Marra G. Katz et al., "Patient Literacy and Question-Asking Behavior During the Medical Encounter: A Mixed-Methods Analysis," *Journal of General Internal Medicine* 22, no. 6 (2007): 782–786, doi:10.1007/s11606-007-0184-6; Mariano E. Menendez et al., "Patients with Limited Health Literacy Ask Fewer Questions During Office Visits with Hand Surgeons," *Clinical Orthopaedics and Related Research* 475, no. 5 (2016): 1291–1297, doi:10.1007/ s11999-016-5140-5.

15. Judith H. Hibbard and Jessica Greene, "What the Evidence Shows About Patient Activation: Better Health Outcomes and Care Experiences; Fewer Data on Costs," *Health Affairs* 32, no. 2 (2013): 207–214, doi:10.1377/hlthaff.2012.1061; Judith H. Hibbard, Jessica Greene, and Valerie Overton, "Patients with Lower Activation Associated with Higher Costs;

Delivery Systems Should Know Their Patients' 'Scores,'" *Health Affairs* 32, no. 2 (2013): 216–222, doi:10.1377/hlthaff.2012.1064.

16. Menendez et al., "Patients with Limited Health Literacy Ask Fewer Questions During Office Visits with Hand Surgeons."

17. "Water: How Much Should You Drink Every Day?," Mayo Clinic, Nutrition and Healthy Living, October 14, 2020, www.mayoclinic.org/healthy-lifestyle/nutrition-and -healthy-eating/in-depth/water/art-20044256.

18. Bruce Y. Lee, "Time to Change the 15-Minute Limit for Doctor Visits," *Forbes*, September 10, 2016, www.forbes.com/sites/brucelee/2016/09/10/time-to-change-the-15 -minute-limit-for-doctor-visits/#7d0fea023477.

19. Mark Linzer et al., "The End of the 15–20 Minute Primary Care Visit," *Journal of General Internal Medicine* 30, no. 11 (2015): 1584–1586, https://doi.org/10.1007/s11606-015-3341-3.

20. Readable's text scoring tool, "Measure the Readability of Text—Text Analysis Tools— Unique Readability Tools to Improve Your Writing! App.Readable.Com," 2020, https://app .readable.com/text/. The readability level of the text on breast augmentation was grade 12.9 by the Flesch-Kinkaid Grade Level, grade 16.2 by the Gunning Fog Index.

21. Francesco Brigo et al., "Information-Seeking Behaviour for Epilepsy: An Infodemiological Study of Searches for Wikipedia Articles," *Epileptic Disorders* 17, no. 4 (2015): 460–466, doi:10.1684/epd.2015.0772; Gildasio S. De Oliveira et al., "Readability Evaluation of Internet-Based Patient Education Materials Related to the Anesthesiology Field," *Journal of Clinical Anesthesia* 27, no. 5 (2015): 401–405, doi:10.1016/j.jclinane.2015.02.005.

22. Wikipedia, s.v. "Cardiopulmonary Resuscitation," accessed February 5, 2021, https:// en.wikipedia.org/wiki/Cardiopulmonary_resuscitation.

23. Remus Ilies et al., "Explaining the Links Between Workload, Distress, and Work– Family Conflict Among School Employees: Physical, Cognitive, and Emotional Fatigue," *Journal of Educational Psychology* 107, no. 4 (2015): 1136.

24. Brandon J. Schmeichel, Kathleen D. Vohs, and Roy F. Baumeister, "Intellectual Performance and Ego Depletion: Role of the Self in Logical Reasoning and Other Information Processing," *Journal of Personality and Social Psychology* 85, no. 1 (2003): 33.

25. "May 18: Disruptive WOMEN in Health Tech- Half-Day Workshop," Meetup, May 18, 2018, www.meetup.com/mHealth-Israel/events/248398573/.

26. Miron-Shatz et al., "Barriers to Health Information and Building Solutions."

27. Both searches were conducted on April 25, 2020, using "Ubersuggest," at https://app .neilpatel.com/en/ubersuggest.

28. Rosemarie O. Serrone et al., "*Grey's Anatomy* Effect: Television Portrayal of Patients with Trauma May Cultivate Unrealistic Patient and Family Expectations After Injury," *Trauma Surgery and Acute Care Open* 3, no. 1 (2018): e000137, doi:10.1136/tsaco-2017-000137.

29. Susan J. Diem, John D. Lantos, and James A. Tulsky, "Cardiopulmonary Resuscitation on Television—Miracles and Misinformation," *New England Journal of Medicine* 334, no. 24 (1996): 1578–1582, doi:10.1056/nejm199606133342406.

30. Rachael A. Record, "Genre-Specific Television Viewing: State of the Literature," *Annals of the International Communication Association* 42, no. 3 (2018): 155–180.

31. Julia Stoll, "Daily Time Spent Watching TV Worldwide 2011 to 2021," Statista, January 13, 2021, www.statista.com/statistics/730428/tv-time-spent-worldwide/.

32. Record, "Genre-Specific Television Viewing."

33. Amir Hetsroni, "If You Must Be Hospitalized, Television Is Not the Place: Diagnoses, Survival Rates and Demographic Characteristics of Patients in TV Hospital Dramas," *Communication Research Reports* 26, no. 4 (2009): 311–322.

34. Beth L. Hoffman et al., "Exposure to Fictional Medical Television and Health: A Systematic Review," *Health Education Research* 32, no. 2 (2017): 107–123.

35. G. Tarcan Kumkale and Dolores Albarracín, "The Sleeper Effect in Persuasion: A MetaAnalytic Review," *Psychological Bulletin* 130, no. 1 (2004): 143.

36. Beth L. Hoffman et al., "It's Not All About Autism: The Emerging Landscape of Anti-Vaccination Sentiment on Facebook," *Vaccine* 37, no. 16 (2019): 2216–2223.

37. Michael Colwill et al., "Cardiopulmonary Resuscitation on Television: Are We Miseducating the Public?," *Postgraduate Medical Journal* 94, no. 1108 (2018): 71–75.

38. Hoffman et al., "Exposure to Fictional Medical Television and Health."

39. Angelo E. Volandes et al., "Randomized Controlled Trial of a Video Decision Support Tool for Cardiopulmonary Resuscitation Decision Making in Advanced Cancer," *Journal of Clinical Oncology* 31, no. 3 (2013): 380–386, doi:10.1200/jco.2012.43.9570.

40. Is it primarily seeing that influences our decision-making, or does listening also do so? Does the format in which one informs a patient matter? El-Jawahri ran another study, this time with advanced cancer patients, who either heard a verbal description of CPR and watched a clip or only heard the description. Of the patients who only heard the description of CPR, 48 percent indicated that they wanted CPR should the need arise. Of the patients who also watched the short explanatory video, only 20 percent were inclined to have CPR. A three-minute video made all the difference. So, yes, seeing—more so than merely hearing—is believing.

41. Retha Rajah et al., "The Perspective of Healthcare Providers and Patients on Health Literacy: A Systematic Review of the Quantitative and Qualitative Studies," *Perspectives in Public Health* 138, no. 2 (2017): 122–132, doi:10.1177/1757913917733775.

42. "Use the Teach-Back Method: Tool #5," AHRQ, Health Literacy Universal Precautions Toolkit, 2nd Edition, page created February 2015, last reviewed September 2020, www.ahrq.gov/health-literacy/quality-resources/tools/literacy-toolkit/healthlittoolkit2-tool5.html.

43. Emanuel A. Schegloff, "Repair After Next Turn: The Last Structurally Provided Defense of Intersubjectivity in Conversation," *American Journal of Sociology* 97, no. 5 (1992): 1295–1345, at 1298, doi:10.1086/229903.

44. Rosemarie McCabe et al., "Shared Understanding in Psychiatrist–Patient Communication: Association with Treatment Adherence in Schizophrenia," *Patient Education and Counseling* 93, no. 1 (2013): 73–79, doi:10.1016/j.pec.2013.05.015.

45. Nancy M. Docherty, Maddalena DeRosa, and Nancy C. Andreasen, "Communication Disturbances in Schizophrenia and Mania," *Archives of General Psychiatry* 53, no. 4 (1996): 358–364.

46. Docherty, DeRosa, and Andreasen, "Communication Disturbances in Schizophrenia and Mania," 74.

47. Rose McCabe and Patrick G. T. Healey, "Miscommunication in Doctor–Patient Communication," *Topics in Cognitive Science* 10, no. 2 (2018): 409–424, doi:10.1111/tops.12337.

48. "Ask Me 3: Good Questions for Your Good Health," IHI Institute for Healthcare Improvement," 2020, /www.ihi.org/resources/Pages/Tools/Ask-Me-3-Good-Questions-for-Your-Good-Health.aspx.

49. Amos Tversky and Daniel Kahneman, "Judgment Under Uncertainty: Heuristics and Biases," *Science* 185, no. 4157 (1974): 1124–1131.

50. Muirean Toibin, M. Pender, and T. Cusack, "The Effect of a Healthcare Communication Intervention—*Ask Me 3*; on Health Literacy and Participation in Patients Attending Physiotherapy," *European Journal of Physiotherapy* 19, no. 1 (2017): 12–14, doi:10.1080/21679 169.2017.1381318.

51. Oana R. Gröne, Ignasi Bolíbar, and Carlos Brotons, "Impact, Barriers and Facilitators of The 'Ask Me 3' Patient Communication Intervention in a Primary Care Center in Barcelona, Spain: A Mixed-Methods Analysis," *International Journal of Person Centred Medicine* 2, no. 4 (2012), doi:10.5750/ijpcm.v2i4.311.

52. Jane Wang et al., "Online Health Searches and Their Perceived Effects on Patients and Patient-Clinician Relationships: A Systematic Review," *American Journal of Medicine* 131, no. 10 (2018): 1250.e1–1250.e10, doi:10.1016/j.amjmed.2018.04.019.

53. "Non-Celiac Gluten Sensitivity," Beyond Celiac, 2020, www.beyondceliac.org /celiac-disease/non-celiac-gluten-sensitivity/.

54. Elizabeth N. Chapman, Anna Kaatz, and Molly Carnes, "Physicians and Implicit Bias: How Doctors May Unwittingly Perpetuate Health Care Disparities," *Journal of General Internal Medicine* 28, no. 11 (2013): 1504–1510.

55. Janet Kaye Heins et al., "Disparities in Analgesia and Opioid Prescribing Practices for Patients with Musculoskeletal Pain in the Emergency Department," *Journal of Emergency Nursing* 32, no. 3 (2006): 219–224.

56. Knox H. Todd, Nigel Samaroo, and Jerome R. Hoffman, "Ethnicity as a Risk Factor for Inadequate Emergency Department Analgesia," *JAMA* 269, no. 12 (1993): 1537–1539.

57. Anke Samulowitz et al., "'Brave Men' and 'Emotional Women': A Theory-Guided Literature Review on Gender Bias in Health Care and Gendered Norms Towards Patients with Chronic Pain," *Pain Research and Management*, February 25, 2018, doi.org /10.1155/2018/6358624; Camille Noe Pagán, "When Doctors Downplay Women's Health Concerns," *New York Times*, May 3, 2018, www.nytimes.com/2018/05/03/well/live/when -doctors-downplay-womens-health-concerns.html.

58. Pierre Bourdieu, "The Forms of Capital," in *Handbook of Theory and Research for the Sociology of Education*, ed. J. Richardson (Westport, CT: Greenwood, 1986), 241–258.

59. Beate Krais, "Gender and Symbolic Violence: Female Oppression in the Light of Pierre Bourdieu's Theory of Social Practice," in *Bourdieu: Critical Perspectives*, ed. C. Calhoun, E. LiPuma, and M. Postone (Chicago: University of Chicago Press, 1993), 156–177.

60. Giuseppe Losurdo et al., "Extra-Intestinal Manifestations of Non-Celiac Gluten Sensitivity: An Expanding Paradigm," *World Journal of Gastroenterology* 24, no. 14 (2018): 1521–1530, doi:10.3748/wjg.v24.i14.1521.

61. Tractate Damages, *Ethics of the Fathers* (*Pirkei Avot*) 2:5. The translation is mine.

CHAPTER 5: THE PROBLEM WITH PERCENTAGES AND PROBABILITIES

1. "China Coronavirus: 83,017 Cases; 4,634 Deaths," Worldometer, 2020, www.world ometers.info/coronavirus/country/china/.

2. Elizabeth Yuko, "13 Ways Coronavirus Is Different from All Epidemics Through History," *Reader's Digest*, September 12, 2020, www.rd.com/culture/ways -coronavirus-is-different-from-other-epidemics/.

3. Calculated using "All People on 1 Page," Worldometers, accessed January 2, 2021, www .worldometers.info/watch/world-population/.

4. The thirty-first conference of the Society for Behavioral Medicine took place in Seattle, April 7–10, 2010. Michael Diefenbach, who organized the conference, studies patient choices and decisions about prostate cancer. The Presidential Symposium was titled "The Future of Genetic Understanding of Disease and the Role of Behavior in Health." My talk was titled "(Mis)understanding Medical Information: Healthcare Professionals and Laymen Alike."

5. Gerd Gigerenzer et al., "'A 30% Chance of Rain Tomorrow': How Does the Public Understand Probabilistic Weather Forecasts?," *Risk Analysis* 25, no. 3 (2005): 623–629, doi:10.1111/j.1539-6924.2005.00608.x.

6. Ulrich Hoffrage and Gerd Gigerenzer, "Using Natural Frequencies to Improve Diagnostic Inferences," *Academic Medicine* 73, no. 5 (1998): 538–540, doi:10.1097 /00001888-199805000-00024.

7. "How Common Is Breast Cancer?," Breast Cancer Statistics, American Cancer Society, accessed February 2, 2020, www.cancer.org/cancer/breast-cancer/about/how-common-is -breast-cancer.html; "BRCA Gene Mutations," Bring Your Brave Campaign, CDC, page last reviewed April 5, 2019, www.cdc.gov/cancer/breast/young_women/bringyourbrave /hereditary_breast_cancer/brca_gene_mutations.htm.

8. When mutated, these genes fail to play their role in protecting cells from DNA damage. As a result, cells are more likely to develop additional genetic alterations that can lead to cancer. "BRCA1 & BRCA2: Cancer Risk & Genetic Testing," NIH National Cancer Institute, April 1, 2015, www.cancer.gov/about-cancer/causes-prevention/genetics/brca-fact-sheet.

9. "Angelina Jolie Pitt: Diary of a Surgery," Opinion, *New York Times*, March 24, 2015, www.nytimes.com/2015/03/24/opinion/angelina-jolie-pitt-diary-of-a-surgery.html?_r=0.

10. Yaniv Hanoch, Talya Miron-Shatz, and Mary Himmelstein, "Genetic Testing and Risk Interpretation: How Do Women Understand Lifetime Risk Results?," *Judgment and Decision Making* 5, no. 2 (2010): 116–123.

11. We had 263 participants and their average age was 40.24. Hanoch, Miron-Shatz, and Himmelstein, "Genetic Testing and Risk Interpretation," 117. The median age of breast cancer diagnosis in women in the United States is 61. However, the rates of breast cancer diagnosis in women is less than 5 percent for women younger than 40, and age 40 is when the rate of diagnosis begins to climb; the highest rates of breast cancer diagnosis in US women occurs over age 70. "Age and Breast Cancer Risk," Susan G. Komen Foundation, September 22, 2015, accessed July 22, 2016, www.komen.org/BreastCancer/GettingOlder.html.

12. National Cancer Institute Fact Sheet, "Genetic Testing for BRCA1 and BRCA2: It's Your Choice," NIH National Cancer Institute, February 2002, accessed April 10, 2009, www .cancer.gov/cancertopics/factsheet/risk/brca. A revised, more recent message from the National Cancer Institute read:

> **Breast cancer:** About 12 percent of women in the general population will develop breast cancer sometime during their lives. By contrast, according to the most recent estimates, 55 to 65 percent of women who inherit a harmful *BRCA1* mutation and around 45 percent of women who inherit a harmful *BRCA2* mutation will develop breast cancer by age 70 years.
>
> **Ovarian cancer:** About 1.3 percent of women in the general population will develop ovarian cancer sometime during their lives. By contrast, according to the most recent estimates, 39 percent of women who inherit a harmful *BRCA1* mutation and

11 to 17 percent of women who inherit a harmful *BRCA2* mutation will develop ovarian cancer by age 70 years. ["BRCA1 & BRCA2: Cancer Risk & Genetic Testing," NIH National Cancer Institute, April 1, 2015, www.cancer.gov/about-cancer /causes-prevention/genetics/brca-fact-sheet#q2.]

13. Option 4 was chosen by 45.2 percent of participants. Hanoch, Miron-Shatz, and Himmelstein, "Genetic Testing and Risk Interpretation," 118. Almost half—specifically, 48.7 percent—chose the correct option, option 1. Hanoch, Miron-Shatz, and Himmelstein, "Genetic Testing and Risk Interpretation," 118. Let me simplify the situation, using numbers from 2016 from the National Cancer Institute: of women in the general population, 12 percent will develop breast cancer, as opposed to between 55 and 65 percent of women with BRCA1 mutation. "BRCA1 & BRCA2: Cancer Risk & Genetic Testing," NIH National Cancer Institute, April 1, 2015, accessed July 12, 2016, www.cancer.gov/about-cancer/causes-prevention /genetics/brca-fact-sheet#q2.

14. "BRCA1 & BRCA2: Cancer Risk & Genetic Testing," NIH National Cancer Institute, April 1, 2015, accessed July 12, 2016, www.cancer.gov/about-cancer/causes-prevention /genetics/brca-fact-sheet#q2.

15. Isaac M. Lipkus, Greg Samsa, and Barbara K. Rimer, "General Performance on a Numeracy Scale Among Highly Educated Samples," *Medical Decision Making* 21, no. 1 (February 2001): 28–36, doi:10.1177/0272989X0102100105.

16. The low numeracy group chose the correct interpretation about 35 percent of the time; the high numeracy participants chose the correct interpretation 64 percent of the time. Lipkus, Samsa, and Rimer, "General Performance on a Numeracy Scale Among Highly Educated Samples," 118.

17. That is, 175 of them, or 84.5 percent, fell into one of these categories. Hanoch, Miron-Shatz, and Himmelstein, "Genetic Testing and Risk Interpretation," 119.

18. Of cancer-savvy women, 59.4 percent correctly chose option 1. Hanoch, Miron-Shatz, and Himmelstein, "Genetic Testing and Risk Interpretation," 120. A sizable proportion (40.1 percent) believed that option 4 was the right one. Hanoch, Miron-Shatz, and Himmelstein, "Genetic Testing and Risk Interpretation," 120.

19. Angela Fagerlin et al., "Measuring Numeracy Without a Math Test: Development of the Subjective Numeracy Scale," *Medical Decision Making* 27, no. 5 (September/October 2007): 681–695 and 672–680, doi:10.1177/0272989X07304449.

20. Michael Diefenbach and I conducted this study but did not publish.

21. Andrew J. Barnes et al., "Tailoring Risk Communication to Improve Comprehension: Do Patient Preferences Help or Hurt?," *Health Psychology* 35, no. 9 (2016): 1007–1016, doi:10.1037/hea0000367.

22. Jonathan J. Rolison, Yaniv Hanoch, and Talya Miron-Shatz, "What Do Men Understand About Lifetime Risk Following Genetic Testing? The Effect of Context and Numeracy," *Health Psychology* 31, no. 4 (2012): 530–533, doi:10.1037/a0026562.

23. Ke Zu and Edward Giovannucci, "Smoking and Aggressive Prostate Cancer: A Review of the Epidemiologic Evidence," *Cancer Causes and Control* 20, no. 10 (2009): 1799–1810, doi:10.1007/s10552-009-9387-y. BRCA mutations and their effect on prostate cancer risk has not been as extensively studied as BRCA mutations and their effect on breast cancer risk. However, according to a study published in the *British Journal of Cancer*, the cumulative prostate cancer risk of men in families with a BRCA2 mutation was assessed to be 7.5 percent by the age of seventy. It is even less clear whether or not the BRCA1 mutation has any effect on

prostate cancer risk. Ephrat Levy-Lahad and Eitan Friedman, "Cancer Risks Among BRCA1 and BRCA2 Mutation Carriers," *British Journal of Cancer* 96, no. 1 (January 15, 2007): 11–15, doi:10.1038/sj.bjc.6603535. One population-based study showed that current smokers, men who have smoked for longer than forty years, and men who have over forty pack-years of exposure had a 40–60 percent increase in risk of prostate cancer as compared to nonsmokers. Lora A. Plaskon et al., "Cigarette Smoking and Risk of Prostate Cancer in Middle-Aged Men," *Cancer Epidemiology, Biomarkers and Prevention* 12 (July 2003): 604–609.

24. Even though the BRCA gene mutations and smoking both contribute to prostate cancer, the numbers in our test statements were slightly inaccurate, because our goal was not to inform but, rather, to test our hypothesis.

25. Our participants ranged in age from 46 to 81, the average being 59.47, and 47.5 percent of our participants had been tested for prostate cancer. Rolison, Hanoch, and Miron-Shatz, "What Do Men Understand About Lifetime Risk Following Genetic Testing?," 531; D. J. Bowen et al., "Prostate Cancer Screening and Informed Decision-Making: Provider and Patient Perspectives," *Prostate Cancer and Prostatic Diseases* 14, no. 2 (2011): 155–161. Almost half our participants had been tested for prostate cancer, which is comparable to larger studies.

26. In the context of genetic risk, under 40 percent—specifically, 37.9 percent—of the men chose option 1, the correct one. In the context of smoking, 37.4 percent of the participants chose this option. Rolison, Hanoch, and Miron-Shatz, "What Do Men Understand About Lifetime Risk Following Genetic Testing?," 532.

27. "Frequently Asked Questions About the American Cancer Society's Breast Cancer Screening Guideline," American Cancer Society, 2021, www.cancer.org/cancer/breast -cancer/frequently-asked-questions-about-the-american-cancer-society-new-breast-cancer -screening-guideline.html.

28. Odette Wegwarth and Gerd Gigerenzer, "US Gynecologists' Estimates and Beliefs Regarding Ovarian Cancer Screening's Effectiveness 5 Years After Release of the PLCO Evidence," *Scientific Reports* 8, no. 1 (2018): 1–9.

29. Sushmita Gordhandas et al., "Hormone Replacement Therapy After Risk Reducing Salpingo-oophorectomy in Patients with BRCA1 or BRCA2 Mutations: A Systematic Review of Risks and Benefits," *Gynecologic Oncology* 153, no. 1 (2019): 192–200; C. Marchetti et al., "Hormone Replacement Therapy After Prophylactic Risk-Reducing Salpingo-oophorectomy and Breast Cancer Risk in BRCA1 and BRCA2 Mutation Carriers: A Meta-Analysis," *Critical Reviews in Oncology/Hematology* 132 (2018): 111–115.

30. Jeff Wise, "How to Hunt Like a Caveman," *Popular Mechanics*, August 19, 2010, www .popularmechanics.com/adventure/outdoors/a6023/how-to-hunt-like-a-caveman/.

31. Leslie A. Real, "Animal Choice Behavior and the Evolution of Cognitive Architecture," *Science* 253, no. 5023 (1991): 980–986, doi:10.1126/science.1887231.

32. Real claims that the bumblebees have probability bias, resulting from short-term calculations or truncated sampling; they rely heavily on the first flowers they encounter. It's comforting to know that bees are also fallible.

33. Stanford Encyclopedia of Philosophy, s.v. "Evolutionary Psychology," September 5, 2018, https://plato.stanford.edu/entries/evolutionary-psychology/.

34. Leda Cosmides and John Tooby, "Are Humans Good Intuitive Statisticians After All? Rethinking Some Conclusions from the Literature on Judgment Under Uncertainty," *Cognition* 58, no. 1 (January 1996): 1–73, at 14.

35. Cosmides and Tooby's paper is seventy-three pages long. Students blanch when I assign it. But then they, too, become converts to the frequentist way of doing things.

36. Cosmides and Tooby, "Are Humans Good Intuitive Statisticians After All?," 13.

37. Cosmides and Tooby, "Are Humans Good Intuitive Statisticians After All?," 1 (emphasis added).

38. Ulrich Hoffrage et al., "Representation Facilitates Reasoning: What Natural Frequencies Are and What They Are Not," *Cognition* 84, no. 3 (2002): 343–352, doi:10.1016/s0010 -0277(02)00050-1; Samuel Lindsey, Ralph Hertwig, and Gerd Gigerenzer, "Communicating Statistical DNA Evidence," *Jurimetrics* 43, no. 2 (2003): 147–163, showing that judges understand DNA evidence better thanks to frequentist presentation. See also Gerd Gigerenzer and Ulrich Hoffrage, "How to Improve Bayesian Reasoning Without Instruction: Frequency Formats," *Psychological Review* 102, no. 4 (1995): 684–704, doi:10.1037/0033-295x.102.4.684; Ulrich Hoffrage et al., "MEDICINE: Communicating Statistical Information," *Science* 290, no. 5500 (2000): 2261–2262, doi:10.1126/science.290.5500.2261.

39. We chose ten thousand to have a round number big enough to save me from having to place half a person in a group, as I would have to do had I instead chosen one thousand.

40. Talya Miron-Shatz et al., "Presentation Format Affects Comprehension and Risk Assessment: The Case of Prenatal Screening," *Journal of Health Communication* 14, no. 5 (2009): 439–450, doi:10.1080/10810730903032986.

41. Cara L. Cuite et al., "A Test of Numeric Formats for Communicating Risk Probabilities," *Medical Decision Making* 28, no. 3 (2008): 377–384, doi:10.1177/0272989 x08315246.

42. If you're interested in delving into these visual formats, see Jessica S. Ancker et al., "Design Features of Graphs in Health Risk Communication: A Systematic Review," *Journal of the American Medical Informatics Association* 13, no. 6 (2006): 608–618, doi:10.1197/jamia .m2115; Isaac M. Lipkus, "Numeric, Verbal, and Visual Formats of Conveying Health Risks: Suggested Best Practices and Future Recommendations," *Medical Decision Making* 27, no. 5 (2007): 696–713, doi:10.1177/0272989x07307271.

43. There was some variation in the way the letters were phrased, stemming in part from the variation in the presentation. But the main difference, as far as we were concerned, was in the way they presented the probabilities.

44. The exact numbers are these: 36 percent of the participants in the 1:181 presentation, 55 percent of those in the visual presentation, and 67 percent of those in the frequentist presentation.

45. Miron-Shatz et al., "Presentation Format Affects Comprehension and Risk Assessment."

46. Jeff and I met over a decade ago, at the first summer school on medical decision-making at Dartmouth College, and it was nice to run into him again via Yash. I love the fact that Jeff answered like a scientist, which he is, not a marketing person, which he isn't.

47. According to Wikipedia: "There are many Arabic editions, e.g. *Nahj al-balagha*, Dar al-kutub al-'ilmiyya, Beirut, 2007, p. 358. This is Askari Jafri's translation from an unattributed online edition. Alternative translations of the main citation are possible: 'knowledge is belief which is acted upon' (Al-Hassanain), 'knowledge is a religion to be followed' (French translation, Beirut 2004), or even 'the intellection of knowledge is an empowerment' (Acevedo, 2019)." Wikipedia, s.v. "Scientia Potentia Est," note 2, accessed March 9, 2020, https:// en.wikipedia.org/wiki/Scientia_potentia_est.

CHAPTER 6: CHOOSING IS A PAIN

1. Barry Schwartz, *The Paradox of Choice: Why Less Is More* (New York: Ecco, 2004).

2. Sheena S. Iyengar, Rachael E. Wells, and Barry Schwartz, "Doing Better but Feeling Worse: Looking for the 'Best' Job Undermines Satisfaction," *Psychological Science* 17, no. 2 (2006): 143–150.

3. Richard H. Thaler and Cass R. Sunstein, *Nudge: Improving Decisions About Health, Wealth, and Happiness* (New Haven: Yale University Press, 2008), 87.

4. Herbert A. Simon, "A Behavioral Model of Rational Choice," *Quarterly Journal of Economics* 59 (1955): 99–118.

5. Schwartz, *The Paradox of Choice.*

6. Adrian Edwards and Glyn Elwyn, eds., *Shared Decision-Making in Health Care: Achieving Evidence-Based Patient Choice*, 2nd ed. (Oxford: Oxford University Press, 2009).

7. Marcel Zeelenberg, "Anticipated Regret, Expected Feedback and Behavioral Decision Making," *Journal of Behavioral Decision Making* 12, no. 2 (1999): 93–106.

8. Itamar Simonson, "The Influence of Anticipating Regret and Responsibility on Purchase Decisions," *Journal of Consumer Research* 19, no. 1 (1992): 105–118.

9. Benjamin Davies and Joshua Parker, "Doctors as Appointed Fiduciaries: A Supplemental Model for Medical Decision-Making," *Cambridge Quarterly of Healthcare Ethics* (forthcoming), https://ora.ox.ac.uk/objects/uuid:512198d1-1637-45ed-b1dc-af2bb2393b6a.

10. Baba Shiv, "Sometimes It's Good to Give Up the Driver's Seat," TEDxStanford, May 2012, www.ted.com/talks/baba_shiv_sometimes_it_s_good_to_give_up_the_driver_s_seat.

11. Roy F. Baumeister and Kathleen D. Vohs, "Self-Regulation, Ego Depletion, and Motivation," *Social and Personality Psychology Compass* 1, no. 1 (2007): 115–128; Andrew J. Vonasch et al., "Ego Depletion Induces Mental Passivity: Behavioral Effects Beyond Impulse Control," *Motivation Science* 3, no. 4 (2017): 321; Anastasiya Pocheptsova et al., "Deciding Without Resources: Resource Depletion and Choice in Context," *Journal of Marketing Research* 46, no. 3 (2009): 344–355.

12. Talya Miron-Shatz et al., "Patient Knowledge of Their Medication Is Low, but Associated with Adherence" (working paper). The cardiologists are Zaza Iakobishvili and Milton Roller.

13. On average, the patients have been on their medication for 3.5 years.

14. Jason Abaluck and Jonathan Gruber, "Choice Inconsistencies Among the Elderly: Evidence from Plan Choice in the Medicare Part D Program," *American Economic Review* 101, no. 4 (2011): 1180–1210.

15. Richard H. Thaler, Cass R. Sunstein, and John P. Balz, "Choice Architecture," *Behavioral Foundations of Public Policy* (2013): 428–439, at 428.

16. Eric J. Johnson et al., "Beyond Nudges: Tools of a Choice Architecture," *Marketing Letters* 23, no. 2 (2012): 487–504, at 489.

17. Jack Hoadley et al., "Launching the Medicare Part D Program: Lessons for the New Health Insurance Marketplaces," Robert Wood Johnson Foundation, June 1, 2013, www.rwjf.org/en/library/research/2013/06/launching-the-medicare-part-d-program--lessons-for-the-new-healt.html.

18. Y. Hanoch et al., "How Much Choice Is Too Much? The Case of the Medicare Prescription Drug Benefit," *Health Service Research* 44 (2009): 1157–1168.

19. Y. Hanoch et al., "Choice, Numeracy and Physicians-in-Training Performance: The Case of Medicare Part D," *Health Psychology* 29, no. 4 (2010): 454–459.

20. Chao Zhou and Yuting Zhang, "The Vast Majority of Medicare Part D Beneficiaries Still Don't Choose the Cheapest Plans That Meet Their Medication Needs," *Health Affairs* 31, no. 10 (2012): 2259–2265.

21. Jonathan D. Ketcham et al., "Sinking, Swimming, or Learning to Swim in Medicare Part D," *American Economic Review* 102, no. 6 (2012): 2639–2673.

22. Jack Hoadley et al., "To Switch or Not to Switch: Are Medicare Beneficiaries Switching Drug Plans to Save Money?," Kaiser Family Foundation, October 10, 2013, www.kff .org/medicare/issue-brief/to-switch-or-not-to-switch-are-medicare-beneficiaries-switching -drug-plans-to-save-money/. Switching was low despite the fact that those who switched were nearly six times more likely to see their premiums fall by at least 5 percent.

23. Daniel Kahneman and Amos Tversky, "The Simulation Heuristic," in *Judgment Under Uncertainty: Heuristics and Biases*, ed. Daniel Kahneman, Paul Slovic, and Amos Tversky (Cambridge: Cambridge University Press, 1982), 201–208.

24. Johnson et al., "Beyond Nudges," 487–504.

25. *Medicare & You 2021: The Official U.S. Government Medicare Handbook*, www .medicare.gov/Pubs/pdf/10050-Medicare-and-You.pdf.

26. סבולג ..,"לארשיב סיליבומה תואירבה יגתומ הלא ?תיללכה וא יבכמ", August 1, 2020, www .globes.co.il/news/article.aspx?did=1001294046.

27. According to the theory of planned behavior, people who have a positive attitude toward a behavior, who feel that their significant others would want them to form the behavior (which would constitute a social norm), and who feel the behavior is within their control are more likely to perform it. Ajzen Icek, "The Theory of Planned Behavior," *Organizational Behavior and Human Decision Processes* 50, no. 2 (1991): 179–211. Note that while organ donation filled the requirements for action according to the theory of planned behavior, some of my students, just like 42 percent of Americans, failed to act upon their attitudes and register as donors. Behavioral economics, with its sobering view of human nature, would chalk that inaction down to laziness, to choosing the path of least resistance, or to status quo bias. If any effort was involved in performing the desired behavior, it was less likely to happen than if it required minimal or no effort.

28. "110,000 People Are Waiting for a Lifesaving Transplant: Register to Be a Donor," Donate Life America, www.donatelife.net/.

29. "Organ Donation Statistics," HRSA Organdonor.gov, accessed June 21, 2020, www .organdonor.gov/statistics-stories/statistics.html; Richard Thaler, "Opting In vs. Opting Out," *New York Times*, September 26, 2009, www.nytimes.com/2009/09/27/business /economy/27view.html.

30. Thaler, "Opting In vs. Opting Out."

31. Eric J. Johnson and Daniel Goldstein, "Do Defaults Save Lives?," *Science* 302 (2003): 1338–1339.

32. Andrew D. A. C. Smith et al., "Live-Birth Rate Associated with Repeat in Vitro Fertilization Treatment Cycles," *JAMA* 314, no. 24 (2015): 2654–2662.

33. Tayla Miron-Shatz et al., "'Luckily, I Don't Believe in Statistics': Survey of Women's Understanding of Chance of Success with Futile Fertility Treatments," *Reproductive BioMedicine Online*, October 4, 2020, https://doi.org/10.1016/j.rbmo.2020.09.026.

34. National Security, "Homepage | חוטיב ימואל," National Insurance Institute of Israel, accessed March 18, 2020, www.btl.gov.il/Mediniyut/GeneralData/Pages/%D7%A9%D7%9B%D7%A8%20%D7%9E%D7%9E%D7%95%D7%A6%D7%A2.aspx.

35. Alice D. Domar, "Quality of Life Must Be Taken into Account When Assessing the Efficacy of Infertility Treatment," *Fertility and Sterility* 109, no. 1 (2018): 71–72.

36. Diana Kurylko, "Model T Had Many Shades; Black Dried Fastest," *Automotive News*, June 16, 2003, www.autonews.com/article/20030616/SUB/306160713/model-t-had-many-shades-black-dried-fastest.

37. Johnson et al., "Beyond Nudges," 489.

CHAPTER 7: DANCE ME TO THE END OF LIFE

1. Brigit Katz, "Chitetsu Watanabe, the World's Oldest Man, Dies at 112," *Smithsonian Magazine*, February 26, 2020, www.smithsonianmag.com/smart-news/chitetsu-watanabe-worlds-oldest-man-has-died-180974283/; Jonah Engel Bromwith, "Pete Frates, Who Promoted the Ice Bucket Challenge, Dies at 34," *New York Times*, December 9, 2019, www.nytimes.com/2019/12/09/us/pete-frates-dead.html?action=click&module=Well&pgtype=Homepage&section=Obituaries; Holly Hedegaard, Arialdi Miniño, and Margaret Warner, "Drug Overdose Deaths in the United States, 1999–2017," NCHS Data Brief, no. 329, November 2018, www.cdc.gov/nchs/data/databriefs/db329-h.pdf.

2. "Teen Drivers: Get the Facts," Transportation Safety, Centers for Disease Control and Prevention, National Center for Injury Prevention and Control, page last reviewed November 18, 2020, www.cdc.gov/transportationsafety/teen_drivers/teendrivers_factsheet.html?CDC_AA_refVal=https%3A%2F%2Fwww.cdc.gov%2Fmotorvehiclesafety%2Fteen_drivers%2Fteendrivers_factsheet.html.

3. "Helping People Share Their Wishes for Care Through the End of Life," Institute for Healthcare Improvement, The Conversation Project, 2021, https://theconversationproject.org/.

4. "Helping People Share Their Wishes for Care Through the End of Life,"; also on "Ellen Goodman Does the Math," The Conversation Project, YouTube video, April 8, 2019, 2021, www.youtube.com/watch?v=eLlYsEU9E1c&feature=youtu.be&ab_channel=TheConversationProject.

5. J. Levenson et al., "The Last Six Months of Life for Patients with Congestive Heart Failure, *Journal of the American Geriatrics Society* 48, no. 5 suppl (2000): S101–S109.

6. C. J. Taylor et al., "Trends in Survival After a Diagnosis of Heart Failure in the United Kingdom 2000–2017: Population Based Cohort Study," *BMJ*, February 13, 2019, https://doi.org/10.1136/bmj.l223.

7. S. Barclay et al., "End-of-Life Care Conversations with Heart Failure Patients: A Systematic Literature Review and Narrative Synthesis," *British Journal of General Practice* 61, no. 582 (2011): e49–e62.

8. J. Zapka et al., "Advanced Heart Failure: Prognosis, Uncertainty, and Decision Making," *Congestive Heart Failure* 13, no. 5 (2007): 268–274.

9. L. J. Brighton and K. Bristowe, "Communication in Palliative Care: Talking About the End of Life, Before the End of Life," *Postgraduate Medical Journal* 92, no. 1090 (2016): 466–470.

10. H. L. Chi et al., "Please Ask Gently: Using Culturally Targeted Communication Strategies to Initiate End-of-Life Care Discussions with Older Chinese Americans," *American Journal of Hospice and Palliative Medicine* 35, no. 10 (2018), 1265–1272.

11. S. Barker, M. Lynch, and J. Hopkinson, "Decision Making for People Living with Dementia by Their Carers at the End of Life: A Rapid Scoping Review," *International Journal of Palliative Nursing* 23, no. 9 (2017): 446–456.

12. Barker, Lynch, and Hopkinson, "Decision Making for People Living with Dementia by Their Carers at the End of Life," 446.

13. S. Lund, A. Richardson, and C. May, "Barriers to Advance Care Planning at the End of Life: An Explanatory Systematic Review of Implementation Studies," *PLOS ONE* 10, no. 2 (2015): e0116629.

14. D. Cortez, D. W. Maynard, and T. C. Campbell, "Creating Space to Discuss End-of-Life Issues in Cancer Care," *Patient Education and Counseling* 102, no. 2 (2019): 216–222, at 216; Barbara Ehrenreich, *Bright-Sided: How the Relentless Promotion of Positive Thinking Has Undermined America* (New York: Metropolitan Books, 2009). The UK version is Ehrenreich, *Smile or Die: How Positive Thinking Fooled America and the World* (London: Granta Books, 2010).

15. Atul Gawande, *Being Mortal: Medicine and What Matters in the End* (New York: Metropolitan Books, 2014).

16. Henry Marsh, "An Oncologist Asks When It's Time to Say 'Enough,'" review of *The First Cell and the Human Costs of Pursuing Cancer to the Last*, by Azra Raza, *New York Times*, October 15, 2019, www.nytimes.com/2019/10/15/books/review/the-first-cell-azra-raza.html.

17. Jessica Schreiber, "BJ Miller '93's Advice for End-of-Life Planning," *Princeton Alumni Weekly*, August 13, 2019, https://paw.princeton.edu/article/bj-miller 93s-advice-end-life-planning.

18. Richard H. Thaler and Cass R. Sunstein, *Nudge: Improving Decisions About Health, Wealth, and Happiness* (New Haven: Yale University Press, 2008): 356–360.

19. Wikipedia, s.v. "Ars moriendi," page last edited January 1, 2021, https://en.wikipedia.org/wiki/Ars_moriendi.

20. G. Gorer, "The Pornography of Death," *Encounter* 5, no. 4 (1955): 49–52, at 50.

21. Gorer, "The Pornography of Death," 51.

22. Ernest Becker, *The Denial of Death* (New York: Free Press, 1973).

23. Joshua Becker, "Why We Buy More Than We Need," *Forbes*, November 27, 2018, www.forbes.com/sites/joshuabecker/2018/11/27/why-we-buy-more-than-we-need/?sh=2120ff986417.

24. Robert B. Cialdini, *Influence: The Psychology of Persuasion* (self-pub., Quill, 1993).

25. D. P. Phillips, C. A. Van Voorhees, and T. E. Ruth, "The Birthday: Lifeline or Deadline?," *Psychosomatic Medicine* 54, no. 5 (1992): 532–542.

26. T. Matsubayashi, M. J. Lee, and M. Ueda, "Higher Risk of Suicide on Milestone Birthdays: Evidence from Japan," *Scientific Reports* 9, no. 1 (2019): 1–7.

27. D. P. Phillips and D. G. Smith, "Suicide at Symbolic Ages: Death on Stocktaking Occasions," in *Life Span Perspectives of Suicide*, ed. Antoon Leenaars (Boston: Springer, 1991), 81–92.

28. T. Miron-Shatz, R. Bhargave, and G. M. Doniger, "Milestone Age Affects the Role of Health and Emotions in Life Satisfaction: A Preliminary Inquiry," *PLOS ONE* 10, no. 8 (2015): e0133254.

29. A. L. Alter and H. E. Hershfield, "People Search for Meaning When They Approach a New Decade in Chronological Age," *Proceedings of the National Academy of Sciences* 111, no. 48 (2014): 17066–17070.

30. B. J. Miller and Shoshana Berger, *A Beginner's Guide to the End: Practical Advice for Living Life and Facing Death* (New York: Simon and Schuster, 2019).

31. "Honoring the Wishes of Those with Serious Illness and Frailty," National POLST, accessed December 19, 2019, https://polst.org/.

32. "Diane Meier, Geriatrician, Class of 2008," MacArthur Foundation, accessed February 21, 2020, www.macfound.org/fellows/class-of-2008/diane-meier.

33. "Palliative Care," HIV-AIDS, World Health Organization, accessed February 15, 2020, www.who.int/hiv/topics/palliative/PalliativeCare/en/.

34. "Palliative Care," World Health Organization, accessed February 9, 2021, www.who.int/health-topics/palliative-care.

35. Elizabeth Weathers et al., "Advance Care Planning: A Systematic Review of Randomised Controlled Trials Conducted with Older Adults," *Maturitas* 91 (2016): 101–109.

36. E. L. Sampson et al., "Palliative Assessment and Advance Care Planning in Severe Dementia: An Exploratory Randomized Controlled Trial of a Complex Intervention," *Palliative Medicine* 25, no. 3 (2011): 197–209.

37. D. W. Molloy et al., "Systematic Implementation of an Advance Directive Program in Nursing Homes: A Randomized Controlled Trial," *JAMA* 283, no. 11 (2000): 1437–1444.

38. Let Me Decide, 2013, www.letmedecide.org/.

39. Ehrenreich, *Bright-Sided*.

40. National Academies of Science, Engineering, and Medicine (NASEM), "Advance Care Planning: Challenges and Opportunities," two-part webinar, October 26 and November 2, 2020: "Advance Care Planning: Challenges and Opportunities: First Webinar," www.nationalacademies.org/event/10-26-2020/advance-care-planning-challenges-and-opportunities-a-workshop; and "Advance Care Planning: Challenges and Opportunities: Second Webinar," www.nationalacademies.org/event/11-02-2020/advance-care-planning-challenges-and-opportunities-second-webinar. The links include workshop agendas, videos of the presentations, and links to articles.

CHAPTER 8: IT TAKES AT LEAST TWO TO TANGO

1. Gerd Gigerenzer and J. A. Muir Gray, eds., *Better Doctors, Better Patients, Better Decisions: Envisioning Health Care 2020*, Strüngmann Forum Report (Cambridge: MIT Press, 2011).

2. Ezekiel J. Emanuel and Linda L. Emanuel, "Four Models of the Physician-Patient Relationship," *JAMA* 267, no. 16 (1992): 2221–2226. Their models are paternalistic, informative (scientific), interpretive, and deliberative.

3. C. Charles, A. Gafni, and T. Whelan, "Shared Decision-Making in the Medical Encounter: What Does It Mean? (Or It Takes at Least Two to Tango)," *Social Science and Medicine* 44 no. 5 (1977): 681–692.

4. "Through the Patient's Eyes: Collaboration Between Patients and Health Care Professionals," Past Program, Salzburg Global Seminar, May 23–30, 1998, www.salzburgglobal.org/multi-year-series/general/pageId/6381.

5. Gary Schwitzer, "'Nothing About Me Without Me'—NEJM Perspective Pieces" (blog), *HealthNewsReview.org*, March 1, 2012, www.healthnewsreview.org/2012/03/nothing-about-me-without-me-nejm-perspective-pieces/.

6. See, for example, Sarah Jackson and Carousel, *Nothing About Me Without Me*, 2016, www.carousel.org.uk/wp-content/uploads/2016/03/NothingAboutMeWithoutMe_WebResource.pdf.

7. Salzburg Global Seminar, "Salzburg Statement on Shared Decision Making," *BMJ* 342 (2011): d1745.

8. Glyn is also my coauthor on two papers, one that points to the fact that patients rarely complain about privacy breaches and one on DelibeRate—a scale we developed for measuring the quality of the deliberation process patients have before reaching a decision. We also, with Glyn's philosopher son, published a chapter on deliberation.

9. Society for Participatory Medicine, accessed September 24, 2019, https://participatory medicine.org/.

10. Nyna Williams, Chris Fleming, and Annie Doubleday, "Patient and Provider Perspectives on Shared Decision Making: A Systematic Review of the Peer-Reviewed Literature," *Journal of Comparative Effectiveness Research* 6, no. 8 (2017): 683–692, at 683. The authors reviewed 290 papers published between July 2006 and December 2016.

11. Bruce Y. Lee, "Time to Change the 15-Minute Limit for Doctor Visits," *Forbes*, September 10, 2016, www.forbes.com/sites/brucelee/2016/09/10/time-to-change-the-15-minute-limit-for-doctor-visits/#7d0fca023477.

12. Robert G. Hill, Lynn Marie Sears, and Scott W. Melanson, "4000 Clicks: A Productivity Analysis of Electronic Medical Records in a Community Hospital ED," *American Journal of Emergency Medicine* 31, no. 11 (2013): 1591–1594, https://doi.org/10.1016/j.ajem.2013.06.028; Christine Sinsky et al., "Allocation of Physician Time in Ambulatory Practice: A Time and Motion Study in 4 Specialties," *Annals of Internal Medicine* 165, no. 11 (2016): 753, https://doi.org/10.7326/m16-0961.

13. Hill, Sears, and Melanson, "4000 Clicks."

14. Naykky Singh Ospina et al., "Eliciting the Patient's Agenda—Secondary Analysis of Recorded Clinical Encounters," *Journal of General Internal Medicine* 34, no. 1 (2018): 36–40, https://doi.org/10.1007/s11606-018-4540-5.

15. Glyn Elwyn et al., "A Proposal for the Development of National Certification Standards for Patient Decision Aids in the US," *Health Policy* 122, no. 7 (2018): 703–706. https://doi.org/10.1016/j.healthpol.2018.04.010.

16. Monica Perez Jolles, Jennifer Richmond, and Kathleen C. Thomas, "Minority Patient Preferences, Barriers, and Facilitators for Shared Decision-Making with Health Care Providers in the USA: A Systematic Review," *Patient Education and Counseling* 102, no. 7 (2019): 1251–1262.

17. "Hypertension," World Health Organization, accessed May 23, 2019, www.who.int/health-topics/hypertension/#tab=tab_1.

18. Rachel A. Johnson et al., "Interventions to Support Shared Decision Making for Hypertension: A Systematic Review of Controlled Studies," *Health Expectations* 21, no. 6 (2018): 1191–1207. To be included in the review, a study had to contain a comparison to some other program, and it had to report an outcome measure.

19. "Injuries, Illnesses, and Fatalities," U.S. Bureau of Labor Statistics, last modified date, November 4, 2020, www.bls.gov/iif/oshsum.htm.

20. Yannick Tousignant-Laflamme et al., "Does Shared Decision Making Result in Better Health Related Outcomes for Individuals with Painful Musculoskeletal Disorders? A Systematic Review," *Journal of Manual and Manipulative Therapy* 25, no. 3 (2017): 144–150, https://doi.org/10.1080/10669817.2017.1323607.

21. Nahara Anani Martínez-González et al., "Shared Decision Making for Men Facing Prostate Cancer Treatment: A Systematic Review of Randomized Controlled Trials," *Patient Preference and Adherence* 13 (2019): 1153–1174, https://doi.org/10.2147/ppa.s202034.

22. Michael Saheb Kashaf, Elizabeth Tyner McGill, and Zackary Dov Berger, "Shared Decision-Making and Outcomes in Type 2 Diabetes: A Systematic Review and Meta-Analysis," *Patient Education and Counseling* 100, no. 12 (2017): 2159–2171, https://doi.org/10.1016/j.pec.2017.06.030.

23. Glyn Elwyn et al., "Option Grids: Shared Decision Making Made Easier," *Patient Education and Counseling* 90, no. 2 (2013): 207–212.

24. Peter Scalia et al., "Online, Interactive Option Grid Patient Decision Aids and Their Effect on User Preferences," *Medical Decision Making* 38, no. 1 (2018): 56–68.

25. Peter Scalia et al., "User-Testing an Interactive Option Grid Decision Aid for PSA Screening: The Divide Between High and Low Health Literacy," chapter 5 in "Encounter-Based Patient Decision Aids: Implementation Experiences and Effects Across Online and Real-World Contexts," by P. Scalia (PhD diss., Radboud University, 2019), 119–140.

26. Talya Miron-Shatz et al., "The Status of Shared Decision Making and Citizen Participation in Israeli Medicine," *German Journal for Evidence and Quality in Health Care (ZEFQ)* 105, no. 4 (2011): 271–276, https://doi.org/10.1016/j.zefq.2011.04.006. See also Orit Karnieli-Miller et al., "On the Verge of Shared Decision Making in Israel: Overview and Future Directions," *Zeitschrift für Evidenz, Fortbildung und Qualität im Gesundheitswesen* 123–124 (2017): 56–60, https://doi.org/10.1016/j.zefq.2017.05.007.

27. Talya Miron-Shatz et al., "Shared Decision-Making in Israel: Status, Barriers, and Recommendations," *Israel Journal of Health Policy Research* 1, no. 1 (2012), https://doi.org/10.1186/2045-4015-1-5; Harvey V. Fineberg, "From Shared Decision Making to Patient-Centered Decision Making," *Israel Journal of Health Policy Research* 1, no. 1 (2012), https://doi.org/10.1186/2045-4015-1-6.

28. Betsy Sleath et al., "Youth Views on Communication About ADHD and Medication Adherence," *Community Mental Health Journal* 53, no. 4 (2017): 438–444, https://doi.org/10.1007/s10597-016-0078-3.

29. Laura Boland et al., "Barriers and Facilitators of Pediatric Shared Decision-Making: A Systematic Review," *Implementation Science* 14, no. 1 (2019), https://doi.org/10.1186/s13012-018-0851-5.

30. Erica M. Carlisle, Laura A. Shinkunas, and Lauris C. Kaldjian, "Do Surgeons and Patients/Parents Value Shared Decision-Making in Pediatric Surgery? A Systematic Review," *Journal of Surgical Research* 231 (2018): 49–53, https://doi.org/10.1016/j.jss.2018.04.042.

31. Carlisle, Shinkunas, and Kaldjian, "Do Surgeons and Patients/Parents Value Shared Decision-Making in Pediatric Surgery?," 52.

32. Catherine Hyde et al., "Process and Impact of Patient Involvement in a Systematic Review of Shared Decision Making in Primary Care Consultations," *Health Expectations* 20, no. 2 (2016): 298–308, https://doi.org/10.1111/hex.12458.

CHAPTER 9: BRAVE-ISH NEW WORLD

1. "Coronavirus Disease 2019 (COVID-19)—Prevention & Treatment," COVID-19, CDC Centers for Disease Control and Prevention, 2020, www.cdc.gov/coronavirus/2019-ncov/prevent-getting-sick/prevention.html.

2. Andy Markowitz, "Does Your State Have a Mask Mandate Due to Coronavirus?," Healthy Living, AARP, accessed December 2020, www.aarp.org/health/healthy-living/info-2020/states-mask-mandates-coronavirus.html.

3. Stefan Becker, "mHealth 2.0: Experiences, Possibilities, and Perspectives," *JMIR mHealth and uHealth* 2, no. 2 (2014): e24.

4. Avraham N. Kluger and Angelo DeNisi, "The Effects of Feedback Interventions on Performance: A Historical Review, a Meta-Analysis, and a Preliminary Feedback Intervention Theory," *Psychological Bulletin* 119, no. 2 (1996): 254.

5. Joshua H. West et al., "There's an App for That: Content Analysis of Paid Health and Fitness Apps," *Journal of Medical Internet Research* 14, no. 3 (2012): e72.

6. Jonathan Shieber, "Plume Is Building a Healthcare Service Specifically for the Transgender Community," TechCrunch, June 18, 2020, https://techcrunch.com/2020/06/18/plume-is-building-a-healthcare-service-specifically-for-the-transgender-community/.

7. Paige Minemyer, "Why Transgender Telehealth Company Plume Is Getting into Employee Benefits," Fierce Healthcare, September 18, 2020, www.fiercehealthcare.com/payer/why-transgender-telehealth-company-plume-getting-into-employee-benefits.

8. Erez Yoeli et al., "Digital Health Support in Treatment for Tuberculosis," *New England Journal of Medicine* 381, no. 10 (2019): 986–987.

9. Ali Hyatt, "Top 10 States to Know About Telehealth," *Amwell Blog*, January 21, 2015, https://business.amwell.com/top-10-stats-you-need-to-know-about-telehealth/.

10. Grand View Research, "Report Overview" for *Corporate Wellness Market Size, Share and Trends Analysis Report...*, December 2020, www.grandviewresearch.com/industry-analysis/corporate-wellness-market.

11. Stephany Carolan, Peter R. Harris, and Kate Cavanagh, "Improving Employee Well-Being and Effectiveness: Systematic Review and Meta-Analysis of Web-Based Psychological Interventions Delivered in the Workplace," *Journal of Medical Internet Research* 19, no. 7 (2017): e271, doi:10.2196/jmir.7583.

12. Karin Ingeborg Proper and Sandra Helena van Oostrom, "The Effectiveness of Workplace Health Promotion Interventions on Physical and Mental Health Outcomes—A Systematic Review of Reviews," *Scandinavian Journal of Work Environment and Health* 45, no. 6 (2019): 546–559, doi:10.5271/sjweh.3833.

13. "Ten Health Issues WHO Will Tackle This Year," World Health Organization, accessed January 2, 2020, www.who.int/news-room/spotlight/ten-threats-to-global-health-in-2019.

14. Dr. Mike, "The Thing About Vaccines," YouTube video, August 6, 2017, www.youtube.com/watch?v=y2WtUMvNjzQ.

15. "Three in Four Adults Globally Say They Would Get a Vaccine for COVID-19," Ipsos MORI, September 1, 2020, www.ipsos.com/ipsos-mori/en-uk/three-four-adults-globally-say-they-would-get-vaccine-covid-19.

16. Sarah M. Bartsch et al., "Vaccine Efficacy Needed for a COVID-19 Coronavirus Vaccine to Prevent or Stop an Epidemic as the Sole Intervention," *American Journal of Preventive Medicine* 59, no. 4 (2020): 493–503.

17. The responses come from government Facebook pages from the UK (www.facebook
.com/UKgovernment/posts/1989273271225090), Ireland (www.facebook.com
/HSElive/posts/1661673554032771), and the United States (www.facebook.com/HHS
/photos/a.577318915631772/3890471307649833), respectively, all accessed on February 7,
2021; spelling as in the originals.

18. Talya Miron-Shatz, "A Decision Scientist's Tips for a COVID-Vaccinated Workplace," LinkedIn, February 12, 2021, www.linkedin.com/pulse/decision-scientists
-tips-covid-vaccinated-workplace-miron-shatz-phd/?trackingId=sbwD43tGYLzY%2
BmC0%2FhHgyA%3D%3D.

19. Talya Miron-Shatz and Scott C. Ratzan, "The Potential of an Online and Mobile Health
Scorecard for Preventing Chronic Disease," *Journal of Health Communication* 16, sup2 (2011):
175–190, doi:10.1080/10810730.2011.602464.

20. "2011 High Level Meeting on Prevention and Control of Non-Communicable Diseases," General Assembly of the United Nations, September 19–20, 2011, www.un.org/en/ga
/ncdmeeting2011/#:~:text=The%20four%20main%20noncommunicable%20
diseases,all%20countries%2C%20particularly%20developing%20nations.

21. "The Coronavirus Pandemic Has Boosted Telehealth; Here's How Existing
Spaces Can Support Virtual Visits," Teri Oelrich and Bryan Langlands, contributors,
Forbes, June 8, 2020, www.forbes.com/sites/coronavirusfrontlines/2020/06/08/the
-coronavirus-pandemic-has-boosted-telehealth-heres-how-existing-spaces-can-support
-virtual-visits/#5184a8137560.

22. Nathan Eddy, "Telehealth Use Rises, but New Trends Highlight Demographic
Divides," HealthcareITNews, May 14, 2020, www.healthcareitnews.com/news
/telehealth-use-rises-new-trends-highlight-demographic-divides; Carrie L. Nieman and Es-
ther S. Oh, "Connecting with Older Adults Via Telemedicine," *Annals of Internal Medicine*
173, no. 10 (2020): 831–832, doi:10.7326/m20-1322.

23. Email to author, July 5, 2020.

24. Alexander Mertens et al., "A Mobile Application Improves Therapy-Adherence Rates
in Elderly Patients Undergoing Rehabilitation: A Crossover Design Study Comparing Docu-
mentation via iPad with Paper-Based Control," *Medicine* 95, no. 36 (2016): e4446.

25. "What Is Predict," NHS Predict Breast Cancer, accessed 2020, https://breast.predict
.nhs.uk/. I sent all my PREDICT material to the Winton Centre, where it was approved and
amended by Gabe Recchia and Mike Pearson.

26. "Cancer Treatment Tool Wins ONS Research Award," Cambridge Network, December 4, 2018, www.cambridgenetwork.co.uk/news/cancer-treatment-tool-wins-ons-research
-award.

27. Michael Hallsworth and Hannah Burd, "Green Means Go: How to Help Patients
Make Informed Choices About Their Healthcare" (blog post), Behavioural Insights Team,
April 20, 2018, www.bi.team/blogs/green-means-go-how-to-help-patients-make-informed
-choices-about-their-healthcare/.

28. Hallsworth and Burd, "Green Means Go."

29. Amir Goren shared this, and many other exciting findings, in an email, July 10,
2020.

30. Christopher P. Bourdeaux et al., "Using 'Nudge' Principles for Order Set Design: A Before and After Evaluation of an Electronic Prescribing Template in Critical Care," *BMJ Quality Safety* 23, no. 5 (2014): 382–388.

31. Anne McElvoy and Philip Coggan, "*The Economist* Asks Richard Thaler," *Economist*, July 21, 2016, www.economist.com/international/2016/07/21/richard-thaler?fsrc=scn/tw_ec/richard_thaler.

32. Julian J. Zlatev et al., "Default Neglect in Attempts at Social Influence," *Proceedings of the National Academy of Sciences* 114, no. 52 (2017): 13643–13648.

33. Nicholas Peters, LinkedIn, www.linkedin.com/in/nicholas-peters-837ab715/?originalSubdomain=uk.

34. Kerry Robinson, phone interview with the author, January 2, 2019; he vetted the interview for release in this book.

35. "Urgent Health Challenges for the Next Decade," World Health Organization, January 13, 2020, www.who.int/news-room/photo-story/photo-story-detail/urgent-health-challenges-for-the-next-decade.

EPILOGUE

1. Aristotle, *Poetics*, trans. S. H. Butcher (Project Gutenberg, release date November 3, 2008, last updated January 22, 2013), VI, www.gutenberg.org/files/1974/1974-h/1974-h.htm.

2. Aristotle, *Poetics*, XIII.

3. Rush Rehm, *Radical Theatre: Greek Tragedy in the Modern World*, ebook (London: Bloomsbury, 2003).

INDEX

Talya Miron-Shatz, PhD, is an international leader at the intersection of medicine and behavioral economics, with over twenty years of experience as a researcher, consultant, and entrepreneur. She uses her uniquely broad perspective to identify psychological barriers that prevent us from making good medical decisions, both minor and crucial ones, and develops ways to overcome those barriers.

Dr. Miron-Shatz (PhD in psychology) did research at Princeton University with Nobel laureate Daniel Kahneman, taught at Wharton, and published dozens of academic papers on how laypersons and doctors—in hospitals, online, at home, everywhere—understand medical information and make health choices. Her clients include Johnson & Johnson, Pfizer, Samsung, digital health companies, and major players in the health industry in North America, Europe, and Israel. She is a senior fellow at the Center for Medicine in the Public Interest in New York, a professor at the Ono Academic College in Israel, and a visiting researcher at the University of Cambridge. She is married, has three children, and divides her time between New York, Cambridge, and Jerusalem.

To learn more and to contact her, visit TalyaMironShatz.com.